THE
HOLY LIVES
OF
THE AZHVARS,
OR
THE DRAVIDA SAINTS

THE HOLY LIVES OF THE AZHVARS, OR THE DRAVIDA SAINTS

ALKONDAVILLI GOVINDACHARYA

GYAN

Published by

GYAN

Gyan Publishing House
5, Ansari Road
Daryaganj, New Delhi-110002
Phone: 011-47034999, 9811692060
E-mail: books@gyanbooks.com

Distribution Network
gyanbooks.com
India, USA, Canada, UK, Australia

ISBN: 978-93-7014-351-7 (HB)

First Published, 1902

2nd Impression 2025

Printed at: Gyan Press, Delhi.

THE HOLY LIVES OF THE AZHVARS, OR THE DRAVIDA SAINTS

Author: ALKONDAVILLI GOVINDACHARYA

THE

HOLY LIVES

OF

THE AZHVARS

OR

The Dravida Saints

BY

ALKONDAVILLI GOVINDACHARYA,

The English Translator of Srî Râmânuja's Commentaries on the Bhagavad-Gîtá; The Author of the Divine Wisdom of the Drávida Saints &c. &c. &c.

1902.

CONTENTS.

ERRATA.

Page	line		for		read
xxvi	22	...	educidation	...	elucidation
xxx	17	...	livese	...	lives
xxxiii	17	...	unwordly	...	unworldly
lii	15	...	condecession...		condescension
lxxii	7	...	qalluvar	...	Va*ll*uvar
5	18	...	retur	...	returned
5	28	...	temple ceremonial		temple-ceremonial
7	3	...	thot	...	thou
27	12	...	become	...	having become
39	5	...	af	...	of
39	12	...	methed	...	method
47	7	...	wear	...	wore
48	18	...	saintes	...	saintess
51	3	...	than He	...	than Him
53	26	...	waste	...	waist
87	22	...	siver-like	...	silver-like
90	10	...	beganto	...	began to
99	9	...	commandad	...	commanded
100	20	...	from	...	for
104	6	...	a real	...	real
114	22	...	they	...	thy
142	23	...	houlders	...	shoulders
144	2	...	surplussed	...	surpassed
148	24	...	wench	...	maiden
151	12	...	costed	...	cost
154	16	...	then	...	them
157	5	...	riner	...	river
160	12	...	anb	...	and
160	24	...	trajic	...	tragic
172	3	...	sang	..	song

177	5	...	teethed	...	toothed
178	5	...	orgin	...	origin
178	18	...	extened	...	extend
182	1	...	Pavilios	...	Pavilions
189	1	...	catalysms	...	cataclysms
191	7	...	Ch.	...	Bk. XI. Ch.
191	8	...	propheysing	...	prophesying
193	6	...	full-moon day		full-moon
196	17	...	dy	...	by
199	9-10	...	gold gem-made		gem-set gold
201	16	...	fell	...	felt
203	14	...	mak	...	make
204	4	...	on His	...	His
208	26	...	head, burst	...	head burst
213	13	...	effective	...	efficient
216	27	...	imparts	...	imports
221	5	...	breaths	...	breathes
221	8	...	stride	...	strode
222	16	...	How	...	Thou

INTRODUCTION

I. Hagiology.

We give a Hierarchic Table. This will give the readers what may be called the main line of the *successio episcoporum* of the Srì Vaishnavas[1] or the stemma of the Visishtâdvaitins,

1. On the superiority of Vaishnavism, M. Barth (*Religions of India*, pp. 216—217) says:—"With the exception of professional devotees, comparatively few *S*ivaites are met with, that is to say, people who make *S*iva their principal God, in the *mantra* of whom they have been specially initiated, and in the faith of whom they hope to work out their salvation. And the number would be still more reduced if we were to cut off the Sáktas from it who pay their vows to Devî rather than to her husband. In all the countries to the north of the Vindhyà, several of which rank among the most thickly inhabited of the globe, the majority wherever local cults of aboriginal derivation do not prevail, belong to Vishnuvite religions. In the Dekhan the relative proportions are different, the Sivites constitute large masses, especially in the south, and the two religions being probably equally balanced. But even there Vishnuism seems to be spreading......if it affords less nourishment to superstitious appetites, on the other hand by the deep glimpses which the doctrine of the Avatáras opens in some degree into the Divine Nature, it allies itself more readily with Vedántic Mysticism, that one of all the systems conceived in India which responds best to its aspirations."

The Amrita Bazar Patrika reports of an American Lady Abhayânanda coming to India to give a new life to that sweet Religion. Vaishnavism (*Theosophist* p.374, Vol. XXIII).

the exponents of the Triune Monism and the Divine Love of the Upanishads,— Srí-Vaishnavas, gathered together organizedly under the leadership of Srî Râmânuja, of the 12th Century. The one hundred pages of Introduction written dy Dr. G. Thibaut, on the Vedânta Sútras, may be said to be one continuous eulogy on the reasonableness of this reputed Reformer's interpretation of the Vedânta.

*S*rì-Vaish*n*avas have since been also called Râmânujas, inasmuch as Râmânuja was, 'that glorious Spiritual Reservoir' into which flowed all the wisdom of the Ancients, both Saints and Sages anterior to him. The present work aims at giving the Holy Lives of the former, the Saints, or those who are called Âzhvárs[1] (*lit*: those drowned in or

---

1. The Âzhvârs or Saints answer to the description given by Emerson:—"A certain tendency to insanity has always attended the opening of the religious sense in men, as if they had been 'blasted with excess of light.' The 'trances' of Socrates, the 'Union' of Plotinus, the 'Vision' of Porphyry, the 'conversion' of Paul, the 'aurora' of Behmen, the 'convulsions' of George Fox and his Quakers, the 'illumination' of Swedenborg, are of this kind. What was in the case of these remarkable persons a ravishment, has in innumerable instances in common life been exhibited in less striking manner. Everywhere the history of religion betrays a tendency to enthusiasm. The *rapture* of the Moravian and Quietist; *the opening of the internal sense of the Word*, in the Language of the New Jerusalem Church; the *revival* of the Calvinistic churches; the *experiences* of the Methodists, are varying forms of that shudder of awe and delight with which the individual soul always mingles with the Universal Soul." (Essays: *The Oversoul*).

maddened with, God-Love) based upon the traditional works we possess. Tired of experimental science and restless speculation, there is great requisition in these days for a knowledge of primitive thought, even though it be had secondhand and with all possible personal and historical errors. To meet this desire is the present attempt and as paving the way for further inquiry, study, and reflection, which, even if they should succeed in disproving facts presented by tradition, must at least furnish us with a mass of information from sources at present untapped or inaccessible.[1] And the Drâvida Field in this respect, *of the Srî Vaishnavas*, has so far been regrettably little explored. The Samskrit-field has almost been covered, and labourers are wanted for the Drávida-field [Vide Preface. p. XXI. Max Muller's Six Systems of Indian philosophy].

The next volume or Volumes (D.V.) will be the Holy Lives of the Achâryas or Sages beginning from Nâtha-Munigal [Vide Hierarchic Table].

The Lord of Queen *Srí** (Mercy) dwells in Vaikuntha. He is surrounded in that Land of Eternal Sunshine and

1. Says S. Johnson :—"I cannot but note that a trustworthy statement of what the non-Christian world has to offer to the eye of thoroughly free inquiry, in matters of belief, is more and more earnestly demanded." (P. 1. Vol. I. *Oriental Religions*). And "It is time the older religions were studied in the light of their own intrinsic values. They are at once spontaneities of desire and faith, and elements in an indivisible unity of growth." (*Ibid* pp. 13-14)

* Are there wives in Heaven? In this connection, Swedenborg's "Conjugal Love" may be read. Emerson (Essays, p: 326-7. Vol 1, Bohn) says of Swedenborg that: 'though the virgins he saw in heaven were beautiful, the wives were in-

(Continued.)

Rapture, with the Celestial Hosts, the Archangels Vishvaksena, Ananta and others, too numerous to count. He dwells there All-satisfied, and Perfect in all the Holy Graces befitting Divinity. The Vaikun*th*a or the "Land of unhampered Freedom and Joy" is described as :—

"That which lies beyond the Sphere of Rajas (or action)"[1]

"That which is Three Parts of the whole, and Nectareous"[2].

"That where Nârâya*n*a—the Centre of the Cosmos—dwells; that which is Imperishable, Transcendental, and Celestial"[3]

---

comparably more beautiful, and went on increasing in beauty evermore." "Sex is universal and not local; virility in the male qualifying every organ, act and thought; and the feminine in woman. (Read Indra's *Srî*-stava. Vish: Pur: I-9 and Lakshmî-Tantra.) Therefore, in the real or spiritual world the nuptial union is not momentary, but incessant and total." "In fact in the spiritual world, we change sexes every moment (cp. *Satya-kâma* and *Satya-sankalpa* of the Upanishads). You love the worth in me: then I am your husband; but it is not me, but the worth that fixes the love; and that worth is a drop of the ocean of worth that is beyond me. Meantime I adore the greater worth in another, and so become his wife. He aspires to a higher worth in another spirit, and is wife or receiver of that influence."

Let those who hate wives in Heaven, first begin to hate their own wives on earth! Do they?

1. क्षयन्तमस्यरजसः पराके (Yajus: Sam: II. 2. 12.)

2. त्रिपादस्यामृतं दिवि (Uttara-Nârâya*n*am or Purusha-Sûkta found in all the Four Vedas).

3. तदक्षरे परमेव्योमन् (Taittirîya Upanishad II. 1. *Ambhas*).

"That Etherial Superlative Realm where the King dwells"[1]

"That which is the Exalted Sphere of Vishnu whom the celestial sages ever see"[2]

Our Scriptures next describe the Glory with which God is there encompassed thus :--

"In the Superb Vaikuntha-Land, the Lord of the Cosmos with His Consort *Sri*, *is*. This Vishnu, of inconceivable Nature *is* there with his Elect, the Loving and the Godly"[3]

"In that Superb Vaikuntha-Land, the Spouse of *Sri*, *is*. The Supreme King is there served by his (minor) Consorts Bhūmi and Nīlā."[4]

"The Celestial Region where Vishnu abides, (listen, O Janamejaya !) shines with its self-radiance of a Thousand Suns, though neither Sun nor Moon nor Fire is there.

---

1. यो अस्याध्यक्षः परमे व्योमन् (Yajus : Sam ; II. 8. 9).

2. तद्विष्णोः परमं पदम् &c. (Âruneya Up : 5. Mukti Up : II. 77 and others.

3. वैकुंठे तु परे लोके श्रिया सार्धं जगत्पतिः । आस्ते विष्णुरचिन्त्यात्मा भक्तैर्भागवतैस्सह (Lainga-Purána I. 2.)

4. वैकुण्ठेतु परे लोके श्रीसहायो जनार्दनः। उभाभ्यां भूमिनीळाभ्यां सेवितः परमेश्वरः ॥ [Pâncharâtra] Read Life of St. *Andâl* for the higher meanings of *Sri*, *Bhû* and *Nîlâ* (p. 40-44).

The effulgence is such that neither Devas nor the Dânavas can gaze on."[1]

"Listen, O King! This region teems with millions of spots and retreats for various delights; and tarns sparkling with crystal-waters and gay with lotus-blooms. To this Elysium, the rest of the Cosmos is Infernum"[2].

"Where, Nârâyaṇa divides Time into Past, Present and Future, but where Time is not Lord"[3].

"Where Time in all its parts of seconds, instants &c effecteth no changes."[4]

"That Region which is Primal, Etherial, Transcending, and Permanent, attaining which, Seers of Wisdom are released from all sin."[5]

"That which is beyond all the Systems in the Universe, the Brahmâṇḍas,—and is Three Parts,—the Fourth Part making the material planes."[6]

---

1. अत्यर्कानलदीप्तं तत् स्थानं विष्णोर्महात्मनः । स्वयैव प्रभया राजन् दुष्प्रेक्ष्यं देवदानवैः ॥ (Bhârata, Araṇya.)

2. आक्रीडा विविधा राजन् पद्मिन्यश्चामलोदकाः । एते वै निरयास्तात स्थानस्य परमात्मनः ॥ (Ibid.)

3. कालं स पचते यत्र न कालस्तत्र वै प्रभुः ॥ (Pâncharátra.)

4. कलामुहूर्तादिमयश्च कालो न यद्विभूतेः परिणामहेतुः ॥ (Ibid.)

5. यत्तत्पुराणमाकाशं सर्वस्मात्परमंध्रुवं । यत्पदं प्राप्य तत्त्वज्ञाः मुच्यन्ते सर्वकिल्बिषैः ॥ (Lakshmí-Tantra XVII. 14.)

6. अण्डेभ्यः परतो नित्यं त्रिपादेन विराजते । इतरेण तु पादेन प्राकृतेण्डे विराजिते ॥ (Pàncharátra.)

While so the Girvâna Scriptures declare, the Prabandhas or the Holy Utterances of the Âzhvârs, called the Drâvida Scriptures, declare :—

"That it is a Country where Joy is Endless"[1];
"His Glory resplendent as the Sun"[2];
"The Spotless Heavens—the Blissful Regions"[3];
"The Expansive Vaikundam"[4];
"The Limpid, Lofty Celestium"[5].

And the Âchâryas or the Sages who followed the Âzhvârs have likewise declared thus :—

"This Sum of Things, manifest and unmanifest, constitute Thee—viz., the Brahmândas, and all their various Contents, the ten-fold larger sheaths enveloping these; the Qualities; the Primordial Stuff; the Sum of Intelligents; the Spiritual Sphere; the Celestials; the Divine Person."[6]

"Thy Essence and Attributes are neither utterable nor conceivable by the highest risen Yogis"[7]

"The Lord of Vaikuntha *par excellence*"[8]

---

1. *Nalam-andam-illad-ór-Nádu* (T. Vây-Mozhi II. 8. 4.)
2. *Sudar-oliyây ninrá* (Ibid: III. 10. 5.)
3. *Telivisumbu* (Ibid IX. 7. 5.)
4. *Mága-Vaikundam* (Ibid IX. 3. 7.)
5. *Telid-ágia sén-visumbu* (Ibid X. 8. 4.)
6. यदण्डमण्डान्तरगोचरञ्च &c(*Yámunáchárya's* Stotra-Ratna. 17)
7. परमयोगिवाङ्मनसाऽपरिच्छेद्य &c. (*Rámánuja's* Saranâgati Gadya.)
8. निरतिशय वैकुण्ठनाथ &c. (*Ibid.* Vaikuntha Gadya.)

"Thy Unfathomable Celestium is Superb and Time-beyond."[1]

"That which is beyond mind, beyond darkness, and ineffably Marvellous."[2]

Scriptures, viz., Vedas, Vedântas, The Âgamas, Smritis, and Ázhvârs and Âchâryas declare thus, *una voce*, the general features of the Spiritual Empyrean, the Divine King, and the Halcyon Bliss; and the Purâ*n*as and the Mahâ Bhârata further add a few details of description to the effect that conuntless domes, and towers and palaces, and enclosures and courtyards and pavements, gay and glistening with precious gems of every quality abound; and in the midst of all this gorgeous splendour sits enthroned the Universal King in the Thousand Columned Pavilion of Precious Stones[3], surrounded by colonnades, arcades, groves and parks; the squares and thoroughfares bedight with arches, festoons, flags and pennons; and "celestials bounding with joy and showering Sâma-gânic praises on the Lord."[4]

There in the Repertory, made of exquisite gold, called Paramapada, sits coronate, the Pure and Infinite Brahman;

1. कालातिगा तव परा &c. (*Kûranâtha*'s Vaikun*t*ha Stava 38.)

2. यद्दूरे मनसो यदेव &c. (*Bhattârya's* Srî Gu*n*a-Ratna-Kósa 21.)

3. सहस्रस्थूणे विचित्रे &c. (Kaushîtakî Brâhma*n*a Up.)

4. नित्यमुक्तैस्समाकीर्णं सामगानोपशोभितम् ॥ (Bhârata, Ara*n*ya.)

and this, Spiritual Seers know as the Holy of Holies, the Glory of Glories."[1]

"There shines not the Sun, nor the Moon, nor the Stars. Why speak of Agni (Fire)? Him, the Ṣhining, all follow; from His Light, all this shines."[2]

"His Glory can only be likened to a thousand Suns, simultaneously shining forth in the sky. Such Great Spirit is He."[3]

"The blossoms and raiments and ornaments which deck His Person, are matchless and only match Himself. They shine with their own light and peculiar light of Intelligence. They vie with each other in beauty and enhance each other in beauty."[4]

"It is a grand river of glory, moving majestic, in rippling whirls."[5]

"An infinite panorama of beautiful pictures rising out of a glory-stream."[6]

---

1. हिरण्मये परेकोशे विरजंब्रह्मनिष्कळम् &c. (Mu*n*d. Up: II.2.9.)
2. न तत्र सूर्यो भाति न चन्द्रतारकम् &c.(Ka*t*h. Up. II.5.15.)
3. दिवि सूर्यसहस्रस्य भवेद्युगपदुत्थिता &c. (Bhârata : Âdi.)
4. स्रग्वस्त्राभरणैर्युक्तं स्वानुरूपैरनूपमैः। चिन्मयैस्स्वप्रकाशैश्चाप्यन्योन्यरुचिरंजितैः ॥ (Pâ*n*charátra.)
5. *Suzhi patt-ódum* &c. (T. V. Mozhi. VIII. 10. 5.)
6. *Sódi-vellattin ulle* &c. (Ibid V. 5. 10.)

And unlike moonlight wasted in wilderness, "This Hari is not alone, but ever, in the delightful company of the Universal Mother Sri,—united like Moon and Moonlight,—*is*, wearing eternal youth (though ancient) and beauty of Person—though He is Measureless and Infinite"[1].

And not alone to Himself and for His Mercy is He; for the countless hosts and ranks of celestials, Eternals and Saved Souls, partake and enjoy the Divine Bliss without satiating; and deeply drunk in voluptuosity of Love and Bliss, they exclaim in fitful ejaculations,—prompted by delirious rapture:— 'Supreme! Salutation to Thee',[2]. 'O, I am conquered',[3] 'Lord! blest be Thou',[4] 'O, will this last!'[5], 'Will any foe snatch this cup of joy from my lips?'[6].

The Lord of Heaven is thus never alone. The Universal Mother of Mercy is inseparably with Him, and numerous 'Heavenly Hosts crowned as God's own'[7], 'Sparkling like million Suns, and shining like billion moons, and holding Empire in the Empyrean,—released from bondage,—free and

---

1. बृहच्छरीरोपि विमानदेहो युवाकुमारत्वमुपेयिवान् हरिः । रेमे श्रियाऽसौ जगतां जनन्या सुज्योत्स्नया चन्द्र इवामृतांशुः ॥ (Pâñcharâtra.)

2. नमो नमो वाङ्मनसातिभूमये &c (Stotra-ratna, 21.)

3. जितन्ते पुण्डरीकाक्ष &c (Jitanta: Rig-veda-khila.)

4. *Pallandu pallandu* &c. (St. Periy-âzhvâr.)

5. & 6. (Read Bhattar's *Srî-Guna-Ratna-Kôsa* 24.)

7. *Madiyudai vanavar* &c. (T: Vây-Mozhi X. 9. 8.)

blessed'[1], eternally *live* circumjacent to the Lord, *strive* by eternal service to Him, and *thrive* by His beatific Presence. His servants are those who have 'reached the Harbour',[2] such as Ananta, Vainateya and Vishvaksena.

This 'King of kings, Vishnu-Brahmam, is the Universal Ruler;— He, who is Sambhu and Prajâpati'[3], holds sway not only over the Celestial Regions but 'Material Regions of the Seven Planes',[4] and even on earth deigns to abide amongst men,

"As Ranga who, sway supreme holds,
O'er earths and seas, and 'xpansive skies,
O'er least of worms—His eye-unmissed—
Aye, dwelling right in Rangam bright."[5]*

---

1. *Ayar-v-arum-amarar* &c. (T: Vây Mozhi I. 1. 1.)
2. *Karai-kandór.* (Ibid: VIII. 3. 10.)
3. राजाधिराजस्सर्वेषां विष्णुर्ब्रह्ममयो महान् । ईश्वरं तं विजानीमः सशंभुस्सप्रजापतिः ॥ (Bhárata: Asva.)
4. *Ezhulókam* &c. (T: Vây-Mozhi IV. 5. 1.)
5. *Pong-odam* &c (Nácchiyár: T: Mozhi XI. 3).

* Thus do the Áryan Scriptures depict God and His Kingdom. Compare this with the Christian Apocalypse of St. John, and Bunyan's Pilgrim's Progress. *Human language must fail to describe spiritual things, but some description, be it ever so vague, is craved for by our hearts. And then, when a description is attempted, it must necessarily be after our best experiences,* based on *ideals, modes and other conditions of embodied existence, to which we are bound.* There are persons who object to *material* picturizations of Heaven. But they may be asked to give us *their spiritual* account of the same! They must, when so pressed, either observe silence, or if they dare make use of their

(*Continued*)

This God of our Scriptures is by natural right the Immanent in both the Spiritual and Material Universes. He is not an extra-cosmic autocrat, but an Immanent Infinite centre

---

material tongue and *material* brain, only a description of what *that* brain and *that* tongue can possibly convey,—and can possibly be intelligibly understood by similarly constituted ears and brains,—can they give; then, what else can it be but a *material* description? Only as *we* are *constituted*, we can know God and His things, and no more. We find a most sensible remark on this point by T. Sadâsivier (P. 445. Christian College Magazine, New Series, Vol. I): "A 'Fact' in another world seen in another plane by a higher vision, when it is translated by the Seer into the words of an earthly language to enable others to understand the said 'Fact', looks sometimes very fantastic and unreal".

Also read Annie Besant's *Avatâras* Pp: 62-64. Says Carlyle:—"How paint to the sensual eye, what passes in the Holy-of-Holies of Man's Soul; in what words, known to these profane times, speak even afar off, 'of the unspeakable'?" (*Sartor Resartus*. Ch: IX.). In his *Doctrine of Representations and Correspondences*. Swedenborg *says*:—"One would swear that the physical world was purely symbolical of the spiritual world; insomuch, that if we choose to express any natural truth in physical and definite vocal terms, and to convert these terms only into the corresponding and spiritual terms, we shall by this means elicit a spiritual truth &c' (Emerson's Essays: Swedenborg). Cp: "यदेवेहतदमुत्र यदमुत्रतदन्विह" (*Kath: Up*:)

Also Emerson says:—"The secret of Heaven is kept from age to age. No imprudent, no sociable angel ever dropt an early syllable to answer the longings of saints, the fears of

round which, and dependent on which, the whole circle of Spirit and Matter, revolves. The God of the Upanishads, of the old Âryans, is God both *in* and *out*, Smallest and Greatest, Nearest and very Far, Easy and Difficult, and Angry and Loving (like parents)[1]. "His one Divine Look imports His Paramount Suzerainty over all the kosmos"[2], says Saint Nammàzhvâr. For the idea of Godhood as proclaimed by this Saint, we refer our readers to the work: *The Divine Wisdom of Dràvida Saints.*

---

mortals. We should have listened on our knees to any favorite, who, by stricter obedience had brought his thoughts into parallelism with the celestial currents and could hint to Human ears the scenery and circumstances of the newly parted soul. But it is certain that it must tally with what is best in nature. It must not be inferior in tone to the already known works of the Artist who sculptures the globes of the firmament and writes the moral law. It must be fresher than rainbows, stabler than mountains, agreeing with flowers, with tides, and the rising and setting of autumnal stars." [*Essays : Swedenborg*].

"Whether or not the Divine Comedy be, as the great seer believed or be not, the revelation of a real material heaven, hell and purgatory, it is, at any rate, a tremendous and impressive embodiment in sensible phantasmagoria of inner and ethical order. * * And may not sense-fantasy body them forth hereafter according to their very essence? For truth in the concrete, in the body, is more real and living than truth in the abstract, remaining uninfluencial without manifold expression of life, without a countenance radiant as from a vision of God upon the mountain."—(Noel. *Essay on Spenser*)

1. See Topics 15, 16 & 18 of *The Divine Wisdom of Dràvida Saints.*

2. *Kanda vàtràl* &c (T. Vài. Mozhi IV. 5. 10)

God is in subtlest contact with every atom of His Universe, whether it be Intelligent Soul, or Non-intelligent Stuff; and yet He is unaffected by the contact, but "remains His own Unique Self, essentially characterized by Infinite Wisdom and Love",[1] and at His side has Eternal Angels possessed of eternal and infinite wisdom,—and "Muktas (Saved Souls), who have inherited Divine Estate, after casting off every species of nescience"[2], all bound to Him in loving bonds of Eternal Service; "living, moving and loving in eternal leigeship with Him, enjoying boundless bliss for endless time."[3] And yet His heart lay close to His children entangled in clay; and that heart bleeding far more, it is said, in His pining love, for these children *abroad*, than the love for His children *at home*. His heart bled[4] :— "My Kingdom is everywhere. O children in distant lands, wandering in the wilderness of God-forgetfulness! Realize your kinship with Me, and join the rank of your Elders at home, and assert your claim on your invaluable heritage viz., Myself and My Kingdom. Return Home, O truants! and sit with Me on the Thrones, and share the exquisite delights of Divine Service with your Elders, and swell their ranks in the féte of beatitude."[5]

---

1. स्वेतरसमस्तवस्तुविलक्षण: &c. (*Saranagati-Gadya* by Rámánuja)

2. *Iyakk-elám-anttu* &c. (T : Chanda-viruttam : 120).

3. *Andam-il périnbam* &c. (T : V : Mozhi : X. 9. 11).

4. Cp: Rig Veda X. 129. 1. The *Nâsadiya* Hymn :— 4. "Love overcame it in the beginning, which was the seed springing from mind."

5. अनुभवजनितप्रीतिकारिताशेषा &c. (Rámánuja's *Saraná-gati Gadya.*)

True, He is Bliss itself, but to Him, His Bliss loses all zest and charm when unshared by His children abroad. "He eateth His full, but the food nourisheth Him not, assimilateth not with His body[1]"— says Saint Nammâzhvâr figuratively. This is exegetic of the voice of the Vedânta viz.,:— "*Alone* God never enjoyeth[2]". God says therefore :—"Like birds devoid of wings are these souls[3]", and "Let Me provide them with body and organs[4]", that by using these instruments in the right direction, as pointed out by My own Word, they may accumulate merit, leading them ultimately to the footstool of God Himself, never more to abandon His

1. *Unda-d-uruk-kâttâde* (T. Vâi: Mozhi: VI. 9. 5.)
2. स एकाकी नरमेत (Brih: Up: I. 4. 3.)
3. त्यक्तदेहेन्द्रियो जीवो लूनपक्षइवाण्डजः (Náradiye)
4. अचिदविशेषितान् प्रळयसीमानिसंसरतः । करणकळेबरैर्घटयितुं दयमानमना: || (Srí Ranga-Râja-Stava: II. 41.)

Sri Râmânuja tells us in his Commentary on Bhagavad-Gîtâ III. 10:—"In the past, Prajâpati (Lord of Creation) intently reflected, at the time of creation, on the entities (*chit*) entangled in matter (*a-chit*) from an immemorial past. They were destitute of a name, of a form, and of a distinction (one from the other), and embosomed in Him. They were fit for fulfiling great aims, but were lying latent like inert or unintelligent substances.

Prajâpati, out of infinite mercy, looked on them, and wishing to work out their deliverance, created them (or projected them into manifestation). With them he inaugurated the institution of Yajnas, so that they may worship Him thereby (and fulfil the end for which they were created).

side. God so willed, because, it is said, He was moved by His love for His own Creatures.[1] "Wonderful is the machinery of the body, made up of hands, feet &c., granted by God for dedication to Him by service, in other words, glorification. For this purpose it was given"[2]. Sang Saint Nammâzhvâr:—"My body is for God,—the hands (for example) are for culling rare blossoms to be offered to the Flowery feet of NÂRÂYANA[3]". But this wonderful body was not properly used for such ends, but prostituted to prohibited purposes. It was not *used* but *abused* as when a knife was given by a master to his disciple to cut sacrificial grass, he used the knife for cutting off a cow's tail; or when a pointed pin was given to pick out weeds, the fool poked his own eye with it; or as when a raft was given to cross the river, he allowed it to drift into the ocean.

The body was thus recklessly permitted to tumble into the ocean of Samsâra and wreck there. The prerogative of free-will was thus allowed the fullest latitude.[4] And yet it

1. There are people who ask: "*Why are we created at all?* The answer to this is!—'*A creature has no right to be consulted about his own creation: and for this reason simply that he is a creature*'. (P. 49. Dr. F. W. Faber's Creator and Creature.)

2. विचित्रा देहसंपत्तिरीश्वराय निवेदितुं। पूर्वमेव कृता ब्रह्मन् हस्तपादादिसंयुता ॥ (Vishnu-Tatvam.)

3. *Nâdâda malar nâdi* &c. (T. Vây. Mozhi II. 4. 9.)

4. Read the interesting rencontre between Rishi Udanka and Lord Krishna, forming Topic 77, pp: 89-90 of *our Divine Wisdom of the Dravida Saints*; and it may be further added

(*Continued*)

was necessary to give it proper direction. Certainly lessons were learned by suffering. Lessons are experiences. Experiences are but the latent powers of the soul roused to activity. The best province for this activity lie in Higher and Eternal Spheres: To make this clear to the soul's vision was the ultimate aim of the *Sâstras*. "These gave God, that darkness, enveloping the souls, may be dispelled and good and evil be rightly discriminated (in its ultimate analysis)."[1] "With the Revelations of yore, the High Lord gave me as my guide, I know how to love Him and serve Him,[2]" said Saint Nammâzhvâr. And yet, these Commandments of God were disregarded, neglected and even held up to ridicule, for pride possessed the soul of man, so much so that he began to think of himself as God, saying:—

" ... ... Look!
Am I not God? Make I not goodly cheer?
Is not my fortune famous, brave, and great?
Rich am I, proudly born! what other men
Live like to me? Kill, then, for sacrifice!
Cast largesse, and be merry!"[3]

---

that if according to Udanka. God Himself co-erced or prompted every thought and act of man, there need be no' such thing as a free-willed being at all; and if there be no such creature, it is all God; and then Udanka's question falls to the ground inasmuch as *Pândavas*, whom God is said to esteem, and Kauravas whom He is said to dis-esteem, are all *Himself*, and Udanka, the questioner himself, has thus no existence

1. हंतुं तमस्सदसतीच विवेक्तुमीशो मानंप्रदीपमिव कारुणिकोददाति.
[Srî-Ranga-râja-Stava II. 1]

2. *Kandè Kamala-malar* &c [T: Vây-Mozhi: X. 4. 9]

3. [Bhagavad-Gîtâ:XVI-14ff]. Also read आघ्रायभ्ररगन्धम् &c.
[Srî-Ranga-Râja-stava II. 38]

And thus, "What was God's own—His own soul and body—and which was to be appropriated for His own ends, the soul misappropriated as his own and misused for his selfish ends. What sin can be more heinous than the sin of this arch-thief who makes away with the soul which is God's"?[1]

God's love is so great he would not let his souls escape from Him thus and be dissevered from him for ever. They disobeyed, resisted, grew impure in their hearts, slided down the wrong decline, and were rolling away into dismal depths, but God would yet arrest them in their headlong course. When a King's command is disregarded, he sets his army against the rebel, and proceeds himself in person. So, it is said, doth the Lord think that time is ripe for sacrificing Himself for love; and this thought actualized, is the great fact of Incarnation,—a fact demonstrating the link between Heaven and Earth. This is the mystery and rationale of Incarnations. God takes on flesh. He becomes Râma, becomes Krish*n*a, and becomes countless other forms in every order of His creation, so as to encompass the run-away souls—millions by one embrace,—and rescue them from the wrong way.[2] But even then His love's cup did not fill, the harvest reaped was but little return for His spacious will. For there were apostatic souls who would not recognize yet the God in the flesh, so much so that the Lord Krish*n*a Himself exclaimed :—

---

1. योऽन्यथा सन्तमात्मानमन्यथा प्रतिपद्यते । किं तेन न कृतं पापं चोरेणात्मापहारिणा ॥ (Bhârata : Âdi : 74. 28).

2. Read : भूयोभूय: &c. (Srî-rang : Sta : II. 45.)

"The minds untaught mistake Me, veiled in form;—
Naught see they of My secret Presence, naught
Of My hid Nature, ruling all which lives.
Vain hopes pursuing, vain deeds doing; fed
On vainest knowledge, senselessly they seek
An evil way, the way of brutes and fiends."[1]

The attitude of the renegado to God, and withal, God's unquenchable love towards him are symbolically depicted thus by Sage Bhattârya:—

God: O Soul, thou art *Mine!*

Soul: Nay I am not *Thine*, but *mine!*

God: How is that?

Soul: But, how is that, (what *Thou* sayest)?

God: What I say is proved by the Vedas, which are My Revelations.

Soul: But list; that: '*I am for me*', is proved by my prescriptive right of timeless enjoyment of myself!

God: But there is an objection to your right?

Soul: Show, Sir, who objected and where is it stated?

God: Find it stated in My Works such as the Bhagavad-Gîtâ.

Soul: But it is *Thy* own statement! Are there witnesses thereto?

God: O Yes.—My beloved wisemen—the Saints and Sages!

Soul. Of course, being *Thy* own, they *must* be *Thy* witnesses; and necessarily do side with Thee!

1. (Bhagavad-Gîtâ IX. 11. ff.)

God: O Unbelieving Soul! May I now solemnly *swear* before all: "Thou art *Mine*, not *thine*"?[1]

Though as men and gods and beasts and plants, God took upon Himself births for the salvation of souls, they shied at Him, shirked from Him, rejected Him, resisted Him and flew from Him, as if He were some strange creature moving with and among them; as if He but *seemed* to be like them, whereas he did deeds beyond their ken, and therefore some devil lurking beneath the human-looking wrapper, must have come to delude them[2]. So they thought.

"I am still foreign to them", God thought. "Let me send out My agents and messengers even more perfectly assuming all the phases of human nature, even to the extent of sharing all their defects and weaknesses. May they then not shy from them as they do from Me." So willing, the Lord commanded the various Symbolized Cosmic Truths imbedded in His Divine Person,—The Kaustubha, the Nandaka &c.—to become incarnate. And

1. त्वंमेऽहंमे, कुतस्तत्तदपि कुतः, इदं वेदमूलप्रमाणात्, एतच्चानादिसिद्धादनुभवाविभवात्, तर्हि साक्रोशएव। क्वाक्रोशः कस्य, गीतादिषु मम विदितः, कोत्र साक्षी, सुधीस्स्यात्, हन्त! त्वत्पक्षपाती स, इति नृकलहे मृग्यमध्यस्थवत्त्वं ॥

2. All Saviours generally of the world, were suspected and persecuted by men. Lord Krishna for example was frequently challenged and maligned by such men as *Sisupála*. Jesus was rejected, and unrecognized in his own days. He was persecuted to the extreme of crucifixion, as we know. Read "*Why men do not believe*", by N. J. Laforet.

these were the Âzhvârs and the Âchâryas, or Saints and Sages,—God's own Sons,—emanating from His Fatherhood, designed to appear among men, and effect their salvation in homely ways and diverse modes.

Thus then did these Saviours, Ananta, Garu*d*a, Vishvaksena &c. (*Read* the Lives) appear among men. And as predicted by Maharshi *S*uka to King Parikshit (Bhâgavata XI. 5. 38-40), most of them chose the Drâvida (Tamil) Land and the banks of the Holy Rivers such as the Kâveri, the Tâmbrapar*n*i &c (*Read* the Life of St. Nammàzhvâr) for their nativity. They were born among all grades of men,—high-caste and low-caste,—and by their holy deeds and holy utterances,—the Prabandhas—fulfilled their mission on our globe.[1]

The lives we have now written are based on the following works:—

(1) Divya-sûri-charitam (by Garudavâhana Pandita, contemporary and disciple of Râmânujâchârya)

(2) Prapannâmrita

(3) Guru-paramparâ-prabhâva.

(4) Prabandha-sâra (by Vedântâchârya)

(5) Upadesa-Ratna-mâla (by Ma*n*avâ*l*a-mâ-muniga*l*)

(6) Pazhana*d*ai-vi*l*akkam.

The Prabandhas of the Âzhvârs teach Sublime Spiritual Truths contained in the Three *Rahasyas*, or Mystical

1. These Holy Souls are otherwise stated to be the flower of humanity, evolved out of them, and chosen as God's vessels to do his bidding. This subject is treated in Part II. of Introduction (*infra*).

Treatises called, the (1) Tirumantra, (2) Dvaya, and (3) Charama-Sloka. These three are distributed among the 4000 verses, thus :—

The First Cluster called the *Mudal-Âyiram*, is comprised of the :—

(1) *Tiru-ppallându*, (2) *Peri-âzhvâr Tirumozhi*, (3) *Tirup-pâvai*, (4) *Nâyechiyâr Tirumozhi*, (5) *Perumâl-Tirumozhi*, (6) *Tirucchanda-viruttam*, (7) *Tiru-mâlai*, (8) *Tiru-ppalli-yezhucchi*, (9) *Amalan-âdipirân*, and (10) Kanninun *siru-ttâmbu*, teach the meaning of Tirumantra, of which (1) to (9) teach its first member, the Holy Pranava, AUM and (10) its second member, NAMAH.

The 2nd Cluster comprising the (1) *Periya-Tirumozhi* (2) *Tiru-k-kurun-dândakam* and (3) *Tiru-nedun-dândakam*, teach its third member, NÂRÂYANÂYA.

The 4th Cluster comprizing the *Tiruvây-mozhi* teaches the Holy *DVAYA* Mantra.

The 3rd Cluster called the *Iyarpâ* comprising the (1) Four *Tiruvandâdis*, (2) *Tiruviruttam*, (3) *Tiruvâsiriyam*, (4) *Periya-tiruvandâdi*, (5) *Tiruvezhu-kûtrirukkai*, (6) *Siriya Tirumadal*, and (7) *Periya Tirumadal* teach the Holy *CHARAMA*-*SLOKA*.

From the Âzhvârs, we thus learn that God is not merely Spirit,[1] not merely Light[2], not merely Love[3], but He is *Grace*[4] *pre-eminently*.

After going over the Holy Lives of the Âzhvârs, the westernized or christianized Hindus of our Land of the Rishis will, it is hoped, take to heart the weighty words of Samuel Johnson when he concludes that: "the Hindus

1. (*John* : IV. 24). 2. (*John* I. 5). 3. (*John* IV. 8 & 16)

4. This idea is foreign to the Bible (?)

can satisfy their desire *through their own sacred books*, legends and dogmatic constructions, *without* resorting to the Christian,"[1] will see like him the wisdom of his remarks:—"It has been common to deny boldly that moral and religious truth had any positive *existence* for the human mind before the Christian epoch; to assume that the Sermon on the Mount actually introduced into human nature that very love and trust to whose pre-existing power in the hearts of its hearers it could itself have been but an appeal. *As if ideal principles could have been imported into man by a special teacher, or be traced back to some moment of arrival, like commercial samples or inventions in machinery*!!";[2] and not to be deceived by verdicts hastily pronounced by even such men as Dugald Stewart that: "the Sanskrit language (*and why not Dravidian as well! and all our Prabandhams*!!) was a mere recent invention of the Brahmans, and Sanskrit literature an imposture"!!![3], and mind his saying:—"I venture the prediction that we shall yet learn of the Oriental Nations many lessons in moral simplicity and integrity &c"[4].

Blest be all Saints.

---

1. (*Oriental Religions Vol.* II. p: 101). 2. (*Ibid. Vol.* I. *p*: 9). 3. (*Ibid. Vol.* I. *p*: 11.) 4. (*Ibid. Vol.* I. *p*: 20)

INTRODUCTION.

2. Incarnation and other Holy Mysteries.

The reader will note, as he peruses the Lives, that the Âzhvâr Saints belong to all grades of Society, high and low; and yet social accidents of birth &c., never formed an obstacle to their elevation to Saint-hood by the door of 'Love to God,'—a door, open to all whose only qualification is their heart open to God. A very high compliment is paid to this catholic feature of Brâhmanism—as yet little realized beyond the confines of India,—by S. Johnson :—

"It was a redeeming element of Hindu Caste itself, that it constituted every Saint an incarnation of Brahma for the preservation of the world, in virtue of his fulfilment of the ideal of sainthood. The equal opportunity, even within the limits of a hereditary class, was at least the recognition that fresh access to union with Deity by discipline and faith could never be wholly foreclosed. Nor was any past form of sainthood regarded as in permanent possession either of supreme and final virtue, or of invincible authority. Its throne was held provisionally, and liable to pass to a stronger master in the sphere of "devotion." This democratic element in Brâhmanical holiness has already attracted our interest. Under favouring circumstances, it would have reconciled incarnation with liberty and progress."[1]

---

1. (Oriental Religions. Vol. II. Pp: 81-82.)

The Saints have all been said to be incarnations of Divinity. Not the whole of Divinity, but several parts of His Divine Person—we are told—and Its (Person's) Paraphernalia such as the Divine Weapons, the Discus, the Conch &c.,—and the Divine Ornaments, the Kaustubha &c.,—and the Celestial Hosts, the Eternals (*nityas*), such as Ananta, Garuda, Vishvaksena &c. In writing the Lives of Ázhvârs, we have for each life recorded the Particular Part of the Divinity, from which each Saint is spiritually said to have emanated. If then the Saints were thus descended as the very Sons of God and became incarnate among men for the work of teaching and salvation, how then are the personal events concerning their lives and personal descriptions they give of themselves, as going tc show that they did not differ from the the general character of humanity,—which is frail, imperfect and depraved,—compatible with the account of their pure sinless descent from the Person of God, and as such having nothing in common with sinful mortals? Granting they were empowered with a vocation from God, and had a mission to fulfil on earth, must not their lives be the very perfection of purity? Have they not to satisfy the conditions of the highest ethical standard which we apply to souls of such extraordinary type? If they are patterns of lives whom God wishes us to follow, could they be like ourselves, and then again be different? Before offering solutions to this problem we may premise that we have no *absolute* criterion first of all, *from our side*, with which to fix the ethical and spiritual perfections, which ought to characterize saints, and make them fit for leading men from earth to heaven. Ethical and spiritual standards of men vary with individuals, with society, with nation and with country. Supposing a uniform standard were yet available, we find that events among men and phenomena in nature constantly tend to upset the standard. There are laws beyond our ken yet, by which God seems to work, and the rationale of which is hidden from our limited understanding and denied to our human judgment. And therefore, even in the lives of actual messengers from God,—actual incarnations of His Own Person as they are said to be,—events do compass such as may seem most outrageous to our moral sense of what is right, and yet they may have their own higher meaning in God's wider vision. When He Himself incarnated as Râma, Krishna &c, He chose to hide His Divine Nature from the evil hearts of men, and behaved Himself often in such a manner as to be ranked with but ordinary mortals. For instance, Râma is said to have eaten and laughed, and fasted and cried &c; (and so did Christ). But this would not by itself constitute a disproof of their Divineship. In this connection, sage Vedântâchârya's theodicial work, called *Virodhi-Parihâra* furnishes us with some information, which will help us somewhat in the educidation of this difficult question :—

(1) Srî Râma's saying :—"I am but a mortal", despite others insisting that "He was Nârâyana Himself", seems to imply that each Avatâra was a distinct soul, and not God Himself directly Incarnate. But that this was a mere seeming, and that God purposely put on Himself the conditions of bound souls (as sign of sacrifice) and that he but imitated them in other ways so as to inspire them

with confidence, is evident from such authorities as: "*Tena vanchayate lokàn*", "*mohayitvá jagat sarvam*" &c. These mean that He was perfectly aware of His Divine Nature but concealed it under the mask of Incarnation, and seemed to be one with men, as only thus, by making common cause with them, there was hope of redeeming the lost sheep unto Himself; for without such necessary masquerading, direct intervention with men was fraught with the danger of being rejected[1]. This mysterious characteristic of the Avatáras is called *Lìlà*. *Lìlá*[2] is literally *drama*, or *sport*, but no English equivalent can adequately convey the philosophical import of this (abused) term. It seems almost sacrilege to translate it by such words as *sport*, which has evidently a sense of objectless frivolity; but God's *sport*, in the design of His Universe, has object and is characterized by a sublimity and beauty, enough at the very sound of Lìlà, —heard by us—to arouse in our Âryan breasts sentiments of deep love and devotion. God's *sport* to us is no other than the chemist's serious work in his laboratory, in which he is intensely and lovingly engaged in disengaging souls from their material dross, and recovering them for Himself in

1. Even in our own little experience, we have strangely realized that as soon as some men, even of the most intellectual kind, saw other men differing from them in religious enthusiasm, or emotion of God-love &c, they at once shied their association. Read Râmânuja's reply to Uyyakkondâr [*Mumukshu-ppadi* part III. by Sage Lôkâchârya.]

2. A proper rendering would be "magic" or "mystery" of God, or that *phenomenal show*, the meaning of which is hidden from our mundane understanding.

their pristine purity. The chemicals, the meanwhile, cannot understand the chemist's treatment of them ! [1]

(2) There are two varieties of Avatâras, direct (*sákshát*), and indirect, by posession or inflation of other souls. Both agree in one respect that the Divine is hidden under manhood, but differ in that the one is constant and the other variable; in other words the *direct* is conterminous with the whole duration of the Avatára, whereas the *indirect* is temporary, or just as long as the Divine suppresses the individual element in the possessed souls and departs after having accomplished some one specific purpose. From such authorities as "*Srishtim tatah karishyàmi tvâm àvisya Prajâpate*", "*Anupravisya kurute yat samihitam Achyutah*", "*Àvishta-mátrás te sarve*" &c, it is easy to distinguish which Avatàras are *sákshat* and which *ávesa*.

(3) But the mere fact of *ávesa* does not constitute a ground for deifying it, and consecrating it as worship-worthy. For we are distinctly told by our Authorities that they are to be eschewed as objects fit for worship ; while, on the other hand, worship is enjoined, even to souls worthy otherwise than by a mere temporary divine inflation ; such souls being sages and saints and seers of God.

(4) And where worship is found enjoined in the case of *ávesa* Avatàras, and even Images of God, it means that

---

1. St. Nammâzhvár says that enquiries into the inner details of these High Mysteries are barred, for ends known to Providence Himself. [T-Vây-Mozhi. I. 3-9. *Valattanan.*]

God elects to be specially present in such media—the *soul* in the former case, and *matter* in the latter case.[1]

(5) All souls are essentially pure, intelligent, blissful, and allegiant to Godhood. These characteristics however are more or less not patent to the souls, in their state of bondage. Wrong use of God-given freedom, and disobedience to dictates of God-given law entails this bondage, which is no other than Divine displeasure incurred by such erroneous conduct. When reparation is made by right conduct based on right principles, this displeasure is re-

1. This latter case has reference to the so-called Idolatry. We Hindus, even stronger than the Christians, repudiate meaningless Idolatry. We do not advocate God-*less* idols or souls, but very God-*full*. We invite our readers to the following science of Idolatry as contained in our Scriptures formulated by Párthasárathi Yogi: "What ought not to be worshiped, is of three kinds:—1. *Mere matter or body*: for it is an entity *inferior* to the worshippers, and is only an inert, unintelligent chattel or instrument, placed by providence at the disposal of worshippers, the latter being "*superior*" thereto. 2. *The mere finite soul*: for, no finite soul has any worth of its own, God alone being the Lord by whom are given and preserved the properties that pertain to every entity in the Universe. 3. *The mere 'sum' too, of matter and the finite soul*: for such *sum* is as valueless for purposes of enlightened worship, as the sum of two ciphers is for purposes of arithmetical calculation. It follows, therefore, that just as cyphers have value, only when they are known to follow figures, the three objects—enumerated above—are worshippable, only when it is realised that they are *bodies having God for their Soul*."

[P. 32. *Universal Religion Formulated*.]

moved. Bondage vanishes, and pristine purity and perfection are recovered. Bondage is thus an adventitious circumstance, like the essential whiteness of the Mallika-flower, acquiring temporarily the color of redness in its association with the Kimsuka-flower.

On such considerations, it may be either that Ázhvârs are souls *celestial*, co-ordinate, co-eval and co-substantiate with God, and directly do emanate from His Person &c, into terrestrial regions as Incarnations, and rendering themselves thus homely to men, circumvent and retrieve them from their perverse ways; [2] or they are souls of the terrestrial kind, in bondage, and passing through the

2. On this hypothesis of Ázhvárs being stainless Sons of God incarnated for work of salvation, there is this question yet. If they were sinless, it may be asked, why they do frequently in their writings confess themselves to be great sinners? Most of them led the holiest lives; how then could sin be attributed to them? The answer is that in the depth of their humility, and when they compared their own nature with the nature of God they found that they deserved to condemn themselves to any extent. This abasement is a natural outcome of their humility and marked the disappearance of the pride of self-will. 'Now mine eye seeth Thee and I abhor myself', is a confession of all Godly and God-ward souls. Really righteous souls do not boast they are righteous. Pascal says in his 'Thoughts':—"There are but two classes of men, the righteous who think themselves to be sinners; and the sinners, who think themselves righteous." Even when thoughts of their real righteousness crossed the minds of the saints, they anon dismissed them as blasphemous and dangerous to their salvation. Their righteousness or otherwise was a thing to be weighed in the balance of God, not in their own self-opinionated balance.

stage of the world's drama like any of them; but relieved from it, restored to the original nature, raised to Sainthood, and so as to serve as teachers and patterns for the rest of humanity to follow.

In either case, they are our leaders, but how in the latter case also can they be said to be emanations from the Divine Person? In one way this also has been established. But we would cite an old authority[1] to confirm our second hypothesis that saints and saviours were first like all other men, and evolved out of them specially in this manner:—

"When by the influence of the wicked (*daityas*), virtue wanes, the Perfect incarnates on earth to re-establish it."

"When again, by the effects of time, God-dear virtue wears away, Three are born in the Krita-age, and Three in the Treta".

"And Three in the Dvápara, and Three in Kali; and these emanate from the *Sankha*, *Chakra*, *Gadà*, *Padma*, *Sárnga*, and Senápati (the Lord of Hosts)."

---

1. बलवद्भिर्महादैत्यैर्धर्मो नष्टो यदा भवेत् । तदावतीर्य भगवान् पुनरुद्धरते क्षितौ ॥ ८२ ॥ क्रमात्कालबलान्नष्टे धर्मे च भगवत्प्रिये । कृतेत्रयस्समुद्भूतास्त्रेतायां च त्रयस्तथा ॥ ८३ ॥ द्वापरेपि त्रयो जातास्तथा जाताः कलौ त्रयः । शंखचक्रं गदापद्मं शार्ङ्ग सेनापतिस्तथा ॥ ॥८४॥ शेषो लक्ष्मीर्योगिनश्च सनकाद्या महौजसः । नीचयोनिषु संजाताः द्विजक्षत्रादिलिङ्गिनः ॥८५॥ अयोनिजा महापुण्याः केचिदत्र च वैष्णवाः । व्यक्तीकुर्वन्तिगाथाभिर्द्राविडेषु विशेषतः ॥८६॥ नाथ प्रशिष्यश्शेषस्तु कलौभूत्वा महायशाः । वेदान्तशास्त्रनिर्णेता भविष्यति

"And Sesha, Lakshmí, and the effulgent Sanaka and others, take birth among all grades of society, Brahma, Kshatra &c"

"Some pure souls of Vishnu descend ex-uterine, and in the Dràvida Land mostly, and proclaim (truths) by (Dràvida) Hymns."

"Sesha, as post-disciple of Nâtha (-muni), takes birth in the Kali age to proclaim the real import of the Vedânta Sàstra"

"The wicked Daityas, who were killed in the Tripura, and those on the Saugandhika-occasion, are born on earth; and they upset the Vaishnava System."

"Mâtarisvâ is similarly born, and battering down evil systems, establishes the righteous one. All these show men virtue."

कलौयुगे ॥८७॥ त्रिपुरेषु हता दैत्या ये च सौगन्धिके हताः । विप्लाव यन्ति ते जाताः धरायां वैष्णवं पदम् ॥ ८८ ॥ मातरिश्वा तथा जातो निराकृत्य च दुस्पृहः । स्थापयिष्यति सन्मार्गमेते धर्मप्रवर्तकाः ॥८९॥ भगवत्सन्निधौ पूज्याः महाभागवताश्शुभाः । पूजया च स्वभक्तानां स्थापनं सन्निधौ पुरा ॥ ९० ॥ तदा वरं ददौ तेभ्यः प्रसन्नो गरुडध्वजः । पूजाऽभावे स्वभक्तानां स्वार्चनं निष्फलं भवेत् ॥ ९१ ॥ नित्यसेवार्थिनां पूर्वं तपतां गन्धमादने । प्रबन्धकर्तृता चापि स्वमाहात्म्यप्रबोधिनी ॥९२ दत्ता ततस्सन्निधौ तु हरेः पूज्या (:) न संशयः । तदिदं सर्वमाख्यातं नष्टधर्मप्रवर्तकम् ॥९३॥(Náradiye, *Srí*-mushna Máhátmye. XI.)

"Pure Godly souls are to be worshipped along with God. And this course was established in the past."[1]

"God (Garuda-dhvaja) granted them the privilege, that unless they were worshipped, His own worship would be fruitless."[1]

"Also God put into them the power of composing the Prabandhas,—treating of His Greatness—when on the Gandhamâdana-mount, they were performing *Tapas*, immersed in His service".

"They thus deserve worship along with God (in His Temples)[1]. Hence (O Bharadvâja), I (Angiras) have related all to thee,—how lost virtue was restored (&c)".

The latter case however (viz, the Saviours were first, men, like ourselves) is the more probable on the evidence of their own sayings. This evidence is to be plentifully had in the sayings of *all* the Âzhvârs. Even the purest and absolutely unwordly of them, St. Nammâzhvâr, conspicuously says so of himself. If then, they have been chosen from the world's circle, it is evidence again of the free grace of God having operated on these souls to its fullest limit of fruition. Grace so exercised on bound souls has more value to us,—bound beings,—than if our saints had been of the celestial order, sent down to us for purposes of salvation, by God's command. For grace in that form is a covenant to us; it is an assurance that release from the state of bondage is as natural a product, as Saints have been a natural product

1. Cp: Plato:—"Oh, we will wait for One, be it a God or God-inspired man to teach us our religious duties, and to take away the darkness from our eyes."

from out of our own ranks. Grace is more enhanced in glory by its operation on sinful souls, than its mere sending down on us a few select agents from High from His own Person. That Saviours have come out of the midst of sinful men is a guarantee that every soul, now in fetters, is ultimately bound to arrive at sainthood and reach Godhood. "Even like the torrent of His Grace on us, on ye, one and all, it poureth", is the unanimous declaration of the Saints.[1] How then are these saints recorded as belonging to the one or the other part of the Divine Person?

In one sense (as already shown) every soul is of God, and is a scintillation from Him. The souls of the Saints need not differ from this conception. Their pre-eminence however as Saints and our Saviours dates from the time when the operation on them of God's Grace became complete.[2] This means, in other words, that God enters into them in a *special* manner beyond his general manner of immanence in all beings and enthrones Himself there in all His Infiniteness, Personal as well as Impersonal[3], and satisfying at once the highest metaphysical ambition of the rational will, as well the highest emotional passion of the craving heart; at once the Object of the all-comprehending

1. Read Topic 139 of our "*Divine Wisdom of the Drâvida Saints.*"

2. Read Topic 142 *(Ibid)*

3. 'Full *Personality* is only possible to the *Infinite* Spirit', says Lotze p: 69: "Outlines of the Philosophy of Religion". *Advaitis*! reflect on this.

wisdom (*jñâna*) of the sage, as well the all-enfolding love (*bhakti*) of the saint.

When God has thus entered, the *all* of Him of course has entered. This means that His entry is the entry of the Person as well as all that pertaineth to that Person—in fine, all the splendid appendage constituting the Paraphernalia of that Person. Saints so entered into, when seen by competent witnesses—whose soul-vision also had opened sufficiently to realise such phenomena of the supernatural order—were found by them to be particularly attached to some one or the other of the Personal belongings of God; and the several saints thus came to be regarded as forming one part of the Divinity more than another; and they were accordingly so designated. The pronouncement then of these seers is our Authority for believing in these matters of Divine Mysteries. Either we believe; or if we do not, we shall not hastily reject, till we can satisfactorily find good reasons for disbelief. To deny from mere lackness of knowledge is not only folly but blasphemy.[1]

---

1. Says N. J. Laforet in his "*Why men do not believe*" p: 238:—"We admit doctrines, it is true, which transcend reason and which reason can only half understand, but we accept them on the testimony of an authority whose title cannot be disputed. Besides, in things of the purely natural order, the human mind meets with obscurities,—with unfathomable mysteries; why, then, should it take offence at mysteries of the supernatural order?"

'There are sacred mysteries connected with the True Religion; and those mysteries are to be found in different garbs in all religions worthy of the name, and form the life and soul of all religions. Sacred history deals with *facts* connected with such mysteries. When the *facts* are distorted by forgeries in the sacred writings, when the mysteries connected with the facts are completely forgotten through the moral depravity and the intellectual indolence of ages, the aspect of Religion *in that particular dress* dies, but there were, are, and will always be sacred guardians of the universal Religious Truths, who can never let Religion itself die out among men', says a most sensible writer[1].

---

1. [T. Sadasivier p. 447. Christian College Magazine Vol I. 1902]

INTRODUCTION.

(3) Miracles and Myths.

As to the question of miracles recorded in this work, their possibility or impossibility may demand some consideration. They are possible with *our* Saints, if they are possible with *other* Saints. They are possible with one religion, if they are so with another religion.

Again the possibility of miracles depends upon a knowledge of nature, which however is not yet the common property of all men. The question of impossibility can only arise when miracles, past or present, do not coincide with laws of nature so far known to present-day men. But which sensible man will assign a finality to the inexhaustible resources of nature? Then again discoveries of past ages are forgotten by the present; and to discredit past facts therefore, because they vary from the present known facts, is the height of the little men's conceit. A writer says :—" It would look as if *Time* is mocking at the futile attempts of modern genius in knowing the mysteries of its duration, and a reflective mind is often faced by facts which show, that they are not called into existence for the first time in the history of the world. As nations have grown and fallen, as the tides have ebbed and flowed, as the seasons have appeared and disappeared, as the night and day have alternated, as men were born and dying, as gases expanded and contracted, so also have sciences professed and degenerated. A child born in the night, and which dies before the next dawn approaches, will hardly have any conception of day and its wonderful physical or mental effects. A child born in the day will have no conception or experience of night if it expires before the evening. ... ... If genius (then) should be credited with the discovery of wonders today, it would be silly to deny its capacity to do so millions of years ago. What has struck us to day (*and what has not struck us to day*) had struck billions of people before and therefore the Vedic precept: "what you have to-day is an imitation of what you had millions of years before", sounds reasonable. The conceit of man makes him revel in the idea that he is the specially gifted one by God to revolutionize the world, and that ancients could not have known what he now sees through the fire of his genius, *and that ancients could not know what he cannot now see through his fire of genius.*" Again the possibility or otherwise of miracles depends upon the temper of the person and other conditions such as environment, association, and development. If he is a believer in God, and God as all-knowing and all-powerfull, and if he has the eye of faith, he sees one thing; but if he is a member of the "*God-less* and *devilish* Society" such as America has now-a-days the fashion and notoriety of organizing, the material eye is still more blinded and disabled to see anything at all.*

Why do not miracles, such as those recorded in the past, happen now before our eyes, is a question often asked?

* Life's peace is found by holy men in the desert, but if holiness is lacking, desert is found in lieu of peace.

Why should they? is the answer. Are miracles to take place for every one for the mere asking, whenever and wherever desired? Were such a happening the sole ground for conviction, then miracles must go on for ever, and everywhere, and there would be nothing in the world but miracles; but then they would no more be miracles. Moreover, is one individual's complaint that he has not been personally witness to a miracle, evidence that others have not witnessed them; and that if miracles have failed to come to the notice of a few men, therefore they have no existence whatever in the present times? If miracles must take place for *every* man, then Krishnas and Christs and Buddhas must be every day born, nay every minute, *ad-nauseam!* We must therefore, in addition to the evidence of our own senses, add the evidence of seers and sages and saints[1], and thus expand beyond our own tiny intellectual cells and wait in patience.[2]

Why are miracles and incarnations confined to certain periods, and not continued through all time? We cannot lay *our* conditions on God's operations. He knows when

---

1. Plato said:—"We must lay hold of the best human opinion in order that borne by it as on a raft. we may sail over the dangerous sea of life."

2. "Says F. Nansen in his Farthest North":—"It is ever the safest plan to expect the least of life. for then one often gets the most" [p: 279. Vol I]. And often does he tell us, in this same book of his dismal voyage to the distant icy North, that sore trials and severe tests to which he was put, proved in the end but precious lessons of patience.

it shall be day, and when it shall be night. As was said before, unbroken continuity of miracles or God's direct manifestations would lose all meaning, and fail in the purpose for which they are intended. And besides, manifestations at particular times is the general law of periodicity which obtains elswhere also in God's government of His Universe. As evolutions and involutions alternate, periods of special manifestations and non-manifestations of God also alternate. And this has the moral effect of training up men in faith, charity and expectancy ; and appetizing them for the sublime beauty and bliss in store for yearning souls. Unless the soul is prepared beforehand by a course of spiritual education beginning with proneness and ending with a burning craving for the Divine, it will not and cannot appreciate God. The fruit must be witheld for a long time before its virtue, deliciousness, &c. are longingly felt. Even when Incarnations actually endured, many disbelieved (like they disbelieved Christ)and even to those who believed in It, *Sri* Krishna for example administered the advice :—"Go home, ye Gopis! for, more when so distanced than when near me, ye will keep your minds better engaged with My thoughts"[1]. "I have disappeared from your sight, that you may better remember Me in your thoughts ; for a thing loved is more doted on in its absence, than when present before one's sight".[2] "Like

1. श्रवणाद्दर्शनाद्ध्यानान्मयिभावोऽनुकीर्तनात् । न तथा सन्निकर्षेण प्रतियात ततो गृहान् ॥ (Bhag. X. 23. 34.)

2. यथा दूरचरे प्रेष्ठे मनआविश्य वर्तते । स्त्रीणां च न तथा चेतस्सन्निकृष्टेऽक्षिगोचरे ॥ (Id: X. 47. 35.)

unto the poor man whose mind constantly dwells upon the money he has lost, I become lost to ye that your minds may dwell on Me; not that I am unwilling to respond to your longings."[1] And Pascal says ;— "Thou wouldst not seek Me if thou didst already possess Me."[2]

But, break in the continuity of Divine wonders is but apparent; for to spiritually developed souls, a continued wonder sustains. For like ourselves, the Âzhvârs had periods of dryness and even emptiness, and they loudly complained of the same in their outpourings. Their patience was sorely tried; but they were rewarded and compensated for in the end; and when their higher percipience dawned, they then wondered that they ever suspected the Universe as God-deserted, or as destitute of ever-increasing wonder. They found that in the fifth Hypostatic Manifestation of God—the Archâvatâra,—all-God (*i.e.* God in *all* and God *all-in-all*) was realized, as if a Cosmos had been confined in an atom (*parisamâpya-vritti*). The seed of *all* Divinity was as it were there. It was for the soul to read its contents. This fivefold Hypostaticity of the Deity, was realised by the Âzhvârs, as for example on Pp: 94—95 of the life of Saint Tirumangai Âzhvâr. But they may be briefly stated here:—They are the (1) *Para*—the noumenal Godhood—, (2) the *Vyûha*—the phenomenal Sonhood of that Godhood *in general*—,(3)

---

3. नाहं तु सख्यो भजतोपि जन्तून् भजाम्यमीषामनुवृत्तिवृत्तये । यथाऽधनो लब्धधने विनष्टे तच्चिन्तयान्यन्निभृतो न वेद ॥

(Bhágavata X. 32. 20.)

2. (Selections from Pascal's Thoughts) No: CXXVIII.)

the *Vibhava*—the phenomenal Sonhood *in particular*—,(4) the *Antaryàmin*—the Ever-Indwelling Presence;—and (5) the *Archâ* is the Worshippable Form in which all the other four are realised by adepts.[1] Thus break in Divine manifestations is but apparent, for in the Archâ is preserved as seed for ever all the anterior hypostates of the Lord. St. Tirumangai Âzhvâr for example had a glimpse of this in the early part of his life, for on page 151 it is written:—" Such is the strength of faith. It will even melt *stones*. For Nambi appeared to Nîlar in his real noumenal *self*, hidden so long by the phenomenal *image*." This has been realised by the Âchâryas who came after the Âzhvârs, and realised by many others, as for example by Govinda Svâmi, recorded in the commentary on Periya Tirumozhi of St: Tirumangai Âzhvâr [V,8.5, *mága-má-nilam*]. How is it possible to record *every* occurence on earth for the mere curious delectation of us faithless moderns, and too when a spirit of unbelief prevails even over the few *recorded* events ? The modern inquirer is so much accustomed to paper and pen and witnesses, that he would have every Saint to have these articles ready with him before he dared exhibit his transcedant powers !! Do we take all saints and sages for mere presti-digitarian tricksters, or something better ? And who are those again who have bequeathed to us the biographies of these saints and sages in *written* form ? Can we trust *them* ? But these writers are to us the legators as well of the Highest truths of religion and metaphysics and other allied sciences.

1 The old Asvattha-tree Symbol may be applied to this also. The root of this Tree is in Heaven as *Para*; the seed with us, as *Archâ*. Whereas *this* is transportable, the *other* is fixed as it were.

If we may then trust them for these, we may trust them for those; and this trust extends up to the very Throne of God; but if distrust begins to burrow at the very threshold, it must end in even dethroning God and overturning His Kingdom. There is no resting place between the two extreme poles of God and Satan, say our Elders. As regards contemporary witnesses also, if there were, what is the criterion that *they* spoke truth? They may be charlatans too for what we know. This reminds us of what Apsethus the Lybian did:—"He wanted to become a God. Well, he collected a large number of parrots and put them all into a cage. For there are a great many parrots in Lybia and they mimic the human voice very distinctly. So he kept the birds for some time and taught them to say: "Apsethus is a God." And when, after a long time, the birds were trained and could speak the sentence which he considered would make him be thought to be a God, he opened the cage and left the parrots go in every direction. And the voice of the birds as they flew about went out into all Lybia, and their words reached as far as the Greek settlements. And thus the Lybians, astonished at the voice of the birds, and having no idea of the trick which had been played them by Apsethus, considered him to be a God." [Simon Magus, p. 12.] Fortunate then if our Saints had *no* witnesses. The safest plan then is to believe in traditions[1] long handed down, and which have been implicitly believed in from generation to genera-

1 Count Leo Tolstoy says:—"The shore is God, the course *tradition*, the oars are the free-will given me &c." [P: 52. *How I came to believe.*]

tion. [*Vide* Introd: *Criticisms* &c.]. To the seers then, God is a continuous miracle, and all His past, they tell us, viz., Incarnations and all, is recoverable in His present Temples, viz., the Inner Temple of man (the *Antaryâmin*) and the Outer Temple (the *Arch-âvatâra*), like the Eucharist of Christ, of the Christians, and realizable in this Form as the ever epiphanous God-star. Hence the Âzhvârs, as their Prabandhams tell us, held firmly to this easily accessible means, the Archá.

"The idea that the ancient nations of the world wished to impose on us, that they wished to appear more ancient than they were, more heroic, more marvellous, more enlightened &c., is an absurd fancy. They did not even think of us, and had no word as yet for posterity.........We must not allow such ideas of fraud and forgery to spoil our faith and our interest in ancient history. The ancients thought much more of themselves than of the nations of the distant future. If, however, what the ancients tell us about their own times, or about the past........., seems incredible to us, we should always try first of all to understand it as *possible*, before we reject it as *impossible* and as an intentional fraud."[1] "While we, overwhelmed with newspapers, with parliamentary reports, with daily discoveries and discussions, with new novels and time-killing social functions[2],

1. Max Muller's Six Systems of Philosophy P: 9-10

2. Read Manu VII. 47 :—मृगयाऽक्षा दिवास्वप्नः परिवादः स्त्रियो मदः ! तौर्यत्रिकं, वृथाटया च, कामजो दशको गणः || = Hunting, games, day-sleeping, gossiping, women, intoxicants, music and dancing, and lazy loitering about, are the ten-fold set of lusting vices.

have hardly any leisure left to dwell on metaphysical and religious (&c.,) problems, the old inhabitants of India...... , at a time when people could not yet think of public applause or private gain, (they) thought all the more of (such) (truths); and hence the perfectly independent and honest character of most of their *writings*."[1]

Rámáyana is full of miracles for example; but they must be explained away as allegories, say our all-wise Indo-Áryan mythologists, whom, unfortunately, the evil spirit of unwillingness to believe *anything* has possessed. But, "how could an epic so dear in India to the memory of the people, so deeply rooted for many centuries in the minds of all, so propagated and diffused through all the dialects and languages of those regions, which had become the source of many dramas, which are still represented in India..........., a poem welcomed at its very birth with such favour, as the legend relates, that the recitation of it, by the first wandering Rhapsodists (Kusi-Lavau) has consecrated and made famous all the places, celebrated by them, and where Ráma made a shorter or longer stay, how, I ask, could such an epic have been purely allegorical? How upon a pure invention upon a simple allegory, could a poem have been composed of about fifty thousand verses, relating with such force and power the events, and giving details with such exactness! On a theme purely allegorical there may easily be composed a short mythical poem, as for example a poem on Proserpine or Psyche: but never an epic so full of traditions and historical memories, so intimately connected with the life of the people, as the Rámáyana.

1, Max Muller's Six Systems cited above (P: VIII)

Excessive readiness to find allegory whenever some traces of symbolism occur, where the myth partly veils the historical reality, may lead and often has led to error......... We have all heard of the ingenious idea of the anonymous writer, who in order to prove how easily we may pass beyond the truth in our wish to seek and find allegory everywhere, undertook with keen subtlety to prove that the great personality of Napolean I., was altogether allegorical and represented the Sun. Napolean was born in an island, his course was from west to east, his twelve marshals were the twelve signs of the zodiac, etc."[1] The Brahmavâdin (P: 299. Vol. VII. 1902) records of a certain scientific friend of theirs having told them that Arjuna, in the Gîtâ represented *Hydrogen*, and Sri Krishna *Oxygen*, and both together water!! It is time now for our very fast-going Indo-Aryan mythologists to begin the converse process of euhemerism.

The reason why nobody has ever answered, or, probably ever will answer, is that each stage of existence can only be apprehended and defined by the powers appertaining to it. Herein lurks the fallacy which has bred such contempt for transcendental speculations (*and things*), because people try to think of what abides beyond (*and what abides in others' experiences*) in terms of their (own and) present experiences."[2]

Present experiences,—science and otherwise—are not all, nor are they final. For we read already of preconceived opinions upset.[3] For example :—

1. R. T. H. Griffith in his notes on Râmâyana. Pp: 562-563.
2. Read Edwin Arnold's Death and Afterwards. P: 24.
3. Vide Astrological Magazine. Vol. VI. pp: 100 ff.

1. Recently special contrivances have been made for weighing thoughts of men. Mind therefore will be weighed and becomes certainly so much of fine matter. When the old Rishis said that mind and passions are objects which could be seen with more developed senses, the European *scientists* laughed outright and paraded their gross ignorance.

2. Lord Kelvin, England's greatest scientist today, has now been able to differentiate between matter of *two* kinds, viz., one that is visible and is subjected to the laws of gravitation and another invisible and which is beyond the sphere of terrestrial gravitation. Westernized India will probably laugh if in an ancient book of India,—the Tattva-traya,—a matter of the kind of Suddha-Satva be found to be dealt with!

3. The atom which was considered by the poor old scientists as indivisible, has now been proved by scientific experiments as a compound having 1000 separate bodies all held together by magnetic or electric currents!

4. M. Flammarion, one of the greatest names in European Astronomy today says that the study of Astronomy gives longevity. He contends that contemplation on sublime and elevated objects always leads to the purification of nervous and blood vessels, and the person, if sincere, will get a long life. If God-contemplation then, made such Saints as Tiru-Mazhisai Âzhvar to live for a very long time, why should we pigmies gape?

Rishis and Saints and Sages then are not such great knaves and fools as the half-educated and English-educated Hindu, or the incredulous foreigner will take them for. The safer position for him is to study them originally in *their* language, literature, religion and philosophy thoroughly well, before he may impetuously venture on a scheme of cold, narrow, and loveless criticism.

'Certain critics of this age, as they style themselves, are displeased with all histories of miracles, not considering that these wonders are, in a particular manner, the works of God, intended to raise our attention (*whenever He thinketh proper*)[1] to His holy providence, and to awake our souls to praise His goodness and power; often also to bear testimony to His truth. Entirely to omit the mention of them would be an infidelity in history, and would tend in some measure to obstruct the great and holy purposes for which they were effected.'[2]

Let all Holy Works then be read with feelings of deference and veneration, thus throwing the soul into the right disposition of receptivity. But if its attitude be one of wanton rejection and stubborn hostility, it is simply profane even to touch these works. Read with faith, even a lie may turn to truth.[3]

Let the soul then approach the fountain of divinity in purity of heart and charity of will; and drink deep the spiritual waters of knowledge; and after fully drinking there,—possessed with holy patience—contain the same, assimilate, multiply, and so that the nectareous fluid may overpour to other thirsty souls, as Manu (VII. 99) says:—

"अलब्धं चैव लिप्सेत, लब्धं रक्षेत् प्रयत्नतः ।
रक्षितं वर्धयेच्चैव, वृद्धं पात्रेषु निक्षिपेत्" ॥

1. Cp: Bhagavadgîtâ: IV. 7. ff.
2. Lives of Saints by A. Butler Vol. II. p. 24.
3. Read *Tiru-vôy-mozhi* V. I. 1.

The adverse attitude is none other than the 'indiscreet effrontery of individualism' and is, what Amiel describes as:—"The modern state founded on the philosophy of atomism. Nationality, public spirit, tradition, national manners, disappear like so many hollow and worn-out entities; nothing remains to create movement but the action of molecular force and of dead weight. In such a theory, liberty is identified with caprice, and the collective reason and age-long tradition of an old society are nothing more than soap-bubbles which the smallest urchin may shiver with a snap of the fingers!"

The conception of God as immanent, as Indian saints and sages have always voiced forth—contrasted with the Western conception that He is extra-cosmic and therefore transcendent only,—has an intimate bearing on the subject of miracles. We will let Amiel speak:—"The supernatural is miracle, and miracle is an objective phenomenon independent of all preceding causality. Now, miracle thus understood cannot be proved experimentally, and besides, the subjective phenomena, far more important than all the rest, are left out of account in the definition. Men will not see that miracle is a perception of the soul, a vision of the divine behind nature; a psychical crisis, analagous to that of Æneas on the last day of Troy, which reveals to us the heavenly powers prompting and directing human action. For the indifferent there are no miracles. It is only the religious souls who are capable of recognising the figure of God in certain given facts."

INTRODUCTION.

(5) Symbolism.

THE whole visible world is a Symbol.[1] Religion which has the function of perpetuating spiritual truths, cannot do so without resorting to symbols. Our book contains sym-

1. In an article on Dante's Symbolism by Miss Cust (Theosophical Review, p : 316 ff. Vol. xxx), we find it written thus :—

"If it be possible that truth embodied is more living than truth in the abstract, then symbols must play an important part in the history of mankind. Carlyle tells us that through symbols men consciously or unconsciously, live, work, and have their being; those ages being counted the noblest which can best recognise symbolical worth and prize it the highest. The sacraments of a religion, which are an "outward visible sign of an inward spiritual grace," or the emblems of some national or individual feeling, are all symbols, and have therefore a double existence, for they belong to the world of fantasy as well as the world of fact, and show what really exists but is intangible to the senses.

"When a visible object represents an idea or feeling shared by a large body of people, it often attains an immense importance, and men will risk their lives for the square of canvas that stands for the honour of their country. Symbols seem to be almost a necessary part of the machinery of religions; each sect possesses its own, easily read by the initiated if unintelligible to the outsider, and rituals survive long after all comprehension of the original purpose of expressing some doctrine has ceased *to exist.* *Another* kind of symbols are the signs used by me *associated together* for definite objects, sometimes preser

bols such as Ranganâtha, Vatasâyin, Chakra (discus), *San*kha (conch) &c.; and it may be useful to add a few notes to let the reader have some idea of what such emblems signify.

1. *Ranga-nâtha or Ananta-Sâyi* (vide St. Tondaradippodi Âzhvâr's life for example):—"Apart from these mythical and more or less historical forms in which Vishnu is represented, there is one other form of great importance and beauty in conception, in which the Vaishnavas worship their one only God of the Universe. The Image referred to is the one that is worshipped in the *S*rirangam Temple, which is the most important Vishnu Temple in South India; the Image of Sri Padmanâbha in Trevandram also is of the same kind. Here we have a sleeping God in human form resting on the well-arranged folds of the long body of a many-headed serpent; and the creating forces of the universe are represented to proceed from the navel of the sleeping God in the form of the four-faced Brahmâ. In the mythologies of the nations of the earth, the serpent has played many parts. As already pointed out, it seems to have had an early phallic significance in India as elsewhere; in the Vedic Myths it is representative of darkness, the enemy of Indra and the other gods; and in the comparatively later Indian cosmogonic myths under the name of *Sésha*, the ever-remaining, and *Ananta*, the endless, it represents Eternal Time. The conception of *Ranganâtha* as the Lord of the Universal Stage, resting on Eternal Time, allowing the cosmic processes of evolution and dissolution

---

with great secrecy, more frequently open to whoever cares to decipher them; as, for instance, figures in mathematics, or badges and coats of arms of families and trades."

to go on freely, and sleeping the sleep which is, in the language of one of our poets, ever wakeful in the cause of the protection of the whole world, or, in other words ever wakeful in watching the progress of the moral law, [1] is indeed a very grand and noble conception of the divine; and it is this conception that is undoubtedly embodied in the Image which is even now the object of worship to many earnest and pious souls. The conception of Sri *Padmanâbha* on the *Ananta-Sayana* is identical with that of Sri *Ranganâtha* on the *Sésha-Sayana*."

(P. 27-28. Function of Religion by M. Rangâchârya M. A.)

2. *Ananta-Sáyí-Nárâyana* (proclaimed by all the Saints; *vide* their Lives) or Lord of Hosts of the Old Testament, *i. e.*, *Leaner on the Infinite*-=the *Infinite Hosts of Naras* according to the *Bahuvrîhi*- [or condecession (*saulabhya*)] denoting etymology of the word. Compare (1) अर्जुनः केशवस्यात्मा, [2] कृष्णश्चात्मा किरीटिनः, as if the *former* deserves *precedence* of *latter* proposition in Krishna's view, so as to lead Him to make Himself Charioteer (*sârathi*) and make Pârtha (or Arjuna) the Rider (*rathi*). The type of all the infinity of saints whereon the Lord thus condescends to lean is *Sésha*, who is hence distinguished as *Âdi-Sesha*, as being उपमानमशेषाणां साधूनां, where साधु (sâdhu) means शेषत्वशाली (or leaner on

---

1. This conception so well fits in with the latest definition of Religion by Kant, viz., "*the representation to ourselves of the moral law as the will of God.*"

2. Or मम प्राणा हि पाण्डवाः.

God. (Pârthasârathi Yogi's Epistle, dated 30th Aug : 1900 Lucknow.)

3. *Vata-patra-sâyi or Vata-sâyî*, (*vide* lives of Peri-y-Ázhvâr) = अघटनघटनां कर्ता (= Miracle-Woker or Wonder-Worker), = अणोरणीयान् महतो महीयान् = Though greater than the greatest = *Infinite*, yet परिसमाप्यवर्नी in each *finite* thing.[1] Cp : Tâtparya-Chandrika (of Vedántâchârya), page 3, line 10 (from Bottom) (Telugu Edition), अघटितंच घटयति, as possessed of Sakti (Power or Omnipotence) or the 5th of the six Primary Gu*n*as (Qualities). Cp : the Mudal-Tiru-v-Andádi, V : 69. (by St : Poygai-Ázhvâr). (*Ibid.*)

2 and 3 : " Brahm with his foot in his mouth (*Vata-sâyi*), and Vish*n*u on his coiled serpent (*Ananta-Sâyi*), or with his necklace of worlds (*vana-mâlâ*) are but mythic sports with the ideal circle, that sacred line which returns into itself ; the natural symbol of the One."

(P. 310 ; Vol. I ; S. Johnson's Oriental Religions.)

---

1. " Cp : The principle of all things entrails made
Of smallest entrails ; bone of smallest bone ;
Blood, of small sanguine drops reduced to one :
Gold, of small grains ; earth of small sands contracted ;
Small drops to water, sparks to fire contracted."
(*Lucretius*)

And which Malphigi had summed in his maxim that "*nature exists entire in leasts.*" This is a favourite thought of Swedenborg.' (Emerson's Essays).

Read St. Namm-âzhvâr's Periya Tiru-v-Andâdi, V. 75 :—*Puriyum &c.*

4. (*a*) *Sri* (*b*) *Bhû* (*c*) *Nîlâ* (vide life of St. *Ândâl*) :—The functions of (these bride-like souls to God) have been thus explained by Vedântâchârya in his Work the(*Dayâ-sataka*):—

(*a*) समस्तजननीं वन्दे चैतन्यस्तन्यदायिनीम् । श्रेयसीं श्रीनिवासस्य करुणामिव रूपिणीम् ॥

(*b*) वन्दे वृषगिरीशस्य महिषीं विश्वधारिणीम् । तत्कृपाप्रतिघातानां क्षमया वारणं यया ॥

(*c*) निशामयतु मां नीळा यद्भोगपटलैर्ध्रुवम् । भावितं श्रीनिवासस्य भक्तदोषेष्वदर्शनम् ॥

(*a*) O Bliss ! Thou e'er rank'st next to God alone
Mother of all alike, sav'st all that groan.'

(*b*) ' O Earth ! Thy very name explains ;
Save specially earth's souls-in-chains.'

(*c*) 'Nîlâ erst as Nappinnai, 'mong us staid,
And Refugees' Kebla, Brindâ-van made.
Goddess in colour Krishna-like Thou wert :
In saving, even more than He, alert.' (Ibid).

5 (See No 55 in the Table of the 108 Divya Desas,—
i. e., Tiru-ppâl-kadal = Kshîrâbdhi = Milky Ocean.)

"*Vide* the commentary of Mallinâtha on the following verse of the Raghuvamsa :—"ते च प्रापुरुदन्वन्तं &c." and Râdhâkânta's Sabda-kalpa-druma, title *Kshîrâbdhi*.

Vide also His Holiness Embâr Svâmi's Preface to the Tattva-traya. We may for the present, identify it as the white Arctic Ocean which surrounds the Earth's North

Pole (Méru) the abode of the Gods who heard the Purâ*n*as there (*Méru-prishthe Maharshayah*).

You may also include the Milky Way (Svâtì-Paddhati) which runs South to North in the direction of the Celestial Pole.

The bands of pure souls waiting on God are called an *Ocean* because of the vastness of their number; and they are called *milk*, because, just as the mother's milk, uniting as it does (1) food (*dhâraka*), (2) drink (*pôshaka*) and (3) condiments or dainties or (*bhôgya*), all in one, is at once the *perfect* and *indispensible* sustenance of the suckling, so likewise, it is the happy privilege of these pure souls to be hungered and thirsted after by the Universal Father as if they were His all, -and this characteristic too of the Universal Father, has been taught us by the Holy name Nârâya*n*a, when taken as Bahuvrîhi Compound, and analyzed as "Nârâh ayanam yasya, Sah."

The waves and spray of this Ocean of Milk are the souls who, from among the general crowd, successively march in companies towards, and are embraced by, God.

Ocean-churning may be esoterically explained as the finding out of the best of each kind of created thing." (Ibid)

6. *Pundarîkâksha*, or the Lotus-Eyed Vishnu. Indicative of (1) attractive beauty and (2) consoling mercy.

(Mukunda-Málá, P. 3, by the said Yogi).

7. *Chakra* (the Wheel or Discus):—Causing *eye*-witnessed movements of bodies, or the *practices* of souls as moral beings.

8. *Saukha* (the Conch):—Causing the *ear*-witnessed "music of the spheres."

7 and 8. Thus, our Lord's Discus and Conch show

Him to be the Lord of two Angels who superintend all we observe in the universe, viz., *matter* (more or less sonorous) in *motion*. Matter and Motion, are, for mathematical purposes, called space and time, which mutually serve to measure each other; for as A. Humboldt well observes: "we measure space by time, and time by space." (Ibid).

For other symbological explanations of Divine Person, Avatâras, Weapons, and Ornaments, consult Vishnu Purâna, Hari-vamsa, and Vishnu-Dharma.

9. *How is God realised by Saints by means of Symbols?*

(*A*). 'Be content with thinking that, to the Yogin who has closed all his outward organs and intensely and lovingly fixt his attention on *remembering* the Múrthi (*i. e.*, any Image dear to the devotee's feelings), which his outward organs have been in contact with, God will appear *somehow within* the devotee's body—where alone the devotee's attention is developed for the time being. Your wretched *Yoga* is not our Gita's *Bhakti-Yoga*. It (the former) is the Yoga which is dealt with by the texts: "*Etena yogah pratyuktah*" (Brahma-Sútra II. 1. 3), for I think according to the Hiranya-garbhas and Pâtânjalas, *Pâshânakalpatva*, (or the being reduced to a stone-like state) is moksha.' Also read द्रुहिणहरगिरस्सोरमं-नारमन्ते ॥ (Sankalpa-Súryodaya II. 89.)

(*B*). In our System, there is but one Dharma (attribute or predicate) of the soul named Jnâna or Consciousness which when *Anukúla* (blissful), is called *Ânanda*. It is neither *two* nor *three* nor *four* (*i.e.* kinds). It has contraction (*sankocha*) or expansion (*vikâsa*) according to the opportunities allowed for its expansion in the four states of bound souls, known as *jâgrath* (waking), *svapna* (dream), *sushupti* (sleep), plus the *turiya* (the ultimate) called *moksha* (liberation). Yogi-pratyaksha (saints' vision) is but the maximum expansion that consciousness is capable of, in the bound state of the *Jîva* (soul). Read Herbert Spencer's Psychology and learn there at least that memory and perception (pratyaksha) are distinguished not in *kind* but solely in *degree* of intensity in the impression.'

(*C*). 'By "spirit," we mean âtmâ (= *âpnôtiti*) or that which pervades bodies. *All* experience or knowledge is spiritual, *i. e.*, is a dharma (virtue) of the soul or spirit or âtmâ. *All* knowledge of an entity *other than myself*, whether such entity be viewed as an embodied *chetana* (conscious soul) or *achetana* (non-conscious stuff), must be derived by means of *organs* and is not intuitive. Lock's aphorism: "There is *nothing* in the mind (*i. e.*, in consciousness) which has not been in the sense, is supplemented by Leibnitz's addition: "except the mind itself, *i. e.*, one's own self (ego or *âtmâ*) and his consciousness (the predicative jnâna). The drift of this is, that when God is realised by a yogî, it is a spiritual experience of the realiser.' (Ibid).

10. *Tulasî* or Sacred Basil:—The following excerpt is taken from the *Capital* (1902):—"The *Tulasi* or Basil plant is a striking illustration of this fact. It is held in the highest veneration by Hindus all over the country and several species of it are recognised. The most common variety, *Quinum Sanctum*, is worshipped in Hindu households. It is not merely as a sacred emblem that the plant has its uses, for medicinally it is much in demand as an expectorant and diaphoretic; while, mixed with lime-juice, it is prescribed for ringworm and other cutaneous affections. The fragrant variety, botanically *ocimum bacilicum*, is valued even more for

its medicinal properties. The juice of the leaves is used for ringworm as well as earache. The bruised leaves are prescribed in cases of scorpion-stings. The seeds are a favourite medicine with Hindu women to relieve the pains attending childbirth. The plant is also commonly used for seasoning curries, and an infusion of the leaves after they have been dried in the shade, is an occasional substitute for tea. Another variety, botanically *ocimum gratissimum*, is also esteemed for its medicinal properties, while the leaves are made into *chutney*. The juice of the leaves of nearly all the varieties is given in various ailments of children. The dried leaves are pulverised and taken as a snuff in certain nasal complaints. The juice of the fresh leaves of one variety, I am not certain which, is administered internally as an antidote to snake-poison." To this we may add that, as a fragrant plant, it is fragrant from root to seed, being thus symbolical of eternal beatitude.* Its leaves are said to be an antidote for fever and a killer of animal desires, and is therefore prescribed for daily use by ascetics. A dead body thrown in a *Tulasi* garden is said to have been preserved from putrefaction for an unusually long time.

11. *Vaikuntha*:—Means "unimpeded", or where God is enjoyed without the impediments (or limitations) of space, time, or conditions. (Pàrthasârathi Yôgi).

12. *Parama-pada*:—That sphere than which there is no higher. (Ibid).

13. *Sênêsa*:—The Commander-in-Chief of the Lord's Hosts. The Director of Archangels. (Ibid).

14. *Garuda*:—Compare the Kerub or Cherub of the Old Testament. (Ibid).

15. *Vâsudeva, Sankarshana, Pradyumna and Aniruddha*:—
Read:—"आमोदे भुवने प्रमोद उत संमोदे च संकर्षणः प्रद्युम्नश्च तथानिरुद्ध इतितान् सृष्टिस्थितीचाप्ययौ। कुर्वाणान्मातिमुख्यषड्गुणवरैर्जुष्टांस्त्रियुग्मात्मकै र्व्यूहाधिष्ठित वासुदेवमपि तं क्षीराब्धिनाथं भजे"; ॥ and Tattva-traya, Part III. (Ibid).

16. *Das-âvatâras* (=the Ten Avatâras of Vishnu).

'The late Theosophist T. Subba Rau used to say that Matsya (fish) &c. correspond to the life-evolution system of evolutionists. But we care not to prove such correspondences. It is enough for us to know that it pleases God to manifest His power to Bhaktas in *all* the four forms under which bound souls are embodied, namely:—
(1) *Deva*, (2) *Manushya*, (3) *Tiryak*, and (4) *Sthâvara*.

Read:—वेदान्वेषण-मन्दराद्रिभरण-क्ष्मोद्धारण-स्वाश्रितप्रह्लादावन-भूमिभिक्षण-जगद्विक्रान्तयो, यत्क्रियाः। दुष्टक्षत्रनिबर्हणं, दशमुखाद्युन्मूलनं, कर्षणं कालिन्द्याः(:), अतिपापकंसनिधनं, यत्क्रीडितं, तं नुमः॥ (Varadarája's Paratv-âdi Pañchaka, V: 3) [Ibid].

INTRODUCTION.

(6) The Age of the Âzhvârs and Criticisms.

1. *The Three First Âzhvârs.*

Mr. S. A. Tirumalai-kkolundu Pillai, in his "Short Sketch of Tamil Literature" (P.162. Vol. IV. Siddhânta Dîpikâ) says:—

" *Poigaiyâr*, the poet who eulogized the military glory of Kocchengannanâr, was, in all probability, identical with one of the twelve Vaishnava Saints, though they claim for their sage a stupendous antiquity which breaks down by the internal evidence in his writings. He is considered by them to have been born in the Treta-Yugam, but he very often alludes to the feats of *Sri* Krishna who lived about the beginning of the Kali-Yugam." As to this we say:—

(1) T. K. Pillay's Poygaiyâr may as well *not in all probability*, be identical with our Vaishnava Poigai-Âzhvâr. His assumption is gratuitous.

(2) Internal evidence on linguistic grounds is at best hypothetical.

(3) We never say our Âzhvâr was born in *Treta*; but *near the end of Dvàpara, i.e.*, 4202 B. C. (Vide Hierarchic Table.)

(4) *Sri* Krishna lived at the *end* of Dvápara, not in the *beginning* of Kali.

(5) Thus there is no anachronism in the First Âzhvârs alluding to *Sri*-Krishna.

(6) Nor are we desirous of exaggerating life-terms of our great men, for we say Krishna lived only *100* years; and St. Nammâzhvâr only *32* years.

(7) Even if the Âzhvârs had been born long before *Sri-Krishna*, there is nothing inconsistent in Yogis like these living till He was born, and even after, and even now. (See Life of Tiru-mazhisai Âzhvâr where these Three pay him a visit, and go on their world-travels). Why deny longevity to the Vaishnava Saints, while T. K. Pillay's Tirumûlar could sit "in contemplation for the *enormous period* of 3000 *years*!" (Vide P: 87. Col. 2. T. K. Pillay's aforesaid sketch: Vol: IV. Siddhânta Dípiká).

2. *Periy-Âzhvâr.*

Mr. M. Seshagiri *Sâ*striar M. A. in his "Essay on Tamil Literature" Page 49, Part 1, speculates on the probable age of Vishnuchittar=(Periy-Âzhvâr), from the fact of Vallabhadeva mentioned by him; but he concludes by saying: "Though we cannot ascertain who this Vallabhadeva was, nor settle his date, *we may rest assured that Vishnu-chitta could not have been born so early as* 3056 *B. C.*!!!" The portion italicised by us shows that Mr. *Sâ*stri does *not like to believe* in this antiquity though he finds he cannot advance reasons for his disbelief! The best answer to the Professor is that by Mr. S. A. Tirumalai Koḷundu Pillai B. A.:—"The Essay on Tamil Litrature by Mr. Seshagiri Sastriyar M. A., of the Presidency College, has irritated the Tamil world to a degree, especially his many hasty and unfounded conclusions in connection with the Ancient Tamil Academy at Madura. The most flagrant of these have been reviewed and rebutted in the body of this work, and I regret my oversight in it of the Professor's view exploding the high antiquity of the Ancient Tamil Classics."

(Pp. i.-ii. *The Age of Mânikya-Vâchakar.*)

Besides, what value could be attached to a speculator like the Anti-Vaishnavite *Sâ*striar, when he dares to make Vishnu-Chittar (Periy-Âzhvâr) to live *after* Râmânujâchârya? Why! he could as well have made *all the Âzhvârs* to have come after Râmânuja in spite of the mass of evidence the Vaishnavas possess to the contrary!! And yet this Professor takes the Hâlâsya-Mâhâtmya for his gospel!!! And then consider the *Saiva*-Legend as reported by Col: H. S. Olcott in the Theosophist for Sept. 1902, p: 706, as follows:—"On the following day we were taken to the Mínákshi Temple and were shown its wonders by the Chief Priest himself. I took the pains to point out to Mrs. Besant that panel in the wall-paintings around the inner tank which depicts the savage cruelties inflicted on the wretched Jain *Digambaras*, who refused to be converted to Hinduism in the time of Kúna or Kubja Pándya, King of Madura *twenty one centuries before Christ.*" Mark the words italicised. And if our Vaishnava-traditions connect Periyàzhvàr with a Kùna Pândya, then the age which we attribute to this Saint is easily believed.

3. *St.* Ândàl.

Professor M. Seshagiri *S*àstri M. A. in his "Essay on Tamil Literature Number I. p: 45" says: "Any one that compares the Nâlâyira-prabandham in point of style and language with the poems included in the Pattuppàttu &c., cannot be struck with the *moderuness of the language and style of the religious hymns of the Vaishnavas in general.*" Apart from the tenability or otherwise of this philosophical (?) criterion (for we believe that a child 10,000 years ago may have lisped exactly in the same style as the Professor's own *modern* child ! '), we call the attention of scholars to such rare antique words as *Ukkam* and *Tattoli* &c. used by St. *Ándál* in her Tiru-ppâvai, Verse 20. Any impartial Tamil scholar may read the Tiruppâvai of *Ándál* and Tiruvempâvai of Mánikka-Váchakar, and he will find that the former is very much anterior, and the latter is modelled after it. (Vide p : 71 Siddhânta Dípiká Vol. I.)

(3) *St. Tirumazhisai-Âzhvàr.*

Mr. Tirumalai Kolundu Pillay writes thus: (P: 163 Vol. IV. Siddhânta Dípiká) :—" Tirumazhisai Àzhvàr, who is considered to be a *Yógi*, seems to have been a contemporary of ' The First Ázhvárs'. The Vaishnavas in delineating his career have made him a man of unbounded egotism ; he is also the most ungracious of the saints. His verses without evincing any high form of divine love show the utmost hatred to *Siva*. In his eyes *Siva* was a stumbling block to Nàráyana's glory and so He is not only lowered below Nâráyana but considered to be a creation of Brahmá."

We reply :—As to the charges of egotism, it is admissible in those who highly feel for their spiritual truths. The *Saiva* Saints are not wanting in this sentiment.[2] As for ' ungraciousness ', instances can be pointed out where *Saiva* St. Mánikya-Vàchakar is more so. To impeach divine love as of a low form, simply because of its ' hatred ' to *Siva*, is unreasonable. As for ' hatred ' to *Siva*, it is not hatred, but the

1. Read any work on the Science of Language.

2. Sundaram *Pillai* M. A. (In " His Milestones,". p : 8) tells us that even after his (Sambandha's) glorious victory over them (Jains and Buddhists) at Madura. the *habit of cursing them* is continued."

unanimous voice of all the Vedas, Vedántas, Smritis, Puràṇas, and Etymological Science[1] which emphatically proclaim that Nârâyaṇa is the Highest Lord. Even if the charge of 'hatred' is maintainable, we would point the readers to only two,out of numerous passages, where Śaiva St. Mànikya-Váchakar's bitterness to Vishṇu is even more pronounced :—

For instance, read the treatment given to Vishṇu by this Śaiva Saint (Tiru-vàchakam, by Dr. Pope Pp : lxii-lxiii),—which even Dr. G. U. Pope characterises as : "*the wild story*", and "*far from edifying.*" It would appear that Śiva drove Vishṇu and Brahmâ :—

"* * * * As the rush of a mighty whirl-wind
The Beauteous One drove them far in whirling course."
(*P. 19, Pope's Tiruvâchakam.*)

And though Vishṇu, becoming Boar, 'dug down through sevenfold regions', "Thy (Śivan's) pair of feet-flowers saw *He not*" !!! (P. 30-31. Ibid). Can bigotry be more rampant ?

As for the longevity of Tirumazhisai-Âzhvâr, it need not be questioned, firstly, because it is a matter which concerns

1. The terms Śiva and Nâràyaṇa belong to the Vedas ; Śiva etymologically expresses but a small aspect of the complete God-head. It simply means '*auspicious*'. Dr. G. U. Pope adds his testimony thus to this fact, for (in his Tiruváchakam : p. lxiv.) he says :—" The original idea of Śivan is found in the Vedas, but the name is simply a euphemism meaning 'propitious' or 'gracious'." This fact is pointed out by the Vedic passage "*Śivas-cha-Nârâyaṇah.*" Whereas, Nârâyaṇa, as all authorities and grammarians agree, gives a *perfect* idea of the God-head. (vide Rahasya-Traya and other works.)

Yogis or developed souls who have nothing in common with worldlings. As for parallels of longevity, they are found among other classes of men, for instance Adam &c., of the Christians, Tirumûlar of the *Saivas*. &c. (Vide T. Ãzhvár's Life.)

In Tirumazhisai-Âzhvár's life, mention is made of Ton*d*ai King, Pallava. Could this give any clue to determine the Saint's age? We think not. For there have been many Pallavas, even though one of that name be found chronologically chronicled, on any stray archœological stone! As to the Ton*d*ai Kings traced by Prof: M. *S*eshagiri *S*âstriar to Kulôttunga Chô*la* (1013—1113 A. C.) [P. 37: Essay on Tamil Literature], we will let our friend Mr. S. A. Tirumalai Kolundu Pillay speak:—"Mr. *S*eshagiri *S*âstriar somehow wrongly assumes that the name Ton*d*amán first appears in history *only* after the time of Kulòttunga Cho*l*a. He leads the reader to think that Tondamãn, the son of Kulottunga, should have been the first sovereign by that name. As there is a wide gulf between Karikãla and Tondamàn, extending over many centuries, the antiquity and genuineness of the authorship of the works break down. This is what he desires the reader to infer. Whence he derived his materials, to arrive at the conclusion that Kulóttunga's son Ton*d*amán was the ancestor of the Ton*d*amán line of kings, is not indicated nor is it known. Whatever the sources, I wish he turn to page 1059 of Devaram A*d*angal Murai (*stalavarisai*) and see that St. Sundarar who flourished about 825 A. D. refers to Ton*d*amàn in a way which leaves no room to doubt that Ton*d*amân preceded the sage by several centuries. Ton*d*amàn seems to Sundarar an antique mythological personage. Pity it is that opinions which are absurd on their very face have been given currency to." (Pp. ii—iii. *The Age of Mânikkavâchakar*). After this, to what age may Pallava-Ráya of our Ázbvár be assigned? After this, our S. A. Tirumalai Kolundu Pillay may himself take care not to call into question the 'historical acumen' or accuracy of the *Vaishnavas* (Pp. *163. Vol. IV. Siddhânta Dipikà*)

Readers, in judging of criticisms, as coming from biassed men, may remember what the Professor in *The Autocrat of the Breakfast Table* tells Jack: "There are three Jacks: Jack as he regards himself, Jack as his neighbours see him, and Jack as God knows him."

5. St. Tirumangai Âzhvàr.

We find in this Saint's life mention made of the religious dispute with the Saiva Saint Sambandhar and his snatching the latter's trident as a badge of victory. "If this be true," says Prof. Seshagiri Sastri M. A. in his *Essay on Tamil Literature*, "it will quite militate against the high antiquity assigned to Tirumangai-Âzhvâr."

But what is Sambandha's age? We find in "*Some Milestones*" by P. Sundaram Pille M. A., the following statements:—

P: 25. Ft: note "Milestones":—"Sambandha had only a pair of cymbals, and never a trident"!

The inference from this is that (1) Sambandha of the trident is probably another,[1]— and as ancient as the Âzhvâr,— but of whom Saivâs have lost all accounts., or (2)

1. Such conjectures are not whimsical when dealing with ancients and ancient history. Why, *two* Auvais have been supposed recently to have existed! [Vide P. 263, Vol.I. Siddh: Díp:]

Sambandha took to cymbals after he gave away his trident to the Âzhvâr. And the 3rd inference is that even if the Sambandha of the cymbals is contemporary with Âzhvâr, how is it Saivas make no mention of this Âzhvâr in their life of Sambandha?

Be this so. Whether it be Sambandha of the trident or of the cymbals, has *his* age been determined? Here are conflicting statements:—

P: 53, "*Milestones*":—"The Hon'ble P. Kumaraswamy of Colombo argues that.........the age of Sambandha ought to be accepted as at least prior to the birth of Christ."

We ask how far back *prior to this Christian Era*? God knows!

Both Sambandha and T. Âzhvâr refer to the famous Chola Prince Kocchengannan. "But when did this Chola live?" is a question put to himself by P. Sundaram Pillay (P. 60. "Milestones"). And turning to p: 162. Vol. IV. Siddhânta Dîpika, this prince is placed about 500 B. C. We ask why not 2500 B. C.? In such nebulosity of historical discussion, we think we had better safely take refuge with our traditional dates!!

We are supported in this conclusion by the statements of a Tamil scholar, Mr. T. Virabhadra Mudaliar B. A. B. L. who accepts the truth of the interview between (some) Sambandha and T. Âzhvâr. He says:—"An investigation of the metres of the Âzhvâr and of Tevâram, is not altogether a hopeless task (P. 138. Siddhânta Dîpikâ). "Tevâram belongs to the 2nd Period, or Period of Ancient Vrittas." (P. 138. Ibid). Tevâram and Periya-Tirumozhi of T. Âzhvâr belong to the same ancient period" (P. 138. Ibid)

We have another scholar who supports the antiquity of the Âzhvâr. Mr. Chelvakesava Râya Mudaliar M.A. who also refuses the astounding conclusion of Prof: Seshagiri Sastri that all the Âzhvârs lived *after* Râmânuja (!!!) [*Ibid*, P.140-1]. This sweeping assertion is only worthy of a madman; of one who draws all his inspiration from a Halâsya-Mahâtmya! Did the Professor ever inquire into the testimonies furnished by Râmânuja himself and his predecessors Yâmunâchârya and Nâthamunigal in *re* the antiquity of the Âzhvârs?

6. *St. Nammâzhvâr.*

The following are our reasons for believing in the traditional date of 3102 B. C., assigned for St. Nammâzhvâr, until we have more substantial proof to the contrary.

(1). The date of the Vedas is still unsettled, though European scholars mostly regard the question as closed. But see Kamesvara Iyer's *Purusha Sûkta* and Tilak's *Orion*. We can well give therefore 4000 or 5000 years B. C., for the Vedas. And the Tamil of Tirumozhi (of St: Tirumangai Âzhvâr) being saturated with the Vedic spirit and containing numerous references to the Vedas, might well be a thousand years, more or less, later than the Vedas, but not still later, because the language of these works is probably the most ancient in Tamil, more ancient than the Kura*l* certainly, and the *S*aiva devotional poets very probably. This is a large question and cannot be discussed here.

(2). The later Puranic Mythology and Sampradâya is not reflected therein at all, which would certainly be if these works (Prabandhas) were later than the Purâ*n*âs.

(3). There is no *prima facie* suspiciousness about the traditional date, and it is existent *as tradition for an immemorial period.* Until our opponents bring very good counter-arguments, our position is safe, and this date must stand.

(4). If *S*aiva critics are to believe in the Three Sanghams going back to 9000 B. C. (in fact we see from the commentary to *Irayavar-Agapporul* that the Sangha members were immortal and continued on for centuries from one *S*angham into another), I do not see why St: Nammâzhvâr's date should (by them) be put very late. We have other reasons, but we reserve them for the present.

(5). As to the authors of Kura*l* copying from St: Nammâzhvâr, it is probable, inasmuch as we find the Commentator to the Kura*l* in many instances supporting the Kura*l* verses with quotations from St: Nammâzhvâr, concluding these by the statement: "*Enru periyôrum panittâr*", *i. e.*, "And the great sage has also laid down likewise," the great sage being St: Nammâzhvâr. The commentator obviously draws from St: Nammâzhvâr as he considers the sage in many instances to have been the fount of inspiration from which the author of the Kura*l* drunk. And the authority of a scholar like Parimêl-Azhagar—the Kura*l* Commentator—is beyond question.

(6). The Kura*l* Metre is the short sententious couplet which probably was one of the last metrical forms to be developed in Tamil. Compare the analogy of *S*ûtra-Literature and the Sûtra-form in Sanskrit Literature.

(7). Why *S*aiva scholars should maintain that the Tol-Kàppiyam (note the name *Kàppiyam*, which is simply the *S*anskrit Kávya, a comparatively late Samskrit name) is the oldest Tamil work extant, is incomprehensible, and still more incomprehensible is the reason they assign for it. The Tol-

Káppiyam is a work on Grammar, and without a most extensive previous literature, such a work could never have been brought into existence, unless *Saiva* scholars are prepared to believe that it is 'a relation', as some of them seem to think of Tamil having been revealed to Agastya in its entirety by the God *Siva*. And again, because the Tol-Káppiyam does not describe some of the metres that occur in prior Tamil works, forsooth it follows that these works did not exist, and all that *did* previously exist have now disappeared. And then why shoud the Tolkáppiyam be like a Census Report, not to omit a single existing metre as the Census Report does not (or at least is not supposed to) omit a single individual, but enfolds all in the meshes of its enumeration ?

(8). It would seem therefore that these fancied facts do not all stand in the way of our finding out a tolerably correct date for St: Nammázhvâr (even though it may be shockingly ancient to the *Saivaites*), which will coincide with the traditional date.

A Kambanáttázhvân is mentioned on page 210. Is this the Kamban who is said to have lived in the 10th century A. C. or Sage Nâtha-munigals' time ? or 11th century A. C. *i.e.*, Sage Râmânuja's time? But these were not the Sangham days ; for the 3rd Sangham is said to have ended 100 A. C., the time of Tiruva*ll*uvar, whose *Kural* was submitted to the Pit*h*a. Saint Nammázhvâr and his disciple Madhura Kaviga*l* lived before Tiruva*ll*uvar, Idaikkádar and Auvai, as is testified to by their praises of our Saint, subjoined below, and therefore during the 2nd Sangham Sittings, which is said to be between 5450 B. C. to 1750 B. C. [Vide P. 17. Vol. IV.

Siddhânta Dípikâ]. The great war of the Mahâbhârata was in this period, and the Pândavas are said to have been entertained by the Pândyan Kings. So then the Kambanâttâzhvân must have been another person altogether, not Kamban of the 10th century A. C. Besides, where was the Sankha-pîtha after the cessation of the last Sangham, 100 A. C.? Probably this was Êkamban? (Vide P. 37. Vol. III. Siddhânta-Dîpikâ). With regard to the confusion of names, it is useful to recall the words of Hunter in his Indian Empire:—"Indeed it is worthy of remark that several of the best Indian Authors, whether Samskrit or Vernacular have left no indication of their names. As it was the chief desire of an Indian Sage to merge his individual existence in the universal existence, so it appears to have been the wish of many Indian men of letters of the highest type to lose their individuality in the School or Cycle of literature to which they belonged. This remark is doubly apt in the case of Tamil Scholars and Poets, from the days of Agastya down to very recent times. The names of Tamil poets are in the majority of cases, after their birth places or after family names. Some names denote the distinguishing features and idiosyncracies of authors. Not one out of a hundred is known by the name by which he was called by those dear and near to him." It is but natural that our Kamban shares the same fate.

The following are the aforesaid testimonies to the greatness of our saint. It will show how opinions held by Tamil Scholars such as Chelva-Kesavarâya Mudaliar, M.A. (vide P: 100, Vol. III. Siddhânta Dìpika) are liable to great modification, as more facts flow in. Tiruvalluva-nâyanâr has certainly quoted from Nammâzhvâr, not the latter from the former. Nammàzhvàr makes mention of Buddha in the Tiruvâimozhi; but this Buddha is not the Buddha of the 600. B. C. of the European Scholars. For there were *24* Buddhas. Even Paràsara Maharshi, the contemporary of Lord Krishna and father of Vyâsa, makes mention of Mâyâmôha Asura's teachings in Vishnupurána III—18. If therefore Parāsara be doubted as the contemparary of Lord Krishna, and evidence here cited of qalluvar, Auvayàr and Idaikkàdar be doubted,—other evidences apart —then only can any question arise against the age of Nammázhvàr being placed 43 days after the beginning of the Kali- age. Read also the footnote 1 (a) (b) (c) and (d), page xxi, Introduction to our "Divine Wisdom of Drávida Saints." At any rate, to us lovers of God, even if our Saint had been born yesterday, like Paramahamsa Ràmà-krishna, no less doth he appear in our estimation. [Umâpati Sivàchárya says in his *Sivaprakàsam* that every thing new is not necessarily false; and we add that every thing old too is not necessarily false]. The ladder of love, the Saint has built up to heaven, is what we care for. Here however are the testimonies :—

(A) *Valluva Nàyanâr*.— *Siru-munivan* &c., meaning :—

"The three kinds of Tamil of the Dwarf Saint (Agastya), as well as my own Kural are the offspring of the child-saint (Nammàzhvàr) born of Nangaiyàr." [1]

(B) *Auvai* :— *Aim...porul* &c, meaning :—

" Some opine that the blessed sayings of the Lord of cool Kurugùr (Nammázhvàr) excel every other kind of Sacred Scripture, expounding the five-fold Doctrine (Artha-panchaka), the four-fold Doctrine (Chaturvidha-Purushàrtha) compressed into the three-fold Doctrine,[2] and

1- See Vinoda-Rasamanjari.
2. *Dharma*, *Artha* and *Kàma*.

yet they are not original, but *derived* Scriptures; but my opinion, in contravention of these opinions, is that Nammâzhvâr's sayings comprise the *Parent* or *Original* Scriptures alone."

(C). *Idaikkádar* (considered by some to be an Incarnation of Vishnu, Vide p: 88. Vol IV. Siddhânta Dìpiká)

Séy-mozhi &c :—meaning :—

"Both the mother language (Samskrit) and the daughter-language (Drâvid) are no doubt both one. The Drâvid sayings (of our Saint) are without question recognized by all as the Vedas. But if any one should say: 'there be many such sayings,' I say at once that these many as well as thy (addressing Valluvar) Kural, are reflections of our Saint's sayings."

The Kamban (?) of the 10th century, (?) as well as Pugaléndi, his contemporary, sang the praises of Nammâzhvâr (Vide P. 133. Vol II. and P. 102. Vol III. Siddhânta Dìpikâ). This work goes by the name of Sathagoparandâdi.

Kamban is said to have sung : *Î-y-áduvado* &c. (Vide Pp. 1 & 10 Tiruviruttam, Edition of Pandit Satha-gopa-Râmânujâchâryâ. 1900)

Pari passu, we may be allowed to say here that the Saiva scholars have a rooted prejudice against Vaishnava traditions and attempt to suppress as much of the references to them as possible. It is said that in Parimel-Azhagar's commentaries on Kural, many passages referring to the Vaishnava-Âzhvârs were suppressed by the Saiva-Editors. One signal instance of this kind has recently been exposed by Mr. Chelvakesavarâya Mudaliar, M. A. on page 133. Vol II. Siddhánta Dìpiká thus :—

"In an Edition of *Tiru-k-kai Vazhakkam*, printed by the late Arumuga-nàvalar, among the many references to Saiva devotees, there is this:— "*Panna-amaitta Vedam oru nânki-naiyum mikka tamizh nàladiyál ódi-y-uraitta karunai-y-óngum kai*", *and this perhaps refers to Nammázhvâr, and this is scrupulously omitted in the edition of Velâyuda Mudaliar.*"

Also V. M. Sathakòpa Râmânujàchàriar, Tamil Pandit, has also recently pointed out in the foot note to page 8 of Tamil Poetry text &c., for the F. A. Examination, of 1901, that Mahàbhàratam written by Villiputtùr-Âzhvàr has been much interfered with by Saivaite Authors and Publishers. He writes thus:—"*Ippadi silar pratiyilulla* ... ... *puttaka-sálaiyilum ullana.*"

We shall now make a few general remarks and notes on Saiva and Vishnava symbols and their moral effect on the development of pure religion, and conclude:—

We have already elsewhere said that truth and faith and God have better foundations in our nature than the time, during which the exponents thereof might have lived. Even their names might have been different from what they are. If for example, *Nammázhvàr* had been *Piravàzhvàr*, and had lived to-day instead of 5000 years ago, the spiritual truths inculcated, and the faith which they excite in our hearts, would remain quite unaffected by such accidents of *names* and *forms*. If however, the modern craze for historicality is any sign that truth and faith and love and God are better established on that account, the failure of such historic merit, which Christians take the pride to assign to their Christianity, is *an* evidence. Dr. Barrows, who came to India to convert it to Christianity by one mighty swoop, said :—*Historical Christianity*, as far as its fundamental truths and facts are concerned, includes the faith in Jesus Christ, His only Son, the Redeemer of the soul, through his life, example, teachings, death and *resurrection &c.*, ... " To this the following excerpts may for the present be taken as an answer ;—"Hindus wage no war against religion of any kind, not even against the noisy *unscientific* dogmatism known as "Historical Christianity ; " let those whom it consoles and satisfies stick to it by all means, and may Heaven's light and grace rest on them ! But we detest the aggressive methods and tactics of most of those who seek to propagate it in this country, and we have it in trust to defend against them the sacred cause of our confessedly *scientific* religion, " [The Hindu 1897. "The Claims of Christianity "].

The *Saturday Review* recently wrote of Christianity :—' In the presence of the scientific religions,—Brahmanism &c.— it has signally failed, and there is no prospect of an eternal victory.':

"Dr. Barrow's definition of historic Christianity bristles with controversial matter, with obscurities and mysteries which it is hopeless to unravel." [The Hindu 1897.]

"Its (Christianity's) gains from among educated Brahmins &c, are few and slight ; its losses from among the scientists and thinkers of Europe are serious." [*Prof : Flint, to the Divinity Students, Edinburgh University.* 1817].

"In the first place it (i. e. evidence for Resurrection &c.) does not come from eye-witnesses, secondly the different accounts do not agree, and thirdly they give a description of the nature and movements of the subject after the resur-

rection which contains in itself contradictory elements."
[*Strauss, the great German scholar & theologian*].

"There is the gravest reason for doubting whether the Sermon on the Mount was ever preached and whether the so-called Lord's Prayer was ever prayed by Jesus of Nazareth. * *. Tell me what Jesus can be *proved* to have been said, or done and I will tell you whether I believe him or in him or not! [*Prof: Huxley*]."

"There is no use blaming honest and outspoken speakers after truth like Huxley and Strauss, when we have the statment of Professor Flint, already quoted, that Christianity is daily losing its hold on the scientists and thinkers of Europe. *The blame rests with those religions which stake their existence on the belief of men in certain* historical occurrences, *instead of basing themselves on truths which are independent of time and place and which will carry consolation and command acceptance because they satisfy man's spiritual nature and its needs and aspirations.*" [The Hindu, 1897][1]. .

As to the Saiva and Vaishnava Symbols, the keen Vaishnava sense revolted against the destructive aspect of the Godhead represented by Siva, and more so against the low form of worship by means of *phallic* emblems. This worship and the awe-inspiring nature of the Destructive, were to them unworthy of a refined intellect, and a love-seeking heart. To draw a heart, a loving Protective Being was required, and to satisfy the moral sense, ennobling—not debasing—symbols

1, Vide also a host of authorities cited by Rev. John MacLaughlin in his book :—*Is One Religion as good as Another*" Pp : 177 ff. (1898).

were required. Thence the highly declamatory style with which the Vaishnavas found it necessary to decry low ideals before they could establish firmly among the masses, the higher and nobler ideals which they offered instead.

Professor M. Rangacharya. M. A., in his learned lecture on 'The Function of Religion in Socil Evolution', points out: "that there is evidence of phallic worship having existed among all early semitic tribes, and the ancient Egyptians also knew it undoubtedly. It has been conclusively proved by modern scholars that both Greece and Rome derived their licentious gods and goddesses, their orgiastic worship and ugly symbols, from the east—from Mesopotamia and the land of the Semites. This kind of religion is far from edifying; religion does good to man individually and socially only when it enables him to curb and control his animal passions; his humanity grows well and safely only when his animality is killed. That progressive religion has largely succeded in killing, as far as possible, man's animality, is well borne out by the fact that orgiastic and licentious cults have existed only as temporary aberrations in the course of the historical development of some poor and incapable religions, and have had soon to die away. Where, however, these degrading cults have not yet become quite extinct, they are, as most of us know, forced to hide themselves in darkness and in shame. The "ape and tiger" in man die hard, but the fiat has now for a long time gone forth that they *must* die."

That phallic worship is against the spirit of the Vedic Religion, the passages of Rig Veda, VII. 21-5, and X. 99-3 distinctly show.

श्रीः

THE LIFE OF

ST. TONDAR-ADI-PPODI AZHVAR.

Saint Tondar-adi-ppodi Âzhvâr or Bhakt-ânghri-renu ranks as No. 15 in our Hierarchic Table. He was born in the country of the Cholas, in Mandangudi (Madras Presidency), in the 288th year after the advent of the Kali Age, or after St Ândâl. He took his birth in a Brâhmana family, claiming his descent from that particular part of Mahâ-Vishnu's celestial Form, known as the Vanamâla[1], the Divine garland adorning His shoulders; in other words an emanation from the five-gemmed Vanamâla. The month of Mârgali[2] or Mârga-Sirsha (= Dhanus or December-January) in which he was born, is specially consecrated to Vishnu, according to the verse:—

'I am Mârgasirsha of the months' (Bh: Gi: X.35).

---

1. This necklace is called Vaijayanti. It is the symbol of the Tanmâtras, or the five Rudimentary elements. (Vide Vishnu-Purâna.)

2. Vide p. 155, Vol: III, Secret Doctrine.

The name, Tondaradippodi, or the "dust of the Feet of the slaves of God" is a later name; the first name given to him being Vipra-Nârâyana. As becomes a Bráhmana, all the Sacraments such as Chaula (Tonsure), Upanayana (the investing with the Holy thread) &c, were each administered to him in due season; and he was well learnt in all the prescribed holy lore consisting of the four Vedas and the six Angas, added to which were other sciences useful for successful utilisation of mundane life. By nature he was a saint, and hence he was keenly alive to the vanities and evanescent character of the world; and remained therefor free from getting himself entangled in such relations as marriage.

Once on a time, he went on a visit to Srîranganâtha the Lord Resident at Srîranga,(between the two branches of River Káveri) and like the four-faced Demiurge Brahmâ of yore, paid his homage to the Shrine on all its four sides, feeding his spiritual nature by a leisurely contemplation of the Divine Beauty as enshrined in the Recumbent Figure of Srì Ranga, revealed as in the shining sapphire of the body, the blooming lotus of the eyes, and all grace and beneficence beaming from the smiling face. To no ordinary eye is the Transcendental Beauty evident: but to the eye spiritually opened like what God did to our Saint, the Vision becomes Beatific and all the soul is thrilled with rapturous exaltation. It is said that Lord Râma by his beauty, entranced men, although a man himself:—

"As fair in face as that fair stone
Dear to the moon, of moonbeams grown,
With noble gifts and grace that took
The hearts of all, and chained each look."
[Râm: II. 3. 28];

And Queen Draupadi fascinated women, though herself a woman[1]. Thus did the grace of Lord Ranga descend on our saint, blessing him with the Divine Vision usurping all his heart; and Vipra-Nârâyana decided to consecrate all the rest of his days to the service of cultivating and supplying flowers to the Deity, the chief being the Holy Tulasi[2] Leaf. Like Pundaríka and Mâlâkâra of yore, did our saint exclusively devote himself to this service; and even like Gajendra of old, of unswerving devotion, and like Saint Peri-Âzhvâr[3] himself who is said to have spun into his floral wreath eight select species of flowers, typical of the eight kinds of mental worship pleasing to Vishnu; viz: (1) Non-injury, (2) Conquest of the senses, (3) Kindness to all creatures, (4) Forgiveness, (5) Prayer, (6) Austerity, (7) Mental culture, and (8) Truth[4].

---

1. पाञ्चाल्याः पद्मपत्राक्ष्याः स्नायन्त्या जघनंघनम् । यास्त्रियो दृष्टवत्यस्ताः पुंभावं मनसा ययुः ॥ [Mahâ-Bhârata.]

2. The Holy sweet Basil. 3. Vide his life.

4. अहिंसा प्रथमं पुष्पं पुष्पमिन्द्रियनिग्रहः । सर्वभूतदयापुष्पं क्षमापुष्पं विशेषतः ॥ ध्यानपुष्पं तपःपुष्पं ज्ञानपुष्पं तथैवच । सत्यमष्टविधं पुष्पं विष्णोः प्रीतिकरं भवेत् ॥

Time was thus fleeing, as if monotonously. To break it, something like recreation having been considered desirable for the fulfilling of some inscrutable purposes of Providence, an event most opposed to the saintly nature of our subject was brought about. Thus :— There lived in a town called Tiru-kkarambanûr, a courtesan of matchless beauty, by name Deva-devi. She is said to be of celestial[1] origin as subsequent events go to prove. She was a visitor frequently at the court of the king Chola, whose capital then was Nichulâpuri (the modern Uraiyûr). Deva-devi was once returning home from the palace escorted by her maids. On the way lay the flower-garden of our Saint. What with fatigue, and what with the inviting garden and its precincts, she could not avoid taking rest under a cool shady tree. It was one tree though, among so many others in the charming park. smiling with ever so many colored sprouts, and blooming with ever so many fragrant flowers. Varieties too were they, mango and jack, fig and lime, plantain and pomegranate. cocoa and areca, and what not ; nor were they standing silent ; for birds of variegated plumes, and all the gamut of music their tiny throats discoursed, swarmed them ; a gay world it was, all music and love,—and utter indifference to the pains and sorrows of existence as is only known to the human kind. Nor did the bees refuse lending the charm of

1 That is: Descended from a celestial Nymph (Divy-âṅgana).

their humming voices to the general concert. Altogether it made a music of the spheres, where the very gods could come, and form the audience, at least as long as no world's complaints reached to force them away from such Elysian banquet. The very air that swept the gladsome grove, did service to the feast of the celestials, by acting the part of a perfumer royal, for through the vistas of wood it pulsed softly and gathered all the delicate odours, which lotuses and lilies, Champaks and what not, held in their tiny cups as loyal offerings, willingly delivered as soon as the messenger came from the royal court. Fancy, what train of thoughts would not enter the mind of a contemplator of such a scene, immediately when sweet repose had succeeded to a tiresome journey? For, a pearly smile playing on her lips, our Devà-devi addressed her maid thus: "Sister! doth not this charming grove rival even the noted pleasure-parks of Indra and Kubera?" "Dear" returthe maid, "how can it be anything otherwise, when odorous blooms, it grows, are considered worthy of finding a place even on our Lord Ranganâtha's holy head, and when it has served to dispel even *his* ennui by giving him repose and recreation after a hard march[1]?" Thus did they chat squatting under the shade, their listless eyes wandering over the voluptuous vistas, in unknown dreams, when they espied our Saint Vipra-Nârayana labouring in the parterres.

1. In our temple ceremonial, God is represented as going a-hunting. It means esoterically: God going in search of hearts.

How did he look? His head and beard were thick and long with hirsute growth. His body too was downy. He was clad in milk-white garments. His brow and breast and arms and neck beamed with the bright vertical insignia of the True Vaishnava[1]. He wore the sacred Tulasi beads and lotus gems. And he was busily employed in building beds for the trees and shrubs, watering the plants, or tending them in a hundred small ways, as the sole service of God fallen to his good share. The eyes of our Deva-devi and her sister wistfully watched all our saint's diligent operations in the garden; but wondered he never lifted his eyes from his work,—even one look for their fair face? No. Even if he was aware of their presence, he was on the one hand deeply absorbed in his divine service, and on the other, had no other than notions of hate and contempt for female charms. This, to *her* unusual—conduct on the part of a man excited her curiosity. For, she inquired of her sister whether she did not think that man either mad or he was no man at all, when he seemed so blindly indifferent to their fascinative presence. But her sister said:—"No Deva-devi. neither is he mad nor is he wanting in the masculine. His whole soul is bent upon his Godly work. His heart is turned away from the world. Thy charms and smiles, thy curves and curls, he

1 This forms one of the Five external acts of Vaishnava Initiation. Here is old 'Free-masonry' for those who would wish to know.

spitteth on. Listen now: if thou couldst melt the stone of this noble creature's heart to flow towards thyself, indeed art thot the best of thy lot. Hear: I make a wager: that if thou succeed, I bind myself to serve thee for six months as thy slave."

"Agreed" responded Deva-devi, and added: 'if succeed I do not, have me *thy* slave for the same period. Anon, she divested herself of all her jewels and other personal embellishments, and sent her sister home with them and all the other maids, bidding them await events. She now placed herself directly before the gaze of our saint, and so near that it was impossible for him not to look. She made this even easier by falling prostrate at his holy feet. "Who art thou? what is this thou doest, my daughter?", asked he. "Lord", cried she piteously, "By birth I am mean. This is due to my past sins. My mother makes me a chattel for every male's satisfaction of lust, that she may make much money by such base bargain. Enough that I am what I am from my past sins. Why should I willingly lend myself to vicious purposes even now and roll myself into a bottomless pit? Hence, Lord, I am once for all resolved to resign that old wretch; hereafter may I trust to you alone for my salvation by serving at your holy feet? See, I am helpless and wayless. Deign to gaze on me, and shower on me your grace. What I ask of you is simply this: Let me look after the garden during your absence at Ranganâtha's Temple to bear your daily burden of flowers intended.

for Him; and bring hither your itenerant charity of food people give ye daily". To a willing helper like her to him in divine service, our Saint had no other word to say but 'yes', simple-hearted as he was, unaware of the guile that lurked behind the veil. His unsophisticated nature admitted a servant, and his kindness to creatures prompted him to share with her his frugal fare after its usual offering to his household God.

Determined as she was to accomplish her purpose, she was possessed with all the necessary patience, for she toiled on in our saint's garden for six long months performing every menial service, a veritable labour of *love*, indeed! She was thus employed one day in the rainy season, when a heavy downpour came. She was wet and shivering, but would not cease from her gardening. Vipra-Nàrayana was in his cottage under shelter. Pity at seeing a creature suffer moved him to ask her to betake herself to his shed. She obeyed. She was instantly at his side, dripping with her wet *sàri*. He saw and gave his own dry garment for her to wear. She obeyed of course; and finding herself thus comfortable and alone with our Saint, thought within herself: "There is rain outside, and here we are snug and secure. The mind is unoccupied. Could a better opportunity than this offer itself? "My Lord", she meekly said, "may not this slave shampoo thy weary limbs?" In all innocence, our saint expressed willingness. As she pressed his limbs, she ejaculated such sweet words and played such coquettish smiles, and cast such furtive glances, that Vipra-Nârâyana's saintliness was by this time banished to the world of zeros, and weak nature's erotic irritation so stole through his frame as to hold irresistible sway over him, so much that he was at the melting point, so to say, as says an old saying:

> 'Female and Male, so Nature's dual,
> The one is fire, the other 's wax.' [1]

Deft at the arts of massage, she succeeded; for he lent himself to her vile embrace, and she of course lost no time in teaching him the higher lessons in the arts of Cupid. She improved upon the occasion too by immediately sending for all her jewels and apparel; decked herself like the very peacock; and displayed her personal charms to such advantage, that he was now her slave. In a new aspect now did all the garden contrivances appear. The shades and seats, the bowers and arches, the glens and glades all invited them to repose and revel. No more were these for God intended, but were all for their flesh and its appetites. To our saint, it seemed a new world unfolded, and thus tempted and transported, he altogether lost sight of his old world. As saint Tirumangai-Âzhvâr exclaimed:—

> "Ah! how I have virtue forsworn!
> Her anklets gingling, me unnerved!

---

1. अङ्गारसदृशी नारी घृतकुम्भ समः पुमान् ।

Oh! how her eye so wide and dark
Has witching spelled my saintly soul!,"[1]

[Tirumozhi I. 6. 2],

Vipra-Nàràyaṇa was completely overpowered. He forgot his Sandhyâ ceremonies and knew no other *ne plus ultra* than our Deva-devi.

Deva-devi had now won the wager with her sister. She stripped her lover of all he had of worldly goods and deserting him went home. Vipra ran at her heels, sat at her doorside and submitted himself quietly to all the injuries and indignities a cast-off lover is indeed subjected by harlot-hussies of this benighted globe.

Day after day went on thus. The Blest Ranganâtha and his Consort *Srì* passed by that street one day in procession; when *Srì*, seeing Vipra moodily crouching under the eaves of Deva-devi's door, smiled, and asked her Spouse: "Who is this"? "Dost thou not know", the Lord answered, "he is our old servant, Vipra-Nàrâyaṇa, who daily brought us buxom blossoms? See, poor soul, he is made penniless, and now spurned by that strumpet indoors!" "What, my Lord", said *Srï*, 'Thou sufferest thy lovers thus to be cast-aways? What, even such saints catchest Thou in Thy unknown snares? Be it, he hath sinned; yet behovest Thee not to chastise him for it if Thou wilt, and redeem him back to Thy holy service?" "Yes", the Lord consoled her, "watch and see how I will contrive".

1. "Silambadi" &c.

A man knocked at the door of Deva-devi. Vipra-Nârâyanâ's knocks had gone unheeded before. But now the knock seemed of a different kind. Deva-devi mused: "could it be by Nârâyana? How, weak as he is, could he have gained so much access of strength into his knuckles, and infused courage into his fainting heart? He has surely got something new for me. Let me open". The door was instantly ajar. "Who art thou?" inquired Devi. "I am Vipra-Nârâyana's humble servant. I am by name Ranga. I am directed by him to go to thee and hand this golden cup." Hearing this, which certainly struck like music on her tympanum, she gladly received the golden cup and earnestly inquired where her dear lover Vipra lay. "Here he is," said the messenger, who stepping on to where Vipra was moaning: "Please, Deva-devi waits for thee at the door, her arms open to receive thee. Enter pray and enjoy as of old." He jumped when he heard this, as if a nectar-cup had been emptied into his ears and found himself once more locked in Devi's embrace to his great glee. But the messenger? He had vanished. He was no other than Ranganátha Himself, who had now quietly retired to his *Sesha*-couch, after His recent mysterious manœuvre.

The next morn, the portals of Ranga's temple were opened as usual for worship, when they found a gold-cup missing among other articles required for the daily ritual. The whole band of the temple-servants was put into consternation. The matter was reported to the manager, and finally reached the ears of the king at Nichulâ-puri. He ordered the apprehension of the priest and his attendants who were most immediately concerned with the loss, and subjected them to punishment. The water-carrier woman of Deva-devi, happened the meanwhile to pass by where the suspected delinquents were suffering, and finding amongst them a lover of hers, inquired of the cause, and was informed of the loss of the golden vessel and all the events which transpired thereon. She at once divulged that a certain Vipra-Nârâyana had brought to her mistress Deva-devi such a gold article, and that she was hiding it safely under her pillow. Acting on this information, the manager apprehended Vipra-Nârâyana and went with him to the woman's house, and sure he found there the gold cup secreted under her pillow. On the report reaching the king, he sent for them all, and questioned Deva-devi: "How couldst thou have stolen God's property?" "Lord, I am thy abject slave", cried she, "I know not to this moment that the article belongs to God. This man here, Vipra, sent it to me by his servant, one by name Ranga. Unaware of the circumstances, I received it." "What do you say, now, Vipra?" thundered forth the king. But he denied all knowledge of the matter. Devi charged, he rebutted. She remonstrated, he vehemently returned the compliment. And so raged the quarrel. The king thought he would levy a fine on Devi and keep Vipra in the lock-up, taking time to consider what condign punishment the law prescribed for stealers of gold. Of course he restored the gold cup to Ranganâtha's sacristy.

Our Queen *Srî*, the Impersonation of Mercy and the Universal Mediatrix between her Lord, the Father, and the souls, her children, now interposed with Him: "Sovereign of my heart," she pleaded, "enough of thy playing fast and loose with Thy poor servant, Vipra. Plague him no longer. Enough for him of this world's illusions. Mercy now." "Well said, my love!, watch what I will next do", so pacified he our *Srî*.

King Cho*l*a had a dream that night. Ra*n*ganâtha appeared to him and spoke:—"Listen, O my faithful! Events are a chain linking the past, the persent and the future. 'Tis not once that man appears on the stage of world's drama. Our servant Vipra is innocent, so far as his persent life is concerned; but in the past lives, there were deeds that he did which now have influenced him for purposes of retribution. Hence did we devise a measure that ends of justice be satisfied. He has been made to suffer though slightly. Enough. We give him discharge, so you acquit him. Next, we do not wish to appropriate Deva-devi's money. Remit the fine. Do in the morn then as We direct, and let our dear Nârâya*n*a be again established in the gardening work, dear as well to him as to Us."

The Ruler of Nichu*l*âpuri oped his eyes as if the dream were still dancing before him: and his astonishment coupled with joy knew no bounds.

He immediately ordered Vipra-Nârâyana's release, narrated to him his dream. and begging his pardon for what had happned unintentionally on his part, showed him every honor and gave him leave to go.

Old recollections came now to our saint like a flood, and a severe conflict ensued between his reformed nature and the defilements to which it by accident had come to be subjected. A severe struggle it was between the new man regenerate, and the old man degenerate. In short, remorse so operated on his heart as to throw in vivid contrast the hell of his lecherous character, when set against the religiosity of his innate nature. "Oh soul, he exclaimed, "hast thou now fully seen the hell of women's society? Only dread, it now excites." "How is my tainted nature to be purified?" he asked himself. "The only remedy is the washings of the feet of holy men to be sipped by me in all faith. This is the Sacrament our Law ordains, through which the holy spirit of God chooses to act on my inmost being"[1]. Thus saying he took the Sacrament and gradually recovered his former sanctity. As a mark that his salvation was solely effected by means of the virtues contained in the dust of Holy Men's' feet,[2] he gave to himself the significant

---

1. एतत्समस्त पापानां प्रायश्चित्तं मनीषिभिः । निर्णीतं भगवद्भक्त पादोदक निषेवणम् ॥ [Bhâradvâja Samhita].

2. यस्य मूर्ध्नि स्थितं यावत् वैष्णवाङ्घ्रिरजश्शुभम् । गङ्गादि सर्व तीर्थानि तावत्तिष्ठन्त्यसंशयम् ॥ [Brahmânda Purâna].

title of Tondar-adi-ppodi (*Tamil*) or Bhakt-ânghri-renu (*Sanskrit*).

Like the Holy Hanumán of Râmâyana who exclaimed :—

> " My heart in Thee is so entwined
> To part is vain attempt.[1] " ;

like Lakshmâna, who declared :—

> " Apart from Thee O Lord !
> Care I for all the worlds ? [2] " ;

and like St. Nammâzhvâr, who confessed :—

> " The honey of Thy Holy Feet once tasted,
> The showy things of all the worlds three,
> To take me fail ; nor I for me I deem.
> All is Thine, 'deed *I* am Thine, O Lord ! [3] " ;

our saint belonged not to the world, belonged not to himself, but belonged to God alone [4]. Nor did he in the depth of his love for God, ramble from shrine to

---

1. स्नेहोमे परमो राजन् त्वयिनित्यं प्रतिष्ठितः । [Uttara : Rám : xi. 15].

2. ऐश्वर्यं वापि लोकानां कामये न त्वयाविना । [Râm: xxxi. 5].

3. *Ulagam mmurinodu* & (Tiru-v-âsiriyam. 2).

4. " 'Tis thine without reserve, most simply thine ;
So give to thee, that it is not my own ;
A willing captive of thy grace divine ;
And loves, and seeks thee, for thyself alone "
(Madame Guyon by Cowper).

shrine like other saints, but pinned his mind exclusively on to the manifestation of God as Ranganâtha in Srîranga, and sang of him in his highly devotional Hymn, the Tiru-mâlai.

Our Archa-form or symbolic representations of the Deity, so that the senses can be held and trained to contemplation, is, we hold, the door-way to Divinity. Enter there, and behold the larger vistas of various visions of God; and joy after joy opening in endless perspective. Ranga then revealed Himself to our saint as Ranga (God) enthroned and hidden in the hearts of all beings(*Antaryâmi*), as Lord Incarnate on earth (*Avatâra*); Lord manifest in various Forms for cosmic work (*Vyûha*); and Lord Supreme and Transcendent as (*Para*) abiding in the Spiritual Universe. Our saint saw God thus in every possible mode. Not only did all his doubt vanish but he ever felt God as if he held Him in his hand.[1]

Turning now to Deva-devi, in whom a reaction had set in, she marked the way her old love went. It astonished her, it set her thinking. Well, such is the virtue of association with the good and holy. Her former association with our saint acted on her heart as a sacrament, and it entered her mind that no less than becoming like our saint himself should henceforth be her worthy end and aim. To such an end she set to work. In real

1. A loving devotion to Personal God is enjoined by the Saints as a sure passport to Endless Felicity.

zest she began, for she dedicated all she had to the Holy Shrine of Ranga, and devoted herself to such menial services in that great Fane, that she felt her former self transformed into a new being.

Love to God, with our saint, now grew into higher and higher stages, and encompassed Him in several folds, as son the Father; friend, Friend; bride, Spouse &c. [1] So risen into companionship with his God, our saint with all the strength he felt of standing on the summit of such godly glory, announced in loud accents thus:

" Whom dare we fear now?
So panoplied are we
With His All-Holy Name,
E'en Death from our door
Oh, ousted, headlong flies [2];

[Tiru-mâlai, verse 1.]

The glory of God's Holy name enabled him, he said, to plant his feet on the heads of Death and its horde; and place his head under the Holy Feet of the godly.

All these and other sentiments of his deep religious feeling, he vented forth in streams of mellow song. And this constitutes the two famous works of his,

1. Read Lokâçhárya's Rahasya, called the *Nava-vidha Sambandha*.

2. Cp: "And when this mortal hath put on immortality, then shall come to pass the saying that is written: *Death is swallowed up in victory.* '*O Death, where is thy sting?*" (I Cor. 55.)

viz; the Tiru-mâlai and the Tirup-pa*ll*i-yezhucchi. The teachings in the former chiefly go to show that the insentient body consisting of the 24 elements is a temporary cage, sooner or later destined to disintegrate (*vide* Verse 6) and that soul is a distinct entity, the 25th; characterized notably by its " dis posability " or subject to the will of God and His Holy Host (*vide* Verse 20). In the Tirup-pa*ll*i-Yezhucchi or the ' Waking of the Lord ', his second work, Saint Bhakt-â*n*ghri-re*n*u shows that the highest aim a saintly soul can aspire to is no more than service to the slaves of slaves of God. (*vide* Verse 11).

For 105 years, the saint is said to have lived in Srîra*n*gam preaching what he *felt* of God and what he *saw* of God[1] and ascended to Eternal Heaven in all saintly glory, leaving to the world the two works of his, viz Tirumâlai, the 'Blest Garland', and Tirup-pa*ll*i-yezhucchi, the 'Lord's Waking'.

Blest be St. Bhaktanghri-Renu

1. Like Thomas à Kempis for example to whom Bishop Ken wrote a Eulogy thus :—

> " His will entire he to God's will resigned.
> And what pleased God pleased his devoted mind.
> Thrice happy saint remote from haunts of ill,
> Employed in hymn, and dispossest of will."

श्रीः

THE LIFE OF

ST. PERI-Y-AZHVAR.

Saint Periyâzhvâr or Vishnu-Chittar is chronicled in our Scriptures as the Image of the Archangel Garutmân, the Eternal, ever dwelling by the side of God. He incarnated in Sri Villiputtûr, the Holy Land of Brâhmana Patriarchs, all whose life being devoted to learning and propagating the Holy Veda, and ever engaged in performing those highly meritorious ceremonies called the Yajnas,—whose ultimate meaning, apart from the several kinds of rewards they are said to procure, is Service rendered to God without expecting a return, *because* He so commands.

The date of his birth is mentioned as Kali 46, Jyeshthâ month, Svâti asterism[1]. (Vide also the Hierarchic

---

1. ज्येष्ठेथ मासे पवमानतारे श्रेष्ठोगुणेनाजनिभट्टनाथः । कृतत्रयीरूपगरुत्मदात्मा कटाक्ष्यलक्ष्यं कमलापतेर्यः ॥ [Divya-Sûri Charitam. v. 33].

Table). Thus our saint was nearly 51 years old when his Divine child Â*ndâl* was discovered in his garden.[1]

He is also called Bhatta-nâtha [2], or Brâhma*n*a chief and is said therefore to belong to the Vêyar [3]-class; *i e* the Bambu-lineage, Bambu being its chief insignia. Kâ*l*idâsa in his Raghuvamsa alludes to this fact by saying :—

" वेणुदण्डमवलम्ब्यशैशवे "—The children prop themselves by their (elders') *bambu*-sticks."

When the Brahma-charya or the student-stage is passed and the Brâhma*n*a enters the Grihastha or family stage the Dharma-Sútra enjoins :—

वैणवं दण्डमादध्यात् ।

'He shall accept the *Bambu* rod ;' and when the Grihastha stage is given up to take up the Sanyása or Anchorite stage, the Bambu Danda, it is well known, becomes the mark of the Brâhma*n*a *par excellence.* Tiruv-arangatt-Amudanâr, the author of Râmânuja-Nútt-Andâdi is said to belong to the Mû*n*gil-kudi or the Bambu-order of descent. Of parents belonging to such high aristocracy, Mukunda, father, and Padmâdevi, mother, our saint was born.

---

1. *Vide* St. *Andâl's* Life.
2. Tamil : Pattar-pirân (the highest canonist stock of India).
3. Vide Periya-Tirumozhi V. 4. 11.

Intuitively he was a votary of Vishṇu[1]. That one has inherited or innate tendencies for virtue is ultima tely attributed to the special grace of God, as was Saint Prahlâda from his very birth. This mighty torrent of divine impulse, not all the demoniac efforts of a Hiraṇya could stem. They say, a saint is born, not made. Having thus the potentiality of such born intuitions, no sensuous proofs nor ratiocinations were needed in his case, nor revelational authority, to recognize the chief end of man. This to him was no other than that life should be entirely appropriated to God's service. Even a little of it not offered by soul to God disenfranchises service of its very essential character of existing for, and serving, God. Púrva-Mịmámsa says thus :—

नाऽकिञ्चित्कुर्वतश्शेषत्वम् । [III. 1. 1].

And St : Nammâzhvâr also sang thus :—

"Of Krishna what beseech I but
That I be used as He hath willed"[2].

Recognizing thus his relationship to God, and therefore the duties implied by such relation, he set about thinking what particular form they may assume.

---

1. Moksha Dharma, Bhârata, says :—"सर्वेषां एवधर्माणां उत्तमो वैष्णवो विधिः". The Upanishads often reiterate :—"तद्विष्णोः परमं पदम्" 'That is Vishṇu's High Estate'.

2. "Tanakkêyága &c (T: V: Mozhi. II. 9. 4.).

Running in his mind over how the *S*esha-couched Nârâya*n*a of the Milky-Sea incarnated in Madhura (north) as Krish*n*a[1], how the Divine Appearance was no other than eternal Truth (*Sanâtana-dharma*) embodied in visible form[2], how the Incarnation was resolved upon for the threefold purpose of saving the godly, destroying the ungodly, and establishing virtue in the land[3]; how Krish*n*a, born of Devakî, and brought up by Yasoda, accepted graciously the offer devout of scented flower-wreathes by MÂlÂkÂra in Madhura on his way to meet King Kamsa[4], our saint resolved upon devoting himself to the duty of supplying flowers daily to Krish*n*a, who to our saint being represented by the Archa-form of Vata-*S*âyin of *S*rivilli-puttûr.

By the way the incident of one like Krish*n*a leaving the High Road of kings and deliberately entering an

---

1. एषनारायणश्रीमान् क्षीरार्णवनिकेतनः । नागपर्यंक मुत्सृज्य ह्यागतो मथुरापुरीम् ॥ [Harivamsa. cxIII-62.]

2. पुण्याद्वारवतीयत्र तत्रास्ते मधुसूदनः । साक्षाद्देवः पुराणोसौ सहिधर्मस्सनातनः ॥ [Bhârata].

3. परित्राणाय साधूनाम् । &. [Bhag : Gîtâ IV. 8.]

4. प्रसाद परमौनाथौ ममगेहमुपागतौ । धन्योहमर्चयिष्यामी त्याह-माल्योपजीविनः॥ [Vish : Pur. v. 19. 21.]

obscure lane in search of a poor flowersman is pregnant with the truth that God never forgets Himself in his High State, but is more condescendingly mindful of His lowest creatures. This truth is illustrated by the whole of Krishna-Avatâr. St Nammâzhvâr alludes to one such event in that Avatâr viz, the butter-stealing, in the following words:—

" Tho' 'loft empyrean in, Thy *Immortals*
With wreaths and spray and scented fumes Thee wait,
Behind the fumes them unawares, adown
To *mortals* fleest, to steal Thy butter dear,
And find thy rest,' midst sturdy sharp horned neat
To win thy coveted prize, sweet Nappinnai" [1].

In our book called "the Divine Wisdom of the Drâvida Saints," Topic 16 gives the philosophy of the butter-stealing incident. The learned gloss on Tirviruttam by Vâdikesari Jîyar says that soured milk represents the union of body and soul. This milk should be churned by means of the rod of contemplation. The latent soul is by this process extracted from the milk as butter. The butter clarified (ghee) represents the soul when glorified in heaven in God's August Presence.[2]

To return to our story. In Madhura (South) called in those days Kûdal, reigned Vallabha Deva, of the

1. "Sâttu-nan-mâlai &c." [Tiru-Viruttam. 21.]

2. As to cloth-stealing incident, read the sense as explained by Annie Besant in her *Avatâra*.

Pâ*nd*ya Dynasty, famous for their wide conquests and righteous rule on earth. On a certain night the king went through the streets of Madhura *incog* on a round of inspection, and spied a Brâhma*n*a sleeping on a pial. He roused him, and asked who he was. "I am a Bráhma*n*a," he said, "returning from my holy pilgrmage to Ga*n*ga (Ganges)" "If thou dost know anything worthy, let me hear thee," begged the King. The pilgrim recited :—

> "Eight months in the year, labour, to happily
> live at home the four rainy months.
> Half the day labour for spending the night happily.
> Work in manhood to provide for dotage.
> Use present birth on earth to secure Moksha hereafter"[1]

The King was struck with the moral contained in this verse and it made him to muse thus: "In all that constitutes the visible, nothing am I in want ; but have I worked for the Invisible ? How may I go about it ?" He sent for his venerable parson Selva-Nambi and asked his counsel as to how he should edify himself as to what constitutes the *summum bonum* for man, and how it is to be secured. Nambi answered:—"According to our Âpastamba-Dharma-Sûtra,[2] king! the pronoun-

---

1. वर्षार्थमष्टौ प्रयतेतमासान् निशार्थमर्धं दिवसंयतते । वार्धक्य-हेतोर्वयसानवेन परत्रहेतोरिहजन्मनाच ॥

2. धर्मज्ञसमय: प्रमाणं वेदाश्च॥ [I. 1. 2. &. 3.]

cements of our virtuous sages based on the Vedas, is our Law. Hence, it is wise to summon a council of wise men, and hear from them the purport of the Vedânta. Then wilt thou know the way to thy desire," The king assented to the proposal and commanded that Pandits be summoned from all parts of his kingdom; and furthur that a precious money-meed for the victor in the intellectual warfare, should be tied up in a cloth and hung up to a festoon to be cut by him after the victory.

The Va*t*asâyin at *S*rivilliputtûr to whom our Saint was rendering daily flower-service resolved that his votary should attend the council and be thus His mouth-piece there to proclaim to the world once again eternal Verities; for mankind is forgetful, and require constant reminding and warning to wean them from evil pursuits and wed them to virtue and God. The Saint had a dream in consequence, and Va*t*asâyin appearing therein commanded him to attend the King's court and win the prize intended. "What" exclaimed Periy-âzhvâr, "boor and illiterate that I am, I am to be deputed to an intellectual tournament! Lord, look at my hands cicatriced by constant plying with the garden implements. To me it seems the height of folly that a poor gardener fit only for humble service to Thee, should dare to appear in the midst of wise-men and throw down the gauntlet! I am unlearned in the Vaidika Lore, and yet Thou desirest me to cut a figure amongst the rare literati that will assemble! How canst Thou have thought of such an impossible thing?" Va*t*asàyin said: "What is it to thee, my son? Thou hast simply to do our bidding. We will do all. Arise and go." [1]

Our Saint opened his eyes in mixed wonder and surprize, and without further ado journeyed at once to the royal assembly convened. On seeing a gem of the hereditary priesthood coming, both Selva-Nambi and the King rose, advanced, fell at his feet and escorted him to the council of wise men gathered together, thus giving our Saint a splendid reception before the eyes of all. This conduct excited surprize and resentment among them. "What," they expostulated with the King, "thou honorest a dullard who

---

1. Cp: (a) 'For wisdom opened the mouth of the dumb and made the tongues of infants eloquent.' [Wisdom. X. 21.]

(b) 'And when they shall bring you into the synagogues, and to magistrates and powers, be not solicitous how or what you shall answer, or what you shall say.

'For the Holy Ghost shall teach you in the same hour what you must say.' (St Luke. XII. 11. 12.)

(c) 'Thus does human weakness become at times the theatre on which the Lord delights to display his power when he chooses the weak and contemptible things of this world to confound and bring to nought the strong and the mighty.' (P. XVIII. Preface Fr. de Sale's 'Love of God').

knows not a letter of the Vedânta!" Selva-Nambi immediately rose and prostrating before our saint, invited him to discourse on the truths of the Vedânta.

Like Vâlmîki whom Brahmâ inspired by saying:

> 'Seek not to trace, with labour vain,
> The unpremeditated strain.
> The tuneful lines thy lips rehearsed
> Spontaneous from thy bosom burst
> Then come, O best of seers, relate
> The life of Râma good and great.
>
> [Râmâyana I. 2.] [1]

and like Dhruva who, become all-knowing by the mere touch of Vishnu's Holy Conch, burst out in sublime praise [2], did our Saint begin:—

"Hear, all ye men! All the Vedas stand before my vision in clearly traced characters. The infallibility of their records is to me self-evident. The letter A (अ) is essentially the begining of all Alphabet. Lord

---

1. Even Schlegel wrote in his preface to Râmâyana: "I congratulate myself that, by the favour of the Supreme Deity, I have been allowed to begin so great a work; I glory and make my boast that I too after so many ages have helped to confirm that ancient oracle declared to Vâlmîki by the Father of gods and men."

2. [Read Vishnu Purâna I. 12. 49. ff.]

Krishna says: 'I am of all the Alphabet A (अ)'[1] 'A(अ) is the Holy Symbol of Vishnu" says the Pâñcharâtra. Vishnu is Nârâyana. 'He is the Para-Brahm, the Uncaused cause from whom all creation flows, endures and to whom returns.'[2] He who aspires for liberation (Moksha) shall therefore meditate on Him, for He alone is the Granter thereof, according to the Scriptures,-the Nârâyana-Anuvâka. Manu, the Legislator confirms the same; [3] and so Rishi Parâsara,[4] and so vociferates the Sesha-Dharma [5]-the end of all the Mahâ-Bhârata.

Enough, O men! By hundreds and by thousands, citatations of this kind are in great profusion spread over the pages of the Srutis, and Smritis, and all the Holy Lore ancillary to them. Are ye satisfied? are ye convinced?"

While thus our Saint discoursed at great length in the midst of the August Assembly, they were all stunned and sat petrified like idols. Not one dared even breathe a word of protest. They were all looking mutely on, when, lo! the precious prize-bag which

1. [Bh. Gi: X. 3.] अक्षराणामकारोस्मि ।

2. [Taittiriya: Up. Bhrigu Valli. 1.]

3. [Manu Dharma Sâstra I. 10 ff.]

4. [Vishnu-Purâna. 1. 31.]

5. [Sesha-Dharma II. 15.]

was hung up, as aforesaid, of its own accord lowered, till it was within reach of our Speaker, who forthwith rent it asunder, and felt inwardly grateful to the *Deus Absconditus*, through whose Divine impulse he was enabled, though an empty vessel himself, to accomplish his Holy Mission.

Miracle thus added to wonder electrified the audience. In one body from the King downward all stood up; and devout and humble, involuntarily threw themselves at the feet of the Inspired Speaker—'He who made manifest to men the Light that shines on the summits of the Vedânta.'[1] In much honer and great pomp, they led the Saint to a gorgeously caparisoned elephant got ready at the portals of the King's Palace; and hoisted him upon it amid acclamations. The Pandits assembled, arranging themselves into a grand procession, some with unbrellas, some with canopies, wreaths, scents &c, doing honor to the Divine Conqueror; and as the procession advanced they exclaimed at the top of their voice: 'Here goes Vishnu-Chittar, the Knower of the Fruits of the Vedas;[2] 'There goes the truth-tongued Hero'[3] and so on, accompanied with blasts of trumpets and blowing of conches. In the midst of such uproarious applause, the King bestowed on him the title of Pattar-pirân' or

1. [Vide Tirumozhi IV. 3. 11.]
2. [Tirumozhi II. 8. 10.]
3. [Ibid IV. 9. 11.]

the Brâhmana-Chief', and thus did the procession, swelled by the King's ministers and retinue, perambulated Kûdal, street after street.

God glorified Himself thus through His chosen vessel, our Saint. He wanted to witness the glorious scene Himself, like parents fondly would the triumphal demonstrations to their child. He came. In all His Devine glory bathed, He appeared in the blue vault. There was His indiscerptible Spouse Lakshmi with Him. The Heavenly Bird Garutmân was His vehicle. So mounted, the vision looked like a huge azure-hued cloud resting on a golden hill. There were the Archangels, the Chakra, and Sankha. There was all the paraphernalia of Gods, Brahmâs, Sivas, Indras, and all the rest of the Heavenly Pantheon. They worshipped Him and served Him in every befitting manner. He manifested Himself thus in His ineffably glorious form, resplendantly girt with the celestial hosts; and the Vision approached nearer and nearer to the dazzled sight of our Saint.

A great lover of God as he was, the sight overwhelmed him; and yet he never allowed himself to swell with pride at the rare fortune which above all mortals fell to his blessed lot. He never allowed his rising emotions to overpower him so as to become dazed and dizzy at sight of this supernatural apparition. He took breath; he did not lose courage; he kept his balance and in the depth of his emotions he kept his wits. For he reflected thus: "Here is my God, the All-knowing, the All-powerful, the All-protecting! The Sapphire-Hued, effulgent with golden lightning! O, Beauty Transcendant! Charm irresistible! Youth Eternal! Thou art above time and its changes. Thou art worthy of dwelling in the spiritual Pañch-opanishan-made[1] Empyrean. Thou art worthy of receiving the adorations of the Ever-seeing Immortals. But here Thou art, in a place under the sway of Time;-here the changing and passing;-here the hell compared to Thy Heaven;-here the regions of the loveless beasts of men whose minds are pervert;-here where Kali reigns supreme;-here where spiritual light is eclipsed. Coming from so high, how mayst Thou render thyself patent to our senses in an atmosphere reeking with the un-divine! Love for Thee makes me not to forget myself, Love for Thee does not strike me down senseless. I recover; I rise above that sentiment; for fear for Thee rises uppermost in my breast, fear for Thy safety; the safety for one so worthy in the unworthy land. This fear is more than love. Love for the beloved begets forgetfulness; but fear supervenes and keeps me above that drowning flood. Oh, let nothing mar Thy Beauty; let nothing steal Thy Strength; let nothing rob from Thy glory. Let me bless Thee thus

1. The five-fold spiritual counterparts of celestial matter, corresponding to the five great elements of the material universe.

my God! Let me bless Thee as the Parent, the child. What moves me is not the love of the lover, not the love of the liege, not the love of the wife, but the love of the mother towards her child." Thus overflowing with sentiments of love peculiar to our Saint alone as distinguished from other saints, the Blest Vishnu-Chittar took the jingling bells of the elephant he was riding: making them do the duty of cymbals, he broke out into a song of blessings, called the Tirup-pallâṇḍu by which he invited all classes of men to join him in the Benedictory.

Intense love begets fear, and evokes a tender benedictory or blessing care for God. In this, the relation of God and man as Protector and protected change places. In this connection the subjoined quotation from that illustrious work of Sage Lokâchârya, beautifully translated by Pârthasârathi Yogi, called the *Srî Vachana-Bhûshaṇa* (The Good-word Jewel) cannot but be a most a valuable embellishment to these pages:—

Explanation of the Faithful soul's God-Blessing or Benedictory Character:—

A Query.

265. Ask you—"Is it not incompatible with the (dependent) nature of the soul to assume the benedictory character?

Answer to the Query.

266. (1.) In the soul's Sage-Mood, the correlations of Protector and Protected, keep their places.

(2.) In the soul's Saint-Mood, these correlations change places.

Elucidation of the last Sentence.

267. (1) When the soul meditates God's Essential—Omniscience, Omnipotence, and Universal Providence, he would be *Protected* by God as *Protector*;

(2) When he meditates on God's Tenderness or Softness (which is the opposite of roughness), he forgets God's Omnipotence and the like attributes and, taking God to be wholly unequal to the rough work of the world, he would feel God to stand in need of being *Protected* by himself as *Benedictor* and *Protector*.

268. This truth is seen (exemplified) in—

(1) the Emperor (Dasaratha—the Lord's father),

(2) Blest Janaka's Blest Daughter (our Queen Sîtâ),

(3) Visvâmitra (the Holy Sage who negotiated the Lord's marriages.

(4) The Holy Sages who dwelt the Blest Da*nd*aka Forest.

(5) The Lord's Blest Footman (Hanumân),

(6) The Mahârâja (of Kishkindha, namely, Sugrîva, whom the Lord Himself honorod as Lord, [*vide* Râmâya*n*a IV—4–18].

(7) The Blest cowherd Nanda (the Blest K*r*ish*n*a's foster-father),

(8) The Blest Vidura (King Pându's step-brother of saintly character),

(9) Pillai Urangâvilli Dâsar (our Saviour Râmânujâchârya's body-guarding disciple), (10) and others.

269. Is it not well known—

(1) that the Lord's own brother was distrusted by St. Guha?

(2) that both were distrusted by St Guha's servants? and,

(3) that thus every soul present, kept separate guard at the gate of the Lord (while He rested under the roof of St Guha as the latter's guest)? [Râmâyana II. 87. 22—23].

270. Thus struck love-blind, were even those who had but a day's sight of the face (of the Lord).

271. But the benedictory love, even of the above enumerated lovers of the Lord, when compared with the love of our Âzhvârs (or Drâvida Saints), falls so far short of the latter, as to seem rangeable almost with the love, of which we (spiritual pigmies) are possessed.

272. And, not like other Âzhvârs, is Peri-Âzhvâr (or "The Great Âzhvâr".)

273. (1) To the former, this kind of love was occasional;

(2) to the latter, it was constant;

274. The very place where the former lose footing from excess of depth (of the grace-stream they are trying to ford), proves shallow to the latter.

275. What (beauty in God's form) sufficed in the former to dislodge them from the states of obedience to God and the Godly, and drawn their essential virtue,—served, in the case of the latter, to stimulate his status of obedience to both, and to enable soul-essence to reach the end of its voyage (without being drowned in the ocean of spiritual confusion) [cp. Aurelius. V. 20. as to changing "hindrance into help"]

276. To *bless* was Peri-Âzhvár's forte, whence he was led-

(1) To *fear* for *fear-removers* too, (Chakra &c. Tiruppallâ*ndu*. v. 1. line 3; and v. 2, lines 2—4.).

(2) To turn even opponents into friends, (Id. v. 4.-5, 7–8, and 10-11.).

(3) to feel heart-burning in subsequent time, for dangers long past, (Id. v. 3. lines 3-4, etc).

(4) to assert that, "to bless is the very goal of faith" (Id. v. 12, line 4.), and,

(5) to warn the sleep-less ever-awake angels, not to fall asleep. (P. Tiru-mozhi, V. 2. 9. &c.)

277. Unlike other Saints and Sages who, in their teaching, sought to remove the solitariness of the teacher and the taught (by bringing them together as the necessary complements of each other), Bhâshyakâra (i. e. our Saviour Râmânujâchârya) and this Saint (namely, Peri-Âzhvâr,) sought by their teaching to remove the solitariness of God Himself (by bringing back to Him His lost sheep), imagining that He Himself "would not appoint *one* faithful servant to

serve Him in a manner suitable to His tender nature."
(Tiru. Vâi. Mozhi, VIII. 3. 3.)

278. (1) Other Saints lived and thrived, by seeing, enjoying, and serving (God);

(2) *This* Saint lived and thrived by blessing (God).

The above is somewhat abstruse to ordinary readers, but it contains a whole philosophy of the "*love of benevolence.*"

"The love of benevolence is one which has been commonly practised by the Saints, and often has seemed childish, or at least mere poetry, to those who love God less fervently. There is a strange pleasure in it from our putting ourselves in an impossible position towards God, in order to confer it on Him. We make ourselves as it were His benefactors, instead of His being ours. We put ourselves on an equality with Him, or even above Him. So it seems. Yet in reality this love of benevolence is the fruit of a holy humility too deep for words, almost too deep for tears. By the love of benevolence we, first of all, wish God to be more perfect, if it were possible, than He really is. Yet what a wild impossibility! But if God's love of His creatures is itself so exaggerated, He must let us love Him with the simplicity of these fervid exaggerations. Moreover this habit of wishing God impossible perfections is not only the result of a more worthy and true appreciation of His perfection and His majesty, but it tends also to produce it, to sustain it, and to increase it. It is at once the cause and the effect of honorable thoughts of God. Another while the love of benevolence takes the form of venturesome congratulations. We wish God all the immense joy of His unimaginable perfections. We know that he possesses it without our wishing it. We know that our wishes cannot swell one drop the mighty sea of his interior jubilation. But it is an expression of our love, not in words only, but in inward sentiment which in his sight is an act, and a meritorious act. We bid Him rejoice. We wish Him countless happy returns of that internal festival which He has in His own blissful self. Or, another while, by the same love of benevolence, we wish Him all increase of His accidental Glory; and our wish is efficacious prayer, and obtains for Him a real augmentation of that particular Glory. The very wish of itself adds to it, and adds immensely when it comes out of a pure heart and a fervent spirit. It also obtains grace of others, and makes the cause of God to prosper in the world. Sometimes we earnestly desire that He may have accidental Glory which He does not receive. We wish that purgatory were emptied into heaven, or that there were no hell, or that all the heathen were converted, or that all wanderers might return to the fold, or that some one day or night there might be no mortal sin in all our huge metropolis. All this, which the saints have reduced to as many practices as there have been saints to practise it, is the love of benevolence." [1]

1. [Revd. F. W. Faber's Creator and Creature. P: 205—209]

To return. Peri-âzhvâr conferred blessings upon the excellent King Vallabha-Deva, and receiving from him an abundance of all marks of honor and worship, retraced his steps home—given wings thereto by true love he bore to Vata-*S*âyin, which, much against his will, was interrupted for a time by this God-bid spiritual expedition. The presents he brought he duly placed before the *S*âyin's Holy Altar and prayed to Him to accept it as His own according to the text:—

> 'The wife, the slave, the son,
> These three, O king, are not their own;
> So all the wealth they earn
> To one, by right as lord, belongs.,[1]"

and gladly renewed his old usual loving service of wreath-weaving and offering the same to his Deity.

Services to God are diverse; it may be mental, verbal or corporeal. As shown at the beginning of the life of our Saint, he chose the corporeal one of flower-growing and offering, after the model of Málâkâra of Madhura during the Avatâra of Krish*n*a. In the same manner that the Holy Flowersman is said to have blessed the mighty arms of our Lord after He came off as victor in His duel with the giant athletes Châ*n*úra and Mush*t*ika set on by Kamsa,[2] did our Saint choose the exploits of

1. त्रयएवाधनाराजन् भार्या दासस्तथासुतः । यत्तेसमधिगच्छन्ति यस्यैते तस्यतद्धनम् ॥ [Pâñcharâtra.]

2. [Read Vishnu-Purâ*n*a V-20]

Krishna to be his theme for composing his benedictory work, the Tirumozhi—in which he imagined himself as one of the Cowherd-race in which Krishna was born, and by the method of imitation (*anukàra*) or portrayal af past events so vividly before the mind as to produce their actual re-enactment, our Saint realized Divine love and beatitude to the stigmate-producing extent. Thus did our Saint end his days, more and more uniting his heart with God, and ultimately the very soul, by ardent love, merging in Him so as to become absorbed in His very substance and essence.

The methed of imitation (*anukâra*) is a natural product of perfervid love: In the case of the Christian saint St Francis, it produced stigmates on his body. Many died by divine love actually consuming them, like the extraordinary death of a Gentleman who died on Mount Olivet (related by St Fancis de Sales, Bk VII. On Love of God). It is the ' supreme degree ' of love, to effect which, it is requisite to ' wound the soul, reduce to a state of longuor, and transfix her.'

Says St Fr : de Sales:—' The soul powerfully attracted by the perfections of her Beloved, endeavours, to the utmost of her power, to *correspond with his sweet attractions* (*anukàra*), and being unable to drag after her the body to which she is united, rather than be retained by it, amidst the miseries of life, she abandons it, and flies like a dove to the bosom of her heavenly Spouse, who seconds her efforts to dart towards him, by raising, and receiving her in his arms. It is written that a man shall quit his father and mother, to cleave to his wife; it is not so with the spiritual union, which is consummated in heaven; the Chaste Spouse then abandons her body, to unite herself inseparably to her beloved.'

So did Chintayantī breathe her last, love-delirious of Krishna. (vide Vishnu-Purâna V. 13.) Our Saint died in love, for *Love is stronger than Death* and attained beatification.

Blest be St. Bhatta-Nâtha.

श्रीः

THE LIFE OF

ST. ÂṆḌÂḶ.

We have twelve Canonized Saints in the Church of the *Srî*-Vaishṇavas. Only one of them is a woman-Saint, the blest Âṇḍâl (saviour) or Godâ-Devî. Find her figuring as No: 14 in our Table of Hierarchy. Hers is a most glorious life It is characterized throughout by such a glowing love for God, as only a female heart can foster. But let us to her life first.

Her spiritual descent is traced back to *Srî*-Devi,—the Universal Goddess—or nearer, to Bhû-Devi. Our Symbology provides Three Queens to God,-the Divine King. They are *Srì*, Bhû, and Nîlâ. *Srî* is the Universal mediatrix, and holds sway over both the Spiritual (Nitya-Vibhûti) and the Material (Lílâ-Vibhûti) Universes. Bhû is the next lady-lieutenant to *Srí*, and holds sway over the Material Universe. Nîlâ, anothor sub-regent, holds rule over one material System (the Brahmâṇḍa). This Nîlâ takes birth, as daughter of Kumbha or Nagnajit—she is therefore patronymically called also Nâgnajitī[1]—and becomes of course the consort of Sri Krishna, when Vishnu so appears on earth as Avatâra, according to the text of the Vishnu Purâna :—

राघवत्वे भवत्सीता रुक्मिणी कृष्णजन्मनि ।
अन्येषु चावतारेषु विष्णो रेषानपायिनी ॥

(This Nâgnajiti is called by the Dravidians Nappinnai.[2] Reference to this latter name frequently occurs in the 4000 Prabandhas.) Nágnajitī is almost identified with Nîlà herself, as Benedictory verse to Ândâl's Tiru-ppàvai will testify. Nilâ as Nâgnajiti thus may be said to rule over our earth. And Ândàl (descended from Bhû) comes nearer home to the Dràvidians as having incarnated in the South of India, in Srî-villi-puttùr[3] (Tinnevelley District, 25 miles West from Sâtur Railway Station, South India. Of yore, it was the Pàndya kingdom with Madhura

1. Read: ' नग्नजिन्नामकौसल्य आसीद्राजातिधार्मिकः । तस्य-सत्याभवत्कन्या देवीनाग्नजितीनृप ॥ [Bhâgavata X-58-32.]

Another account states that Kumbha, the brother of Yasoda had two issues, one Sri-dhàma, and the other Nílá or Nappinnai [Read commty : on Benedictory verse: "नीळातुङ्गस्तनगिरि-तटी " &c to Tirup-pâvai]

2. Mean; : ' the beautiful-tressed '.

3. In Sanskrit " Bhanvi-narya-pura "

as capital.) So is our saintess's spiritual descent traced.

It may not be out of place here to enlighten our readers with what the Three Female Divinities, Srî, Bhû and Nílá represent. The *S*akti or energy of God is personified as Female. It is the love-energy that manifests as the Cosmos, in other words the Principle of mercy ordering all things towards a blessed goal. This Energy is three-fold, or the energy called Mahâ Lakshmi divides herself into Three Energies, called:—

(1) Icchâ *S*akti (Energy of will),
(2) Kriyâ *S*akti (Energy of act),
and (3) Sâkshât *S*akti (Essential Energy).

And Icchâ *S*akti subdivides herself into *S*rí, Bhû and Nîlá[1]. There are authoritative Scriptures for these Three Goddesses The Srí-Súkta[2] is found in the Rig-Veda [Max Muller's Rig Veda], and Bhû-Sûkta and Nilâ-Sùkta are found in the Yajur-Veda. A learned friend of ours who belongs to the Madhva community tells us that the three energies of *S*ri, Bhù, and Nîlâ

1. Read: "महालक्ष्मीर्देवेशस्य भिन्नाभिन्नरूपा चेतना ऽचेतनात्मिका............सा देवी त्रिविधा भवति शक्त्यात्मना । इच्छाशक्तिः क्रियाशक्तिः साक्षाच्छक्तिरिति । इच्छाशक्तिस्त्रिविधा भवति । श्रीभूमिनीलात्मिका ।" [Sîtopanishad.]

2. (D. V.) We may give English versions of these, one of these days.

severally preside over the three energies of Nature: the Satva, Rajas and Tamas.

Thus is our Saintess Ândâl related to the Economy of the Cosmos. Now to enter on our story. There lived in Srî-Villiputtûr Periy-Âzhvâr, or Vishnu-Chittar, one of our Twelve Canonized Saints (whose life is separately written), born in the patriarchal Bráhmana clan. He had a hand-garden where he grew the sacred Tulasi, which he daily wove with other fragrant flowers into handsome wreaths and offered to the Lord-Resident of the place, Vata-patra-Sàyin[1]. One day Vishnu-chittar was digging his garden when to his astonishment, he found a glorious child covered with sod, just in the manner that king Janaka discovered Sîtâ:—

> "Once as it chanced, I ploughed the ground,
> When sudden, 'neath the share was found,
> An infant springing from the earth,
> Named Sîta from her secret birth." [2]
>
> [Râmayana I. 66. 13.]

---

1. 'The Sleeper on the Fig-leaf' at time of Deluge. [Read Bhágavata XII. 11 & 12.]

2. Read the parallel:

> "Great Erectheus swayed,
> That owed his nurture to the blue-eyed maid,
> But from the teeming furrow took his birth,
> The mightly offspring of the foodful earth."
>
> (Iliad Bk II).

The date of her birth is recorded in the Holy Books, (of which Divya-Sûri-Charita is one), Kali, 97, Nala year, Âdi month, Pùrva-phalguni asterism. Vishnu Chittar thus becomes our Saintess's father, like Janaka of Sità. He gave her the name of ' Gôdâ of the sweet curls '. or simply Gôdâ[1]. He found her a most fascinating beauty, slender-waisted, sweet-curled, divinely beaming mien, bewitching eyes, and what not. He took her up, as a Divine child, and brought her up as a fond parent would, bestowing on her every mark of his tender care and affection.

We said before that Vishnu-Chittar's sole occupation was to present daily his beautiful wreaths of blossoms to the Vata-Sâyin. The child had now bourgeoned forth into girl, and bloomed into maiden. She was gamboling about at will in gaeity and mirth, never once checked by the aged father in his almost revered love for the divinely born wonder. In his absence, she would, in her uncurbed freedom, meddle with her father's things and arrangements, and in these frolics, she used to take advantage of her father's absence at the Holy Fane of Vata-Sâyin and take up the wreaths of flowers which he had intended for the Lord, wear them in her locks, place herself before a mirror, and admire herself thus :— "How do I look with these blossoms on, with my gay glittering necklace, chiming wristlets, rosy lips and in

1. Meaning "she who presented her garland of Hymns" to God. 'Go' means speech=Hymn.

short, the whole of myself so adorned ? Don't I match Him (God) ? ". She was thus ever busy at her toilet, and her father's floral arrangements were victimized for the purpose. She would wear the wreaths, unwear, and put them by in balls. Vishnu-Chittar one day discovered her coqueting with the Divine wreaths[1], and chiding her severely for her sacrilegious trifling, laid the flowers away as unsanctified, and hence unworthy for presentation to the Va*t*a-Sâyin. That day went with the Lord without flowers.

Saint Vishnu Chittar had a dream. Va*t*a-Sâyin appeared and questioned him as to the cause of his failing to bring Him the daily wreaths. The explanation was given that as those that were set apart for Him as usual were discovered desecrated by his daughter, by her unwittingly wearing them in her own tresses, he laid them by as unworthy of his acceptance. 'Desecration ?" frowned the Lord, "rather say consecration ! We regard thy odorous wreaths rendered more odorous by thy daughter having worn them. We like them. We will have no others but they." The saint woke up in astonishment, and his wonderment of the already wonderful damsel, knew no bounds. 'May she not be *Srî* herself, or Bhû, or Nîlâ, under this guise ? ' he mused, and from that day forward, he not only worshipped his daughter as God's

1. *He found a lock of her head tangled with the flowers.*

own spouse, but made it a point to carry garlands to Vata-sâyin, after they were first used by her. It is said that God alone can know the excessive flavour which articles first used by His elect receive and as such all the more grateful to Him. From this day onward, Ândâl received the blessed epithet of 'Sûdik-kodutta-Nácchiyár' meaning the *Queen that wore and gave.*

Our worthy Periy-âzhvâr watched his growing daughter. As she grew, he remarked that her love for God also grew,-Love,-Love passionate,—Love disconsolate! It became intolerable to be without Him. The very life of the lover is imperilled, unless the lover unite with the Beloved. In the stage when love for the Beloved becomes so furious, as can no more be kept under cover of secrecy, or bounds of decency, or dictates of reason, its exuberance whips the lover into acts not unlike those of madmen. So enamoured of God did our young Saintess become, she could not brook her existence in separation from her Lord. In her ardour to realise Him as in the most personal intimate relations with her, her imagination carried her beyond all reasonable bounds, and she pictured before her fancy, all the exploits of God in His Krishna-Avatâra as if they were being enacted anew for her. Spiritual visions of past events is possible under altered conditions of time and space, produced by the ecstatic state into which the heart is whirled. Our saintess then began to imitate[1] Krishna's exploits. She imagined, like

1. Read this imitation (*anukâra*) explained. Pp. 39 ff.

the Gopis of old in Brindâvan and Gokul, to be herself Krishna, when Krishna had deserted them on an occasion. Said they :—

> 'O, vile Kâliya! stay,
> See, I am Krishna's self' &c. [1]

In this manner pangs of separation from the Spouse, were crossed; else life was insupportable. Ândâl, likewise, found consolation during her night-time of separation from God, by resorting to such practices as Vrata, and its auxiliaries such as Ablution, and Invocations to Kâma-Deva &c, (of purely Oriental description), as measures mediatorial and propitiatory to join her with her Lord. (Vrata is the punctilious performance of a self-imposed festive vow of a certain orthodox description, having for its final aim, the realisation and possession of God's August Presence. The way to go about this is religiously sung in the 30-versed Poem of our Saintes, called the Tirup-pàvai or the 'Sacred Vow.' The Imploration to Káma-deva (the Indian Cupid) and other cognate modes are caroled in the 143 vari-versed Hymnal called the Näcchiyâr-Tirumozhi' or the 'Queen's Blest Speech.' These comprise a portion of the 4000 Prabandhas.)

Ândâl was thus deceiving time. Her love-pourings *then* are our weapons of salvation *now*. Father

---

1. दुष्टकालिय तिष्ठात्र कृष्णोहमितिचापरा ।

[Vish: Pur V. 13. 27.]

Pery-âzhvar became anxious about her. She was ripening into full bloom of youth, and was becoming more and more love-lorn and pining for her Divine Spouse. Like Janaka of yore,

"Then as he saw the seasons fly,
And knew the marriage-time was nigh,"

Periyâzhvâr was:

'On trouble's billowy ocean tossed
Like one whose shattered bark is lost.'

[Râmayawa II. 118].

And he was like:—

'The father knowing how I came,
No daughter of a mortal dame,
In all the regions failed to see
A bridegroom meet to match with me.'

[Ibid].

"Whom indeed of mortals, wouldst thou marry, my darling daughter?" asked he of Ândâl. Ândâl grew wroth at the bare mention of mortality, and said in accents of grief and anger:—

' Mark! ' if to man I am' e'er noise abroad
That moment would my life forsooth depart.'[1]

[Nācchiyâr-Tirumozhi I. 5.]

1. Cp: "* * * * I am the soldier
Of the God of Battles; to no living man
Can I be wife * * * "
* * * * * * * *
* * * * Woe, woe to me,
If bearing in my hand th' venging sword
Of God, I bore in my vain heart a love

(Contd: on page 50)

'Pardon me, proud dame, for my careless suggestion', ventured Âzhvâr to say, 'certainly thou shalt wed a God., But whom wilt thou, of the One-hundred and Eight ?' Ândâl bid her father to name them, and give a description of each. (Readers are invited in this connection to the brilliant description of this event sung in the Samskrit Kâvya, called the Divyasûricharitam. We append a list of the 108 Holy Shrines). The father began with the Lords of the Pâ*nd*ya Country, the Lords of the Mountains of the West, the Lords of the North, the Lords of Tonda Circle, the Va*t*a-*S*âyin of Srí-villi-puttúr, the Beauteous Lord Azhagar of Tiru-mâl-iru*n*-joli-Hill, and ended with *S*ri Ranga of *S*rirangam.

As she listened with rapt attention, her heart melted, eyes, moistened, the frame thrilled, and in strains bewitching, sang forth :—

> 'Judge ye, the beauteous locks and looks
> And fruit-red lips, my Rang-Nectar's ?'
>
> [Ná-Tirumozhi xi. 2],

(Contd : from page 49)

> To earthly man ! Woe to me ! It were better
> That I never had been born. No more.
> No more of this ! Unless ye would awake the wrath
> Of Him that dwells in me ! The eye of man
> Desiring me is an abomination
> And a horror * * * * * * * "
>
> [Schiller's 'Maid of Orleans' by Carlyle.]

Thus showing how her heart was made captive by the graces and glories of Ranga-Nâtha alone, and therefore no other than He would she wed,. she said, and became more and more love-sick; and raved[1], ever thinking and dreaming and singing of Rañga :—

> " Will Ranga come, or will he not?
> So pining I, my wristlets drop."
>
> [Tiru-mozhi v-5-9].

Seeing Â*n*dâl love-mad, good Vish*n*u-chittar could not think. He was in a fix. In his perplexity as to how really it was possible to consummate an event of such marvellous description as that of marriage between a human being and a Divine being, he pensively dropt into sleep. There came to him a Divine vision. *S*rï Ranganâtha Himself appeared and solved his dilemma by announcing that He Himself would propose for his daughter's hand and heart. Âzhvâr was rejoiced and felt as if a great weight had been lifted off him, and blessed himself for having been chosen an instrument in these divinely miraculous proceedings.

Here in *S*riranga, a Divine afflatus came over the officiating priest of the Holy Fane there; and he spoke:- "Go ye all, good servants, with all our Insignia : the Umbrellas, the Chowries, the fans, the maces and all,— to Srî-villi-puttúr—to where our affianced is and escort

1. Nâcchiyâr Tirumozhi describes in detail all the love-doings.

her thither with all royal honor." The fiat went and forthwith started *S*rî Ra*n*ga's retinue from *S*rîrangam to *S*rî-villi-puttûr, and arriving there in due time, secured the audience of father Âzhvâr, and reverently delivered to him the Divine message concerning his holy daughter, Â*n*dâl.

At this happy coincidence, our Âzhvâr's surprize was beyond measure. He proceeded to his own tutelary Deity, the Va*t*a-*S*âyin, and related to him all the wonderful occurrences and awaited his sweet pleasure and permission how to act. Va*t*a-Sâyin bade him do as Ranga directed. Overjoyed, he returned home and addressing Â*n*da*l* said:—"Divine Virgin, all is as thou dreamed and raved. Here are glad tidings for thee from thy would-be Spouse. See His envoys and all the godly insignia waiting for thee. Prepare and we shall depart". So saying, in accents of mixed joy and trembling, he made ready a celestial-looking jewelled sedan; and carefully screened her from public gaze, for no more dare sinful mortals gaze on one who was now beyond doubt God's own Bride—she was now the Vestal, solely consecrate for Ra*n*ga-nâtha:—

> 'The bride eyes not her garment,
> But her dear Bridegroom's face;
> She will not gaze at glory,
> But on her King of Grace."[8]

8. [Last words of Rev: Samuel Rutherford], adapted.

In great pomp and glory, trumpets blowing, music discoursing and followers acclaiming in deafening notes: "Here is our *Ândâl* come; 'tis she who wove and gave; 'tis she of the odorous tresses; 'tis she the Chanter of Tirup-pâvai; the Glory-Queen of Rangam she, comes," a triumphant entry was made into *Sri*-rangam. In grand procession the sedan was conveyd into the Inner Sanctum, and there the screens covering it were removed.

There was the great assembly and the huge concourse of the faithful gathered together in the halls, corridors, courtyards, and transepts of the Minster and close-packed, breathless waited they as to what was going to happen. A stir, a rustling. The Glorious Virgin softly descended from the litter. She dazzled the eyes of all men. King Vallabha-Deva, of Madhura, the devout disciple of our Saint Vishnu-Chittar was also there wrapped in holy fear and astonishment. There was the Virgin-Glory presented to their stupefied vision, softly descending, softly stepping and softly pacing towards where Lord Ranga was, expectant, waiting for her. What with her silken attire wafting soft zephyrs with its movement, with *Sengazhunir* blooms redolent, with the musk Tilak on her brow setting off the moon-beam face, with the gazelle eyes kissing the ears and casting side-long glances; with welkin-waste and dancing breasts, jingling bracelets, and tinkling anklets, and swan-like gait, she was a fairy scene, a divine vision, a celestial dream, which in a moment seemed to flash between the sedan and the shrine; and there the apparition-like figure stood before His Majestic Presence drinking Him in with love-filled eyes, and gliding towards His Lotus-Feet (and thereby acquiring the title, Kesava-Nambiyai *kkâl* pi*d*ippâ*l* (Kesava's Foot-serving Maid) and ascending the soft *Sesha*-bed of the Lord, more and more pressed on to His side; and lo, where was she? she had passed into Him. Her distinct person was no more cognizable to mortal ken. Glory merged in Glory. The two poles of sentient existence, soul and God met. It flashed and was fused. The spiritual transmutation was now complete. The Saintess was beatified. They were struck mute, and paralyzed; our Saint father-Âzhvâr was especially dumb with amazement. He had cherished and fondly loved his Divine child. He could not restrain his emotions. He burst into tears. Were they tears of joy or what? judge you readers.

There was a Voice from within, commanding Vishnu Chittar to be conveyed to his Presence. They did so. "Even thou hast been raised to the position of our Father-in-law, even like unto the Lord of the Milky Sea giving us his *Srî*. May we honor thee!" Said the Voice. And the attendant priests wreathed our Father Saint, gave him the Holy Fluid, and other honors of the Pañcharâtra kind; and he was commanded to return to his father-land *Srî*-Villiputtûr, and there serve out the Va*t*a-Dhâman the rest of his days, in his usual avocation, and bide his time for ascending into Heaven.[1]

As with the world-Saviours of men, specially deputed by God for the purpose, so with our Saintess, the facts of Incarnation and Resurrection are extraordinary events, or super-normal, which should not be attempted to be reduced to any 'law' so far known. Like the Immaculate Conception of Christ, even more immaculate (i.e birth in a Tulasi-Garden) is the appearance of our Saintess on earth; and like Christ's Resurrection, even more spiritually eminent is the Transfiguration of our Saintess. No more incredible need be such miracles as it

1. We visited Sri-Villiputtúr in March 1901, and bought a copy of the Sthala-Máhâtmya. The origin of Andál's Avatār is thus given: Bhû asked her Lord of the milky ocean:—"You have your Vainateya born on earth as Vishnu-Chittar, executing your commands there as your apostle by his teachings and doings. Permit me also to take birth there as his daughter and share in the ecclesial work of your Holy Church." The Lord smilingly approved of the plan and said: "By all means, do. While you are there, we shall be pleased to wear the flowers rendered fragrant by your wearing. You shall in Drávida-verse enlighten the world with the saving truths of the Vedánta; and a Lay to us it shall be. You shall of course behave as my spouse even though veiled in mortal guise, and finally attain myself as your Lord. You shall then be installed in all my temples on earth as Archa, and all who shall serve you in that form shall be eligible for moksha."

[Page 23].

pleases God to manifest to mankind now and then as signs of his love and assurance for its eternal welfare than the occurrences recorded by modern sciences. Says Sir Edwin Arnold M.A. [pp: 14-15. Death and Afterwards]:- "There is positively not a single prodigy in the ancient religions but has its every-day illustration in Nature. The transformation of classic gods and goddesses are grossly commonplace to the magic of the medusa, which is now filling our summer seas with floating bells of crystal and amethyst. Born from the glassy goblet of their mother, the young hydrozoon becomes first a free germ resembling a rice grain; next a fixed cup with four lips; then those lips turn to tentacles, and it is a hyaline flower; which presently splits across the calyx into segments, and the protean thing has grown into a pine-cone crowned with a tuft of transparent filaments. The cone changes into a series of sea-daisies, threaded on a pearly stalk; and these, one by one break off and float away, each a perfect little medusa, with purple bell and trailing tentacles. What did Zeus or Hermes ever effect like that? Does anybody find the Doctrine of the Incarnation so incredible? The nearest rose-bush may rebuke him since he will see there the aphides which in their wingless state produce without union creatures like themselves; and these again, though uncoupled bring forth fresh broods, down to the tenth or eleventh generation, when on a sudden winged males and females suddenly result, and pair."

As for the Doctrine of the Incarnation, eminent men like Cardinal Newman have declared it to be essentially Indian. We invite our readers, amongst others, to read Yogi Párthasârathi's reflections, [pp: 126 *ff.* "Tatva-Traya or The Three Verities]; and append the remarks of Samuel Johnson [pp: 78-79, Vol: II, Oriental Religions]:—"Emile Burnouf (in his Science of Religions) thinks that incarnation in the complete sense is pre-eminently an Aryan belief; that it is easier for an Aryan to conceive God as incarnated in man than to conceive prophetic inspiration in the Hebrew sense."

"Burnouf fails to appreciate this philosophical scope of the fact he has attempted to state, when he ventures to infer from it that the dogma of the *divinity of Jesus* will stand permanently for all Aryan races as a truth of positive religion. It is mainly from *Aryan* idealization indeed that the dogma in question has proceeded. Jesus himself was of *Semitic* descent: the earliest records of his life are of similar origin, and form no exception to the instinctive reluctance of the Semite to ascribe pure deity to the human. To effect this, they required to be clothed in purely Aryan conceptions from Greek and Oriental sources. And they were in fact so transformed, in the Christian consciousness."

Here are his conclusions well worth noting by all Truth-seekers:—"The discovery by Christian scholars in their study of Hindu religion, of what they may regard as faint heathen "foregleams and dim presentments of Christian truths,"—such as trinity, atonement by the saint for the sinner, and salvation by the merits of the saint,—justifies no expectation that the *Christian* forms of these beliefs, as "based on truth instead of dream," must be recognized by the heathen mind as that for which it was yearning, and for which its way has been prepared. The resemblances simply show that, even as believers in such conceptions and doctrinal forms, the Hindus can satisfy their desire through their own sacred books, legends and dogmatic constructions, without resorting to the Christian." (*Ibid p : 101*).

And one such wonderful Incarnation then is our Saintess's.

Benedictory Verse.

I. "Hail Gôdâ sweet : for all immortal time
Be blessed thou, who roused of yore
In melting strains—the Vedas' deeper sense
'That souls of ours, for Him and His
For ever are'—a lovely wreath of lays,—
Which, when He woke,—Srikrishna Sweet—
From beauteous sleep on Nila's breasted slopes,
Did chain Him fast in links of gold."[1]

Blest be St Âṇḍâḷ.

---

1. नीळातुङ्गस्तनगिरितटी &c, referred to in page 42.

The 108 Holy Shrines referred to on Page 50 of the "Holy Lives of the Àzhvärs" favored by Sri S. Pärthasàrathi Yogi.

Serial Number.	Name of the Holy Shrine, alphabetically arranged.	Number according to the different Circles	The Nearest Railway Station, &c. Rwy : Station.	Approximate Distance in Miles.	Direction.	Remarks.
1	A*tt*a-puja-karam.	75	Kánchipuram (or Conjeeveram) ...	1	South	
2	Árimeya-vi*n*-nagaram.	32	Do Do ...	1	Do.	
3	Anbil	4	Búdalûr	8	North	North of Kolladam (Coleroon)
4	Ádanûr	9	Kumbhakó*n*am.	10	N.	
5	Inda*l*úr.	22	Máyavaram	4	N.E.	
6	U*r*aiyûr or Nichu*l*âpuri. ...	2	Trichinopoly Fort. ...	$1\frac{1}{2}$	W.	Nativity of St Prâ*n*a-Nâtha.
7	Ûragam	81	Kànchipuram	$\frac{1}{2}$	S.	
8	Ka*n*diyûr.	15	Tanjore	5	N.E.	
9	Karambanúr (or Uttamarkóil). ...	5	Trichinopoly Fort ...	5	N.	North of Coleroon.

Serial Number.	Name of the Holy Shrine,	Number according to the different Circles.	The Nearest Railway Station, &c.			Remarks.
			Rwy : Station.	Approximate Distance in Miles	Direction.	
10	Kapisthalam (or Sundarapperumal Kòil) ...	28	Tanjore	13	N. W	
11	Kàragam.	83	Kànchìpuram	½	S.	
12	Kírvánam.	84	Do Do	½	S.	
13	Kàvalambádi (Gopi-pati). ...	38	Shiyáli (Sirkáli) ...	7	E.	
14	Kázhi-cchīrāma-vinnagaram ...	24	Do Do	½	E.	
15	Kúdalúr	25	Pāpanásam ...	4	N.W	
16	Sálagrámam	100	Janakpur (North India) ...	...	...	
17	Singavézh-kunram (or Ahóbilam) ...	97	Kamalàpuram ... or Erragundala ...	50 40	N. N.	
18	Sittira-kúdam	23	Chidambaram ...	1	N.W	
19	Sirivaramangai(or Vânamàmalai) ...	51	Tinnevelly ...	18	S.	

Serial Number.	Name of the Holy Shrine.	Number according to the different Circles.	The Nearest Railway Station &c.			Remarks.
			Rwy : Station.	Approximate Distance in Miles.	Direction.	
20	Siru-puliyûr	11	Mâyavaram ...	9	S.	
21	Srî-villi-puttur	48	Sâtûr ...	22	W.	Nativity of Sts Bhattanâtha and Ândâl (Godà-Devi).
22	Srîvaikuntam	54	Tinnevelly ...	16	E.	
23	Sem-poñjai-kóil (or Mahâkárunya.)	35	Síyàli ...	5	E.	
24	Tañjai-mámani-kkôil.	3	Tanjore. ...	3	N.	
25	Talai-cchanga-nânmadiyam. ...	13	Siyâli. ...	10	S.E.	
26	Tiru-kkacchi (or Hastigiri) ...	74	Kánchípuram. ...	3	E.	
27	Tiru-kkadal-mallai (or Mahàbali-puram)	93	Chingleput. ...	18	E.	Nativity of Bhûta-Yogi. 10 miles from Kovalam.
28	Tirukkadigai	95	Solingipuram(Bânavaram?)	9	N.W	
29	Tiru-kkadi-ttánam	79	Tinnevelly ...	4?	...	Travancore State.

Serial Number.	Name of the Holy Shrine.	Number according to the different circles.	The Nearest Railway Station &c.			Remarks.
			Rwy : Station.	Approximate Distance in miles.	Direction.	
30	Tiru-kkan*d*am-ka*d*i-nagar (or Deva-Prayāg)	102	Almora ...	152	Miles	
31	Tiru-kka*n*nan-gu*d*i	26	Kivalúr. ...	1	E.	
32	Tiru-kka*n*na-puram	17	Nannilam ...	4	E.	
33	Tiru-kka*n*na-ma*n*gai	27	Tiruvàlúr. ...	4	N.W	
34	Tiru-kka*l*vanur.	85	Känchipuram ...	½	W.	Within Kámâkshamma's Temple.
35	Tiru-kkât-karai.	61	Tinnevelly ..	40	S. ?	
36	Tiru-kku*d*andai.	14	Kumbhakô*n*am ...	2	N.W.	
37	Tiru-kkurugúr(or Ázhvâr-Tirunagari)	49	Tinnevelly ...	19	E.	Nativity of St : Parānkusa.
38	Tiru-kku*l*andai	56	Do ...	26	N. E.	
39	Tiru-kkuru*n*gu*d*i	57	Do ...	26½	S.	

Serial Number.	Name of the Holy Sbrine.	Number according to the different Circles.	The Nearest Railway Station &c. Rwy : Station.	Approximate Distance in Miles.	Direction.	Remarks.
40	Tiru-kkûdal	47	Madura ...	½	E.	
41	Tiru-kkôttiyûr	42	Do ...	32.	E.	The Madura-Mutupet Railway (now in progress) will almost reach it.
42	Tiru-kkóvalùr	73	Tiru-kkòvalúr ...	3	S.W.	River to be crossed.
43	Tiru-kkôlùr	58	Tinnevelly ...	20	E.	
44	Tiru-cchengunnûr	64	~~Do~~ (A sanitarium) ...	[illegible]	w. of No. 80	TravancoreState.
45	Tiru-cchèrai	12	Kumbhakonam ...	7	S. E.	
46	Tiru-ttangâ	76	Kânchipuram ...	2	E.	
47	Tiru-ttan-kâl	45	Sâtúr ...	13	W.	
48	Tiru-ttetri-yambalam (Raktámbaka)	36	Sìyâli ...	5	E.	

Serial Number	Name of the Holy Shrine.	Number according to the different Circles.	The Nearest Railway Station &c. Rwy : Station.	Approximate Distance in Miles	Direction.	Remarks.
49	Tiru-ttevanâr-togai (Mâdhava) ...	33	Styâli. ...	4	S.E.	
50	Tiru-naraiyur(or Näycchiyär-kóil) ...	20	Kumbhakonam ...	6	S.E.	
51	Tiru-nâgai. ...	19	Negapatam ...	$\frac{1}{4}$	W.	
52	Tiru-nâvây.	65	~~Tinnevelly~~ ...	...	...	Travancore(Pattambi P.O.)
53	Tiru-ninra-vûr.	89	Tinnanûr ...	1	S.	
54	Tiru-nîr-malai	91	Pallävaram ...	$2\frac{1}{2}$	W.	
55	Tiru-ppäl-kadal	107	The North Pole (The Milky Sea)? ...	...	N	
56	Tiru-ppiridi (or Nanda-prayäg?). ...	103	Almora(Joshimath)? ...	135	Miles	Said to be near Mânasarovar.
57	Tiru-pput-kuzhi	88	Känchipuram(or Pälúr) ...	9	S.W.	
58	Tiru-ppuliyur.	63	~~Tinnevelly~~ ...	...	...	Kuttanâdu (Travancore.)

Serial Number.	Name of the Holy Shrine.	Number according to the different Circles.	The Nearest Railway Station &c.			Remarks.
			Rwy : Station.	Approximate Distance in Miles.	Direction.	
59	Tiru-ppull-ā*ni*	44	Madura ...	60	S.E.	
60	Tiru-ppu*l*i*n*gudi	52	Tinnevelly ...	17	E.	
61	(Ten)-Tiru-ppérai	53	Do.	24	E.	
62	Tiruppèr-nagar(or Appakkudattân)	8	Búdalûr ...	6	N.W.	Kôvila*d*i
63	Tiru-ma*n*i-kkû*d*am(Ratna-kûtâdhipa)	37	Sìyāli ...	$5\frac{1}{2}$	E.	
64	Tirumál-iruñ-jòlai	41	Madura ...	12	E.	
65	Tiru-mùzhi-kka*l*am	62	Cochin state, Cranganore. Local Post called Anjal	...	...	
66	Tiru-meyyam.	43	Madura ...	40	N.E.	
67	Tiru-mògûr	46	Madura ...	10	N.E.	
68	Tiru*van*-parisâram	60	Tinnevelly ...	40	S.	

9

Serial Number	Name of the Holy Shrine.	Number according to the different Circles.	The Nearest Railway Station &c.			Remarks.
			Rwy : Station.	Approximate Distances in Miles	Direction.	
69	Tiru-va*n*-va*nd*ûr	67	~~Tinnevelly~~ ...	...	...	Travancore.
70	Tiru-v-ananda-puram	59	~~Do~~ ...	~~40~~	E.	~~Trivendram~~(Travan-core)
71	Tiru-vayindira-puram	72	Tiru-pâ-puliyûr. ...	4	W.	
72	Tiru-v-ayôtti (or Ayodhya) ...	98	Fyzabad. ...	6	...	
73	Tiru-v-ara*n*gam (or Srirangam) ...	1	Trichinopoly Fort. ...	4	N.W	Head Qaurters.
74	Tiru-valla-vâzh	66	~~Tinnevelly~~ ...	...	...	Travancore State.
75	Tiru-vallikke*n*i	94	Madras Central Station ...	2	S.W.	Triplicane.
76	Tiru-vazhu*nd*ûr(or Tèr-azhundûr)...	10	Kuttâlam ...	2	S.E.	
77	Tiru-vâ*tt*âru	68	~~Tinnevelly~~ ...	60	S.W.	Travancore.
78	Tiru-v-âyppâ*d*i(Gokul)	106	Muttra (Nandagao) ...	6	...	

Serial Number.	Name of the Holy Shrine.	Number according to the different Circles.	The Nearest Railway Station &c.			Remarks.
			Rwy : Station.	Approximate Distance in Miles.	Direction.	
79	Tiru-vàli	18	Sìyá*l*i ...	6	E.	
80	Tiru-vâ*r*an-vi*l*ai	71	~~Tinnevelly.~~ ...	...	...	Travancore State.
81	Tiru-vi*d*a-vendai(or Śinga-pperumâ*l*-kôvil)	92	25 miles by boat from Triplicane (Madras) ...	...	...	
82	Tiru-vi*n*-nagaram	16	Kumbhakô*n*am ...	2½	E.	
83	Tiru-vevvu*l*	90	~~Tiruvàlùr.~~ ...	2	N.	
84	Tiru-ve*ll*a-kku*l*am(Nàrâya*n*a) ...	39	Sìyâ*l*i ..	4	S.E	
85	Tiru-ve*ll*-a*r*ai	6	Trichinopoly Fort ...	14	N.	
86	Tiru-ve*ll*iya*n*gudi	29	Tiru-vi*d*ai-marudúr ...	5	N.	
87	Tiru-vehkà(Yathôktakàri) ...	82	Känchìpuram ...	2	E.	Nativity of Saro-Yogi.
88	Tiu-vê*n*gadam	96	Tirupati ...	7 miles over hill		

Serial Number.	Name of the Holy Shrine.	Number according to the different Circles.	The Nearest Railway Station &c.			Remarks.
			Rwy : Station.	Approximate Distance in Miles.	Direction.	
89	Tuvarai (Dvâraka.)	104	Porbandar ...	74	N.	(Dvâraka, Kattiawar Peninsula) reached in 24 hours by steamer from Bombay.
90	Tolai-villi-mangalam	50	Tinnevelly ...	21	E	
91	Nandi-pura-vinnagaram	21	Kumbhakònam ...	3	S.W.	
92	Nilà-ttingal-tundam	80	Kánchípuram. ...	1	W.	Within Ekàmresvara Temple.
93	Niragam.	79	Do ...	½	S.	
94	Naimisàranyam	99	Misrikh (Sitäpur) ...	12		North India.
95	Paramapadam	108	The Spiritual Regions ...	$x + o$	...	Lord's Blest Heaven.
96	Param-ècchura-vinnagaram. ...	87	Kánchìpuram ...	½	S.	
97	Pavala-vannam	86	Do	½	N.	
98	Pâdagam	78	Do ...	1	W.	

Serial Number.	Name of the Holy Shrine,	Number according to the different Circles.	The Nearest Railway Station, &c.			Remarks.
			Rwy : Station.	Approximate Distance in Miles	Direction.	
99	Pârtan-pa*ll*i(Kamalân*á*tha) ...	40	Sîyâli	7	S.E.	
100	Pu*ll*am-Pûda*n*gu*d*i	7	Kumbhakô*n*am	6	N. W	
101	Ma*n*i-má*d*a-kkóil	30	*S*îyâ*l*i	5	E.	
102	Va*d*a-madurai ...	105	Muttra(Madura North) ...	...	...	Nativity of *S*rî Krish*n*a.
103	Va*n*-puru*d*óttamam	34	*S*îyá*l*i ...	5	E.	
104	Vadari-y-â*s*ramam	101	Badrinâth (Garhwâl) ...	174	N.	From Haridvâr.
105	Vara-gu*n*a-ma*n*gai	55	Tinnevelly ...	18	N.E.	
106	Vittuva-kkó*d*u.	69	Pattambi P. O.(Malabar)	...	...	
107	Vé*l*u-kkai	77	Kâ*n*chîpuram ...	2	E.	
108	Vaigunda-vi*n*nagaram (Vaikun*t*hes-vara) ...	31	*S*iyâ*l*i ...	5	E.	

ABSTRACT.

Chòla-Land Circle Shrines		... ...	40
Pändya-Land	Do	Do	18
Malai-nâd (Malabár)		Do	13
Central Land Circle		Do	2
Tonda-Land	Do	Do	22
North	Do	Do	12
The Land Transcendant		... ...	1
		Total	108

श्रीः

THE LIVES OF

St. Poygai Âzhvâr
St. Pûdatt-Âzhvâr.
St. Pey-Âzhvâr.

Saints Poygai-Âzhvâr (Saro-muni), Púdatt-Âzhvâr (Bhûta-Muni), and Pëy-Âzhvâr (Mahad-áhvaya) are the most ancient of the Âzhvárs, and were contemporaries. Âzhvâr has the meaning of "Drowned in God-love" or "Sunk deep in Divine ecstasy;" or "Bhaktas or Lovers of God by *God's Grace*". This means, they were not self-constituted lovers, as when so constituted, it would involve the danger of spiritual intumescence, more dangerous than worldly pride, and tending to separate one from God beyond all reconcilable bounds, (like for example an angel behaving more like Satan than Christ).[1] True liberty of soul

---

1. Says Párthasârathi Yogi in Tatva Traya [P. 174]:— "Even after the pitfalls of avarice and amorousness have been escaped, there remains a pitfall which is more dangerous still, namely, Ambition, with which false ideas of greatness too have

consists in humble obedience to the dictates of God. Opposition begets bondage; in other words, liberty hoped to be obtained by opposition is virtually liberty lost. "He knows to command, who knows to obey" is a maxim of even worldly utility. This law extends to the spiritual universe and subtler operates there.[2] The Triad of the Âzhvârs then whom we are chronicling here were of the order coming under this Law. They had no will of their own, to express differently. God's will was their will, for as a poet of the Vedas says:—

स वा एषब्रह्मनिष्ठ इदं शरीरं मर्त्यमतिसृज्य ब्रह्माभिसंपद्य
ब्रह्मणा पश्यति, ब्रह्मणा शृणोति ब्रह्मणैवेदं सर्वं अनुभवति ॥

[*Mâdhyandin-âyana Sruti* cited by the Dvaitins.]

Which means in the words of Jelal-u-din, in Masnâvi [Engl: Tran: P: 174]:—

been associated by large numbers even of the comparatively better classes of mankind. This greater pitfall is Ambition, or that treason-inducing vice which makes Shakespeare put into the mouth of the patriot Brutus the following speech:—'As he was my benefactor I love him, but as he was ambitious, I slew him.' Thus God slays *the ambitious*, or those who attach undue or sole virtue to their own efforts with which God, they think, can be purchased."

2 Cp: "For he that is called in the Lord, being a bond-man, is the freeman of the Lord. Likewise he that is called, being free, is the bondman of Christ." [1 Cor; vii. 22.]

"God says: 'whoso is God's, God also is His'."
"God says: 'I am his Eye, his Hand, his Heart'."

Or as Hadis says:—"My servant draws nigh to me by pious deeds till I love him, and when I love him, I am his eye, his tongue, his foot, his hand, and *by Me* he sees, hears, talks, walks and feels."

The first of our Triad, the Blest Saro-muni was born in a golden lotus in the Holy Tank situate in the precincts of the Holy Vishnu Fane of Kânchi-puram (Conjeeveram). From this fact, the Saint is also called Kâsâra-Yogi. He was born in the Dvâpara age Siddhârthi Year, Âsvayuja month, *Srâvana* asterism,[2] shadowed by *Sri* Vishnu's Pâñchajanya. We shall leave Saro-Muni for a while.

Púdatt-Âzhvâr (St. Bhúta-Yogi)

This Saint took his birth in Mallâpura,[3] out of a Mâdhavi[4] blossom. Proceeding from *Sri* Mahâ-Vishnu's Holy Club, the Kaumódakí, his date of birth has been fixed in the same Dvâpara age, and year and

1 Meaning *Hemáchala* or where Brahmâ worshipped Lord Varada.

2. See Hierarchi Table No 4. and Divya-Súri-Charitam 11.10.

हेमाब्जिनी हेमसरोजगर्भो च्छ्रीपाञ्चजन्योऽजनितत्रयोगी । तारे हरेराश्वयुजाख्यमासे समस्तजीवावनकर्म हेतोः ॥

3. Known as Mahábalipura (Seven Pagodas), Madras, called *Tiru-kkadal-mallai* in Tamil. (Vide 108 Divya Desas)

4. Called *Kurukkatti* in Tamil, *Bot*: Gartnera Racemosa.

month as Saro-muni, but only a day younger than he, born in *S*ravish*th*a asterism.[1] We shall now state Pèy-âzhvar's date and return.

Péyà-Âzhvâr (St. Bhrântha–Yogi.)

This Saint was born in Mayûra-puri (Mailápùr) in the Holy Fane of Âdi-Kesava-Pperumâ*l*, in a Red-Lotus blossoming in the Holy Well there. He is said to be inspirited by *S*ri Mahâ-Vishnu's Holy Sword, the Nandaka ; the same Dvâpara age, year, and month as Saro-Yogi and Bhûta-Yogi is his ; but one day later, in the asterism Prachetas (*S*atabhishak).[2] He is called Bhránta-Yogi because demented by love of God.

Saro-Yogi was thus born on Tuesday, Bhûta-Yogi on Wednesday, and Bhrânta-Yogi on Thursday. They were all thus immaculate-conceived ; aye more, not even the semblance of a woman is connected with their birth (like Mary), but were all flower-born ; even like unto the lotus-born Demi-urge Brahmâ, or the mind-born Kûmâras. The mode of birth by coupling male and

---

1. See Divya-sûri charita II-12 :—

मासेथतस्मिन्वसुभे ऽजनिष्ठ पारेसमुद्रं पुरिमल्लनाम्न्याम् । लता गृहान्ताद्भुविभूतनामा कौमोदकीशक्तिमयोमुनीन्द्रः ॥

2. Vide Hierarchic Table and Divya-sûri-Charita :—

तन्मास एवा विरभूद्विपश्चित्प्राचेत सर्क्षे ऽथमयूरपुर्याम् । महाभि धानोमणिकैरवान्तात् श्रीनन्दकात्माश्रितभक्तिरूपः ॥

female natures came as a fact of evolutian long after the androgyne-period,[1] and Brihad-Âranya Upanishad says;—[III-4-3.][2]

"He did thus not feel delight. Therefore alone he feels no delight.[3] He desired a second. Like unto male and female in close embrace—as one—he was. This one he burst in twain. Thence were husband and wife produced. Thus was each a half of himself as a split pea is of the whole. So declared Yâjña-Valkya. (Undivided) it is ether. (When divided as half male)

1. Sir Edwin Arnold says: "The nearest rose-bush may rebuke him (the skeptic), since he will see there the aphides, which in their wingless state produce, without union, creatures like themselves, and these again, though uncoupled, bring forth fresh broods down to the tenth or eleventh generation, when on a sudden winged males and females suddenly result and pair (P. 15. Death and Afterwards)

If God can create *out of nothing*, He can no doubt create saints from flowers, even as Eve from Adam's rib.

2. सवैनैवरेमेतस्मा देकाकीनरमते सद्वितीयमैच्छत् । सहैतावा-नासयथास्त्रीपुमांसौ सम्परिष्वक्तौ । स इममेवात्मानं द्वेधापातयत् । ततः पतिश्चपत्नीचाभवतां । तस्मादिदमर्धबृगलमिव स्व इतिहस्माह याज्ञवल्क्य स्तस्मादयमाकाशःस्त्रियापूर्यत एव । तां समभवत्ततो मनुष्या अजायन्त ॥

3. Greek Plotinus said that the One could not dwell alone but must for ever bring forth souls from Himself (P. 325. Vol I Johnson's Oriental Religions.)

it is complemented by female. He (Demiurge) coupled thus (his two parts). Then were men born."[1]

The highest state again, they say, will be the androgynic, or as our Vedànta tells us that in Moksha (spiritual state) one becomes *Kàma-rùpa* or can assume *any form desired.*[2] No wonder then that the three Holy Commissioners from God were flower-born. Indeed were they in their age three Spiritual flowers sent out to perfume the mundane atmosphere somewhat. By God's Free Grace, these Saints were endowed with a habit of the purest water; *i e.*, the precious case of clay, in which their soul-gems were for a time enshrined, was formed of the pure Sàtvic part of material nature, that so to the soul within, the tenement acted as a translucent medium, helpful not obstructive, to its designs. The gross parts of material nature, the Rajas and Tamas did not enter into their grain. It was all Satva which enableth souls to right apprehension of things, as said in Bhagavad-Gità [xviii-30.]

" That is Sátvika-Reason, Pártha! which discerns

1. Vishnu-Purána says: 'तथोक्तो ऽसौद्विधास्त्रीत्वं पुरुषत्वंतथा करोत्'. Bhàgavata :—' ताभ्यां रूपविभागाभ्यां मिथुनं समपद्यत'।

2. God's Seraphs and Cherubs are like unto God Himself. Cp: [John I. 32] "the spirit of God descending like a dove. and angels appearing as men, like Raphael to young Tobias (Tobias. V.)

action and inaction, duty and non-duty, fear and non-fear, bondage and release."[1]

As the Saints knew what 'bondage' was, the worldlings, in chains of bondage, shunned them. As they knew what 'release' meant, they were slaves to God. Always so are the Godly, wherever lie their vocation either in Heaven or on Earth.[2] 'God is our Proprieter and we His property'[3], thought they, and acted they. Such thought and act were compatible with their essential soul-nature, that of its innate intelligence and bliss, being solely employed to subserve His Sovereign Will.[4] Knowing as they did the delights of Divine Service, they were perfect in all the chief three-fold elements which constitute ripe spirituality, viz :—

---

1. प्रवृत्तिंच निवृत्तिंच कार्याकार्ये भयाभये । बन्धंमोक्षंच यावेत्ति बुद्धिस्सापार्थसात्त्विकी ॥

2. (a) दासावयमिति ब्रह्ममानिनो लोकवर्जिताः ॥

[Vishnu Dharma.]

(b) दासभूतास्स्वतस्सर्वे ह्यात्मानः परमात्मनः । नान्यथा लक्षणं तेषां बन्धेमोक्षे तथैवच ॥ [Isvara Samhitâ]

3. (a) स्वत्वमात्मनि सञ्जातं स्वामित्वं ब्रह्मणिस्थितम् ॥

[Vishvaksena Samhità.]

(b) आत्मदास्यं हरेस्स्वाम्यं स्वभावञ्च सदास्मर ॥ [Ibid.]

4. नाहन्देवो न मर्त्योवा नतिर्यक्स्थावरोपिवा । ज्ञानानन्दमयस्त्वात्मा शेषोहि परमात्मनः ॥ [Jñâna Sára.]

(1) Knowledge (of God.) = Jñâna.
(2) Love (to God) = Bhakti.
(3) Dispassion (or Aversion for world)=Vairâgya.

Physically Satva-constituted, mentally God-absorbed, ethically world-weaned, and emotionally God-enamoured, our Holy Triad needed neither food nor water. All their manna was God, and all their senses revelled in seeing, hearing, feeling, scenting and tasting Him. Said St: Namm-Âzhvâr :—

'In Thy milk of Grace, grew I ripe'[1]

Seeing that with the worldlings, 'to eat was to live and to dress was to thrive' [2], and that what was light to them was night to the saints, and night to them their light, as Bhagavadgîta [II-69] says :—

'In what is night to all, the Saint is awake;
Where awake they, 'tis to him night." [3] ,

they avoided their company as uncongenial to their spiritual nature, but roamed in the world from place to place, sojourning there a day, a night, an hour, just as long as the humanity of the place was prepared to tolerate their angelic temperament, and benefit themselves by their celestial virtue. "Roofless, and will-

1. "*Unadu pâlé-pôl sîr* &c (Periya-Tiruv-andâdi. 58.)
2. '*Undiye udaiya*' &c (Perumâl Tirumozhi III 4.)
3. Cp: "But the sensual man perceiveth not these things that are of the spirit of God: for it is foolishness to him" (1 Cor: II. 14).

strong'[1] they spinned over the land each in his own direction, even themselves not knowing each other. 'They sought sequestered spots, and shunned the passion-infuriated *hoi polloi*'?[2]

God's very soul[3] then were this Triple. God's soul bleeds for His children tethered in clay. By sending the Elders, the wisdom-ripe Eternals of His Family, He sends His own soul (like the Father sending His own Son, who is one with the Father [4]). So long

---

1. 'अनिकेतस्थिरमतिः' [Bh: Gi XII. 19]

2. 'विविक्तदेशसेवित्वं अरतिर्जनसंसदि ॥ [Bh: Gi: XIII.10]

(Cp:) Thomas a Kempis says: "The most emiment saints, where Providence has permitted it, have shunned all intercourse with men, and chosen to live wholly to God in retirement and solitude."

"It is the declaration of Seneca, that 'as aften as he mingled in the company of men, he came out of it less a man than he went in'; and to the truth of this our own experience, after much free conversation bears testimony; for it is much easier to be wholly silent than not to exceed in word; it is much easier to keep concealed at home than to preserve ourselves from sin abroad; he, therefore, that presseth forward to the perfection of the internal and spiritual life must, with Jesus, 'withdraw himself from the multitude.'

(Imit: Christ: Bk I. Ch: XX).

3. ज्ञानीत्वात्मैवमेमतम् । (Bh: Gi: VII-18).

4. 'I and my Father are one' (John X. 30)

the Holy Triple were occupied in the passive phase of love to God. The active phase, or service, begot of love, was to come next. Service[1] to God is service to His children in the manner His Providence planneth. His Children of clay, He wisheth to redeem, and 'rouse them from their immemorial lethargy'[2]. For such service then it pleased Him to employ these Three Flowers. He wished, through them as His chosen vessels, to drive the darkness of ignorance enveloping His clayey creatures and impart to them the light of knowing and loving Him. To carry out His purpose in a way of his own, he inspired each one to turn towards the Holy spot, Tiru-kkôvilûr[3]. Saro-Yogi came on a night to an open plain. A tempest with gusts of wind and pelting rain overspread the heavens. To shelter himself, the Yogi repaired to a narrow crevice close by with a small shutter. Bhûta-Yogi chanced to come to the same place. Finding the little crevice closed, he cried:"Any one in? open pray." "There is just space for one", said Saro's voice. "If one could *sleep* there, it could admit of two *sitting*. Open pray," came the re-

1. 'All privileges are given with a view to service. Daily bread is given that the kingdom may come.'

(*Science and Providence*, by D. S. Cairns, Pp: 364-5: *Contemp, Review*: March. 1900).

2. 'अनादिमायया सुप्तः' । (Mândûkya : Up..)

3. See the table of 108 Divya Desas. It is called Vâmana-Kshetra.

tort. Who says this, thought Saro, cannot be an ordinary person, and he readily opened the wicket and admitted the stranger. It was pitch-dark and the rain was pouring in torrents. Before the two made themselves snug in the narrow enclosure, a third came and knocked. It was no other than our Bhrânta-Yogi. "No space can be spared for a third", said the two, "for we have just enough to sit together." "If two could *sit*, three could certainly *stand*", rejoined our Bhrânta. "This seemeth certainly an extraordinary personage[1]", consulted the two, "let us admit him." He now walked in and the three stood shoulder to shoulder, in perfect suffrage and amity, conversing on Godly Themes and Mysteries[2]. When asked 'who are you'?, the one Saint said: "Different I am from non-soul; I am for God; for Him alone I am[3];" the other said: "To Vâsudeva sole I am thrall"[4]; the third said: "Slave to the Kosala-King am I"[5].

1. *Extraordinariness* consists in the act of unselfishness displayed even at the risk of convenience at a time of trial; thus contrasting with the *ordinary* selfish world which cannot endure "even each other's breath." as sage Appillâr says in his Introduction to the three Andâdi works of these three Saints.

2. Read Bh: Gi: X. 9: मच्चित्ता &c.

3. भगवच्छेषभूतोहं अनन्यार्होऽचितः परः || [Pâñcharâtra.]

4. दासोहं वासुदेवस्य सर्वलोकमहात्मनः || [Nâradiye.]

5. दासोहं कोसलेन्द्रस्य रामस्याक्लिष्टकर्मणः ||

[Râmâyana: Sund: 43-9.]

"Ah! now I have got them;—what a fine sight, my three elect joined together thus—", was the holiday thought of Providence, "How long and weary have I each of them chased. At last clubbed!—are they not?" was His rejoicing. "Now let me feast myself in company with my beloved gems, of such rare water, set together thus." So consulted He with His Queen Consort Sri—Mercy's self.

Now, each of the Three standing Saints felt some, as yet invisible, body squeezing Itself between them. For, they had themselves hardly an inch of space to spare standing as they were. And it appeared hard and heartless that a Ghost also should have taken into its head, at such hard times, to forcibly insert Itself between them. They felt the wedging-in tighter and tighter becoming. "What shall we do? broke out Saro after all. "Wait, I shall light a lamp and see who this Mysterious Being can possibly be". But where is the light to come from and oil and lamp, the rest of it all? 'Here', said St Saro exultingly:—

"The solid land, the lamp; its girdling liquid main the oil[1]; and light, the shining Sun. . And thus I shall discover the Stealing Stranger."

[1st Tiru-v-andâdi. 1.][2]

1. Cp: देवायज्ञमतन्वत वसन्तोऽस्यासीदाज्यम् ॥

(Tait. Up: Purusha-Sûkta.)

2. "Vaiyam tagali-y-ây &c."

"Here", joyously said St: Bhûta, "let me add my light":—

> "With love the lamp,—longing the oil,—
> The frenzied heart the wick—the soul melted,—
> The light of wisdom, light I to Nâr"*na*,
> In meet Tamizh, I know so well."

(2nd Tiru-v-andâdi. 1)[1].

And our third Saint Bhrânta said:— "Here is my quota, brothers, to your lights." Ye have lighted no doubt. But my nature, as one inebriate of God-love, is not even susceptible of that effort. My very name Bhrânta denotes 'The Crazed'; 'for my furied love for Padmâ-Rama*n*a's Lotus-Feet drives me mad^2; and my affection for Vish*n*u makes me thrill and sweat; my eyes stream as if flood-gates of joy did burst; my voice fluteth in ambrosial speech; and I dance with joy, rid of all fear and sure of my Beloved[3]. And, when ye

---

1. "*Anbe tagaliyâ r-ârvame neyyâga &c*"

2. पद्मारमणपादाब्ज प्रेमभ्रान्त्या मनोज्ञया । भ्रान्तयोगीति विख्यातं मुनिं वन्दे गुणाम्बुधिम् ॥ Padmâ-Rama*n*a = Lord of Srî.

3. Cp (*a*) नियतपुळकिताङ्गा निर्भरानन्दबाष्पा गळितनिखिल-सज्जा गद्गदस्तोत्रगीतिः । अमृतलहरिवर्णा हर्षनृत्तोपपन्ना विगतनरक भीति र्विष्णुभक्तिर्विभाति ॥

(Vedântâchârya's Sa*n*kalpa-Sûryodaya X. 26)

(*b*) *Read* Pp: 67—69. Part II. Oriental. Lectures on Inspiration Intuition and Ecstasy. &c.

For (*c*) (*d*) (*e*), *vide page* 84.

shall therefore strike your light and show to my vision a Surpassing Spectacle, I can only rave thus:—

"Lo Her—Mercy—I see; & His Form of Gold I see;
And Their sun-effulgent hues blending, indeed I see—
Proud daring Discus, and the friendly Conch I see;
All this, this blesséd day, in Him the Ocean-hued."

(3rd Tiru-v-andádi. 1)[1]

On lighting the lamps, the Charmer of hearts, with His Mercy,— The *S*riman-Nârâya*n*a—, who cannot abide alone without His lovers, as light cannot without the sun[2], and fragrance without the flower, was disclosed to their startled view. This was the Ghost—the Invisible Wedge--The Divine Figure--which indeed pressed them asunder in the dark. They were dazzled with the Beatific splendour[3]. They were deluged in Its

(c) *'Péyanáy ozhindeṇ &c'* (Perumál T: Mozhi. III. 3. 8.)
(d) *'Azhuran tozhuran &c'* (T-vái-mozhi. V. 8. 5)
(e) *'Kálázhum neñjazhigum &c'* [Peri T: Andádi 34].

1. *'Tiru-kkandén pon-méni kandén &c'*

2. भास्करेण प्रभायथा || (Râmáya*n*a, Yud: 121. 19)

3. *(Man's perception of God sensible as well as mental)*:—
"For not only can he *think* God, he can also *see* God, the mind with which he does the first being a mind purified from obscuration by Matter; and the eyes with which he does the last being of a more or less regenerate self. Of the seers of all ages the supreme beatific experience—that which has constituted for them the crowning confirmation of their doctrine concerning not only the being but the nature of Deity—has been

(Continued on page 85)

glory. The Three burst out in song: Poygai Âzhvâr with his *First* Tiru-v-Andâdi, Pûdatt-Âzhvâr with his *Second* Tiru-v-Andâdi, and Pèy-Âzhvâr with his *Third* Tiru-v-Andâdi.

Thus, the One Saint began his Hymn by defining God as represented in His Manifested cosmos; the Second Saint began his Hymn by describing Him as Nârâyana; and the Third began his by adding '*Srî*'[1] to Nârâyana. All the Three Hymns brim with Knowledge of God (*Para-bhakti*), Love of God (*Para-jñâna*), and Sight of God (*Parama-bhakti*); but in each, one of these three elements notably predominates. These three stages of God-love are realisable to their fullest extent in Heaven alone; but by His grace, the Saints realised them all even while tarrying on earth.

It is these three stages that our Spiritual King *Srî* Krishna adverted to in His Celestial Song, the Bhagavad-Gîtâ (XI-54):—

---

the vision of God as the Lord. For those to whom this vision has been vouchsafed, hope the most sanguine is swallowed up in realisation the most complete; belief the most implicit is merged in sight the most vivid; and knowledge most absolute is attained, that the "Kingdom of Heaven" is in very truth "within", and that the King thereof is—where alone a King should be—in the midst of His Kingdom."

(P: 288. The Perfect Way or the Finding of Christ.)

1. 'As living Substance, God is One. As Life and Substance God is Twain. *He* is the Life, and *She* is the Substance'.

(Pp: 53-54. Ibid.)

"To realise me like this. Arjuna!—to know me,—to see me,—to enter into me—is only possible by unequivocal love"[1]; and,
Vishnu Purâna in *verse* Eighty-seven, and *Amsa* Six[2].

We have these Three Works (Prabandhas), each a Lotus of one Hundred petals (verses,) enlightening, edifying and illumining the world, ever since Providence vouchsafed them to us through His Elect Saviours[3].

Reference to our Three "First Âzhvârs" is made in Villi-Bhâratam, Introduction, in the stanza:—

'Pâvarun tamizhâl' &c.

Blest be the Âzhvâr-Triad.

---

1. भक्त्यात्वनन्ययाशक्य: || &c.

2. संज्ञायतेयेन &c. Read commentary on this by *Sruta-prakâsikâchârya* (P: 29. Bhagavadvishaya, Vol I. Telugu Ed:)

3. Read Tiru-mazhisai-Âzhvâr's life following, where our Holy Triad appear again.

श्रीः

THE LIFE OF

St. Tiru-mazhisai-Âzhvâr.

---

*"Bow we, Bow we, to Bhakti-sâr,
Of five-fold Spir'tual Forces[1] strung;
Who, shell-and-silver-error", xpelled,
To Saviour Murâr's Feet, e'er clung."[2]

Thus runs the Adoratory Verse sung for our Saint, the Blest Tiru-mazhisai-Âzhvár, so called from the place of his nativity Tiru-mazhisai near Púnamalai (Madras); and called Bhakti-sâra or "Essence of God-

---

* शक्तिपञ्चमयविग्रहात्मने शुक्तिकारजतचित्तहारिणे । मुक्तिदायकमुरारिपादयो र्भक्तिसारमुनये नमोनमः ॥

1. According to our Scriptures, there are spiritual bodies which are said to be. the 'Five-Upanishad'-composed. Cp: "But God giveth it a body as he will: and to every seed its proper body." (1. Cor: XV. 38). "And there are bodies celestial" (Ibid: XV. 40).

2. *Murári* is 'Foe-Queller'. Mura is the demon-foe whom Krishna cut to pieces. *Shell-and-Silver-error* is the erroueons misapperhending of a siver-like shining shell for silver itself. This is a Vedántic analogy, finding its applicaziou in the *apparently* real world taken to be not *virtually* real.

love". Our Scriptures,—the Brahmâ*n*da-Purâ*n*a—tell us that the place is the old Mahîsâra-Kshetra, which was sanctified by the Videha-Line of Kings dwelling in that country for the performance of Holy works. It would appear that Rishis Atri, Bh*r*igu, Va*s*ish*t*ha, Bhârgava, Angiras and others went to Brahmâ once, and prayed to him to determine for them the best locality on earth where they could take their lodging and pursue their spiritual avocations undisturbed. Brahmâ, it would appear, put Mahîsâra in one pan and all the rest of the earth in the other pan of a scale, and finding Mahîsâra weighing more, he assigned it to the suppliant Rishis. Glad, the Rishis returned and occupied the Sacred spot. Time went on thus.

Of these, Bhàrgava Rishi, who occupied the West End of the Holy spot and was spending his days in the celebration of what is known as the *Dìrgha-Satra*; by which ritual he but long worshipped the Ancient of ancients, the Blest Vâsudeva. His wife conceived, and bearing twelve months long, she gave birth to a child. It was but a lump without features chiselled, or limbs divided, and enwrapped in the amnionic bag. Divya-súri-charita records that, of the spiritual essence of Sudarsana (= Mahâ-Vish*n*u's Discus) was our saint born, in Magha Asterism, Taishya month (January-February), Dvâpara Age, year Siddhârthi.[1] Both

---

1. सागर्भमाधत्त मुनेश्चपत्नी सुदर्शनांशो नतदानुविष्टम्। पपातगर्भो भुवितैष्यमासे मघाभिधाने महनीयतारे ॥ Vide Hierarchic Table.

husband and wife knew not how to deal with this apparent monstrosity. It had to be disposed of somehow. Living in the woods as they did, they took the fleshy lump and consigned it to the shade of a bamboo-clump and went their way.

The shapeless being was however taken care of by Mother Earth. For gradually, the lump developed into form, limb and features, and began to breathe; and then to wail, probably pinched by the first beginnings of hunger. Abandoned and left forlorn and in such a deserted region, who indeed could answer the cry? Certainly He,—the Friend of the Distressed (Âpad-bándhava). The Lord[1] of Mahísára, Vishnu, heard the plaintive voice, approached the curious child, and eyeing it with affection, blessed it and willed that all hunger and thirst may cease. Child though it was, its eyes first opened to see the Ambrosial sight of Vishnu's Divine mien; but in a wink, the Vision vanished from its view, and set it crying all the bitterly to the weird silence around.

Aroar weeped the child at the unbearable severance from God's Divine Presence but a moment before vouchsafed. At first faintly, then louder and louder fell the cry on the ears of a woodman, Tiruvâlan, who had betaken to the forest with his fellow-laborers to fell timber. They set out in search and following the

1. Called Jagannâtha.

direction from which the sound came, at last reached the child. Wonder seized the forester, and joy following, shook his being. He tenderly raised the child, and carefully carrying it in his arms, flew to his wife Pangayacchelviâr (Pankaja-Selvi) and delivered it. She received it with her open arms, for she was childless. All the mother's emotions overran her frame; and ended even in sensibilities. For indeed the anatomy of her breasts underwent change; they moistened and living milk beganto drip. She put them to the child, but lo! the child would not be nursed thus. Though a child, it was a Blessed Child,a Divine Wonder. It would not feed on human breasts, but on the Blissful Graces of God. It felt no wants and therefore no more did it cry. Neither bladder nor entrails had any function to perform with this rare infant. And yet it grew and fine developments came in the most mysterious manner. Altogether it was a most marvellous piece of workmanship turned out by the Great Architect of the Universe.

News spread. Of course. Even silence will begin to whisper over prodigies of nature. It reached the townsfolk of Mahisâra. Belonging to the Fourth grade of society (*Sûdra*), and childless, a venerable old man lived his quiet days in the town with his lady. He was dowered though with wisdom. For, not the other inhabitants of the place but him alone, it struck that he should visit the marvellous little infant in the woods. Early on a morn he rose, and his wife accompanying, journeyed they together to the spot; and there, on seeing the spiritual glory of the infant and the wondrous celestial nature of its composition, were awe-fixed and joy-filled. With milk too they had come. Both joined their hands in divine fear and fervour and besought the infant—their hearts—melting to deign to accept the offering of milk they had so lovingly brought, and satisfy their spiritual craving. So, the infant responded, and granted their fervid prayer by drinking the milk. For many days the couple came and went, with unfailing supply of milk. And too, the infant would no other milk or nourishment have. It thrived thus much better than the too-much cared for ordinary children of the worldly world.

Our superhuman kind of young saint divined the intention of the old couple, so unremitting in their visits and attentions. One day he drank their milk, but leaving some over. He opened his mouth and bid the couple to drink the remainder and said: "Ye shall have a good son born." They did so, and wondrous to relate, old as they were, they felt youth bubbling in their veins. The good huswife conceived, and when nine months were gone past, a divine kind of child was born, whom, finding Vidura-like, they named Ka*n*i-kka*n*nar. The child was going to be one who,

'Would never for mortal's praise abuse his tongue'.[1]

1. "Nâ-kko*n*du mâ*n*idam pâdâda."

[4th T: Andâdi. 75.]

The parents carefully educated their son in all the sacred lore permitted to their social rank'.

The first influx of God's grace, while yet the child was in the woods screened by the bambu-clump, steadily gained strength, and our Young Saint felt its sensible effects within his inner consciousness. Not alone *spiritual* were these inner workings. They left no desire for milk or any kind of food for *material* sustenance. He was now seven years of age. Though young, he had inclinations to practise the eight-fold Yoga, for remember, he was born of Rishis. He mused how he should decide for himself the best course. He would examine the existing systems of thought, he thought. He set about it. There were systems expounded by Śâkya, Aulûkya (= Vaiseshika), Akshapâda (= Nyâya), Kshapaṇa, Kapila and Patañjali.[1]

1. For these, or some of these systems, and as to the points in which they differ from the true sense of the Vedânta, consult such works as the *Sarva Darsana Sangraha*; Max Muller's *Six Systems of Indian Philosophy*; Râmânuja's *Sri Bhâshya*; *Bhagavad-Vishayam Vol 1.* [The Mahâ-Pravesa]; and others too numerous to mention. The main point is this that some of the systems are atheistic, some skeptic, some agnostic, some inferentially theistic, some hypothetically theistic, some partially theistic, some absurdly pantheistic; the complete Vedântic theism being that expounded by the Drâvida Saints as summarized for example in our Saints' perception of the God-head as shown in the life *infra* Bhâtta and Prábhâkara belong to the ritualistic School of the Pûrva-Mîmâmsa; whereas Yâdava and Bhâskara (who came a good deal after our saint) are of the Uttara-Mîmâmsa school.

which did not recognize the authority of Scriptural evidence in matters of Divine Science, and conflicted with each other on points. There were again systems which recognized Scriptural evidence as proof of transcendental verities, such as the *Saiva*, Mâyâvâda, Nyâya, Vaiseshika, Bhâtta, and Prâbhâkara. These again were found dissenting on points. Neither was there universal agreement, nor did they strictly teach how real knowledge of the Divinity may be gained. He found them all dry and dreary, and after weary traversing over all these waste fields of speculation, he felt his position somewhat as described by St. To*n*d*ar*-a*d*ippo*d*i Âzhvâr :—

"Those noble souls well-ground in Veda's Lore,
Refuse e'en minds to Buddh and Jin to lend;
Much less would ears t' their heretic tenets bend."[1]

Seven Hundred years[2] elapsed thus. After rejecting many systems of thought as unsatisfactory and incomplete, he examined the Vedas and the Vedântas, and found that the Parabrahmam or Paratatvam, which the latter treated, was the Sole Truth,—the Sole Light

1. "Kalai-yara-kkatta mándar." [Tirumálai : 7.]

2. Extraordinary longevity of course excites our suspicion and surprize, because we are modern pigmies. But compare:—
Adam lived 930 years, (Gen. v. 5.); Seth, 912 years; Enos 905; Cainan 980; Malaleel 895; Jared 962; Lamech 777, and Mathusala 969.

shining on the Summit,—the One Father of whom Brahmâ and Îsa were born—and He alone was worthy of our love and worship. The difficult paths of Reason and Yoga were relinquished for the happy one of Bhakti—Love to God.[1]

As love increased, nearer did it carry the soul to the Source of all Love, to the God-head. Gleams and flashes, visions and revelations of Divinity followed, till out of his Grace, attracted by the receptive attitude of the yearning Saint, the complete Nature of God was revealed to his blessed consciousness—complete Nature consisting of His Essence (*summum genus*); His Attributes such as omniscience and omnipotence, depending on the Essence; the Person, which is the Beatific Envelope,—the Person, which serves to proclaim the Beauty of the Essence and the Attributes (or Graces)—; the Adornments such as the Crown, Club, Conch and Discus depending on the Person; the Weapons which also depend on the Person and rival the Adornments, and in addition serve the purpose of defending Creation against the Hordes of Evil; the Universal Mercy and Mediatrix, *Srî* and her

1. Cp: "Go on in the Right Path; and contemplate the One Ruler of the world.
He is One and Self-Proceeding. From Him only are all things born.
He works in all unseen by mortal eyes, yet seeing all.
[*Orphic Hymn of the Mysteries.*]

celestial Maids ever basking in the Moonshine of His Eternal Presence; the Several Hosts of Angels, ever engaged in Service Divine, as if, if that were for a moment deprived, their very life was in peril; the Great Empire of the Empyrean Country, which hath neither limits to its extent nor end to the joy it, in infinite measure, affordeth[1]; and the Theatre of the Manifested Cosmos, on which scenes of Evolution, Progression and Involution were enacted in unending succession—the Cosmos manifested with the Three-fold Elements of the Matrix (matter), Intelligence (soul) and Time[2]. Thus did our saint perçeive and realize God in His fullness of Essence, Character, Beauty, Environment, and Display, both in spheres Spiritual as well as Material[3].

As for that aspect of God, in which He is Father of Brahmâ, and Grand-Father of Rudra, which was vouchsafed to our Saint as a fact and which he sensibly realized, he but found confirmation of the same which he had read in his studies of the Scripture-Revelations. For in regard to the first, Brahmà (the demi-urge for

1. 'Ńalam-andam-illad-òr-Nàdu' [T: Váy-mozhi. II. 8. 4].

2. *Prakriti-purusha-kâlâtmaka.*

3. We cannot refrain from making a remark here that foreigners have allowed themselves to be misled by the Advaitic view of God imposed upon the Vedânta, and even that misunderstood. If Râmânuja were only more broadly known and studied, not only a complete conception of the God-head but a complete view of the Vedânta will be gained.

Creation), the Svetásvatara-Upanishad [VI. 8.] declared thus :—

> ' He, Who, of old did Brahmâ make;
> And Who, of the Vedas, made him gift'.[1]

And in regard to the second Rudra (the demi-urge for Destruction), the *S*ata-patha-Bràhma*n*a declared :—

> 'Salutation to Rudra,—Thousand-eyed,—
> The eldest son of Brahmâ,—th' eminent'.[2]

Not the Upanishads alone, but authoritative works which are exegetic of the same, such as the Mahâ-Bhârata [*S*ánti-parva] corroborated this Truth by proclaiming ;—

> "On the *sacra prescriptive* examined,
> The same again and again reasoned out,
> This final decision is arrived at,
> That Nàràya*n*a alone is worship-worthy".[3]

---

1. योब्रह्माणं विदधाति पूर्वं योवैवेदांश्च प्रहिणोति तस्मै ॥

2. सहस्राक्षाय ब्रह्मणः पुत्राय ज्येष्ठाय श्रेष्ठाय ॥

3. आलोड्यसर्वशास्त्राणि विचार्यच पुनःपुनः । इदमेकंसुनिष्पन्नं ध्येयोनारायणस्सदा ॥

Cp : (*S*esha-Dharma II. 15-16.) सत्यं सत्यं पुनस्सत्यं. उध्दृत्य-भुजमुच्यते । प्रमाणं नापरंवेदान्नदैवं केशवात्परम् ॥ For fuller information on this subject, consult 1. Kuresa-Vijaya by Kuranàtha; 2. Tatva-*S*ekhara by Lokâchàrya; 3. Bhagavad-

(*Continued on page* 97.)

This pronouncement of Vyâsa was the decision of our Saint; and firmly holding on to it with all his heart and soul, sat down for deep meditation for seven hundred years by the side of Gajendra-Tank at Kairavani (Tiruvallikke*n*i, Madras);—past all controversial opinion—and truth found,—its eternal memorization alone remaining for him.

While so engaged, Rudra and his consort Rudrà*n*i, wishing to put our Saint's faith to test, paid him a visit. He rode the Nandi, held the Trident and other marks peculiar to his office. Our Saint, while constantly lovingly keeping his mind ever on Nârâya*n*a, was yet found employed in sewing up an old rag. Rudra came sailing in the air; and our Saint saw him. Fearing lest Rudra's shadow fall on him, he moved aside to avoid it. Pârvati asked her husband who could be this personage, so fastidious. Rudra answered:— "Dear, this is a Great man; he will not even deign to look on us." "And for that very reason, Lord, I wish very much to see him", said the wife, as women are always curious. "Very well", granted Rudra, and both approached our Tiru-Mazhisai. He remained perfectly indifferent, and paid them not the least regard. Rudra led the conversation: "Why art thou so inatten-

---

Vishaya. 4th Volume. [illegible] '*Oarum técum*'; 4. Tatva-Nirnaya by Varadarája (Ammâl) 5. Vishnu-tatva-Rahasya by Ràma-Subrahmanya Sástri (the latest) edited by Govardhana Rangàcharya. 1873; and others too numerous to mention.

tive to us"? "What have I to gain from thee"? the Saint replied. "I have come to confer on thee a boon", Rudra said. "I want nothing", the Saint retorted. "But let our visit to thee not go in vain; do ask some boon, pray", Rudra rejoined. Our Saint smiled and returned the answer:— "But tell me, sir, if thou canst grant Moksha? If thou canst, do grant it me then." "Nârâyana alone has that power Excepting that, pray, ask of me any other boon"[1] returned Rudra. "Well then, canst thou postpone by one day, say, the death of a person destined to die to-day?" questioned our Saint. "Ah, that goes according to the person's Karma", responded Rudra. "I understand", said Mazhisai-ppirân, and in mockery added: "but thou seemst determined to do me a favour. Please thyself then. Grant, Great Rudra! that this thread do follow the needle". Rudra felt piqued, his anger was roused and he thundered forth thus:— "I will consume thee to ashes even as I did Ananga". Thereon he opened his third eye on

1. (a) Srikantha in his Bhâshya on Srí-Sûkta cites:—

ऐश्वर्यमीश्वरादिच्छेन्मोक्षमिच्छेज्जनार्दनात् ॥

[P. 4. Telugu Edtn: Madras, 1881]

(b) In Harivamsa Ch CCLXXI-31, Rudra says:- मुक्तिंप्रार्थयमानं मां................मुक्तिप्रदातासर्वेषां विष्णुरेवनसंशय: ॥

I.e, They may pray to me for Mukti, ...but actual Giver of it to all, is Vishnu alone, no doubt."

his brow, and smoke and fire issued, going forth in streams and columns as if the whole world was going to be burnt down. Tiru-mazhisai-Âzhvâr watched his opportunity and let one eye in the thumb of his right foot open. Fire came forth, like unto the universal conflagrating fire, blazing up like a million Vaisvànaras combined. Before this fire, which burned as if a million suns collided, Rudra's fire was but a fire-fly. To put down the scorching fire of the Saint, Rudra commandád the Pushkal-âvartaka Storm-clouds to empty their liquid contents. They came, over-spread the skies, flashed, and roared. Torrents poured down. The fire was quenched and lands were converted into oceans. But the Saint remained firm like :—

> "Mountains, tho' hard battered by rain,
> Get in the least not injuréd,"[1]

Rudra obsérved the exemplary character of the God-absorbed Saint, expressed his wonder and admiration, and applauding him, approvingly conferred upon him the title of *Bhakti-Sâra*, or "Love-Juice". And looking at his Consort, chidingly said: "Look to what lengths hath thy female curiosity led; into what disasters hath thy quidnunc-disposition landed us. Even like the Rishi Durvâsa confounded by the Godly Ambarisha, we have been discomfited in our mischievous meddling with an innocent recluse. Learn at least now the

1. गिरयोवर्षधाराभिर्हन्यमानानविव्यथुः [Bhâgavata.]

lesson that the Godly (Bhâgavatas) are invulnerable." So lecturing to his Lady, the Blest Rudra left our Saint and wended his way.

The Âzhvâr continued undisturbed for a time in his Yoga. But a certain *S*ukti-hâra, a spirit of the ether happened to pass that way. He bestrode a tiger. All of a sudden, the tiger stopped. It could not proceed a pace further, do what he will. *S*ukti-hâra was startled. He looked around but found nothing. Bending his eye downward, he discovered our Saint seated deeply absorbed in Yoga. So, it was his spiritual influence which would not permit his passing the Saint directly over the zenith. The ether-traveller wondered, got down from his vehicle, and softly approaching Bhakti-sâra: "O Bhârgava[1]-Muni", he addressed, "canst thou not cast away this rubbish of a rag thou wearest? Here is a celestial-woven vesture for thee". So saying he presented one. Bhârgava rejected it, and creating another of his own with glistening gems, and shining like the sun, showed it to him. At seeing it, the spirit lowered his head from shame. And yet he would try the Saint once more. He removed a necklace he wore, and begged the saint to wear it as his Rudra-âksha[2]-mâla. But the saint took the Padm-âksha and Tulasi[3] necklace he wore and

1. *I.e.* Descended from Bhrigu Rishi.

2. The berry of the tree *Eleocarpus Ganitrus*, used for rosaries &c by Saivaites.

3 The Lotus seeds, and beads made of the Basil stalks, used by the Vaishnavaites.

said: "Just look at this." *S*uktihâra to his surprize found it a radiant wreath of all the nine precious gems strung together. "Ah, he is too groat and noble a person to be trifled with by beings of my kind", exclaimed the air-farer, and falling at the Saint's feet, begged of him to pardon his pride, and betook himself away.

Tiru-mazhisai-ppirân continued in his meditations for another period, when another incident happened. There was a magician by name Ko*n*ka*n*a-siddhan (probably belonging to the Ma*l*ayâ*l*am country) who had heard of the fame of the Saint. He wished to test him. He came, and telling him he was versed in the arts of alchemy, offered him a magic-pill (*rasa-gulikâ*)[1], which had the virtue of converting the 80th part of a copper coin into gold of fabulous value. But with utmost disregard, the saint regarded the pill and said: "O Master of magic, we do not need thy pills. Hero take this. It will not only give thee a crore, but a crore of crores". So saying, he rubbed off the dried-up sweat on his golden body, and mixing with it a bit of wax which he scraped out of his ear, and making a bolus of the whole, gave it to the alchemist. He took it and put the same to test. Lo, it worked miracles. He had now

---

1. An alchemical compound with mercury as base, probably the Indian Philosopher's Stone. A base metal such as iron touched by it will convert it into gold. *Rasa-vidu* is the Indian Science of the transmutation of metals.

ocular demonstration of the fame of the Saint. He approached the Saint in due love and loyalty, prostrated to him, and receiving his blessings, returned home.

Our Âzhvâr now changed his abode, to avoid these interferences with his retirement and meditation. He swiftly departed to a cave, and hiding himself there, controlled his senses and concentred his mind on the Universal Spirit.

Time was thus smoothly gliding on. When the Three First Âzhvârs, Poygai, Pûdam, and Péy, who, we have said, were ever on the move, came near the spot where Bhakti-Sâra sat drowned in introvision,—in the course of their peregrinations. They had not approached quite near, but were yet at a distance. But even from there they could see a marvellous spiritual glory beaming forth. "What could this be?" they wondered within themselves, "let us search it out." Following the lead of the glory, they came nearer and nearer, and at last approached the cave. They discovered some one sitting entirely oblivious to all surroundings. Retiring into their Yogic consciousness, they divined that the personage before them must be no other than Bhârgava-Muni. "Holy Sire," they addressed "art thou well?" "O Holy Sires Trio," came a voice in response, "Padma[1]-born! Mâdhavî[1]-born! Kairava[1]-born! are ye three well?" They met, saluted each other, and love at the meeting of saints with saints

1. The Flowers Three (*Vide* their Lives).

brought tears of joy, and their bodies thrilled and trembled with rapturous sensations. They embraced each other, spoke of God and His Infinite Glories; and all four thus, drinking deep the wine of God, fell into Yogic delirium.[1]

It is said, "they were united one with the other, as milk with milk, and honey with honey." Having but one pursuit and one aim, they had one interest, viz, the "imbibing of the nectar of the loving contemplation of God's Holy Feet". After spending some time thus in ecstatic enjoyment of God—their minds united and dissolved in the ambrosial waters of His love—love overmastering and maddening their brains—, by consent the Triad left the place together for another tour, and arrived at Mayúra-puri, the birth-place of Bhrânta-Yogi (*vide* his Life), and there were rejoiced to see the Holy well (Kairava-tírtha) where he was born. They tarried by its side for a length of time engaged as usual in Divine meditation. This Triad was ever on the trot. They left Mayúra-purí, and again visited Bhârgava-Muni, and tasting of God there again with him, took his leave, and again went out on their untiring tramping over the globe.

Bhárgava left his cave in order to visit his native place Mahisára. Going there he found he ran short

1. आह्लादशीतनेत्रांबुः पुळकीकृतगात्रवान् ॥ सदा परगुणाविष्टो द्रष्टव्यस्सर्वदेहिभिः ॥

of Tiruman[1]. He dug the earth, but failed to come across a vein. With Vaishnavas, it is a serious matter to miss even a day, after bath, wearing these holy marks. Without it they could not read Scriptures, perform Prayers (Sandhyâ), worship God, nor eat food. Our Saint—a type of a real Vaishnava—may therefore be imagined how he fared in such circumstances. He was in grief and laid himself down in anxious thought. He had a vision, in which TiruVêngadam-Udaiyân[2] appeared and led the Âzhvâr to a spot where his holy clay lay. He started. Of course the vision had vanished. He rose and tracked the spot; behold, he found his Tiruman. In triumph he wore it on appropriate parts of his body. By this incident his vigour in God-contemplation gained in strength as days went on.

He would visit Kâñchî, he thought, for a variety. It was where his friend Saro-Yogi (Poygai) was born.

---

1. The white earth, cleansed, perfumed &c. used by the Vaishnavas for wearing as vertical marks on the forehead and various parts of the body representing the Holy Feet of God, with Goddess Mercy between them in red. [Just as this was being penned, a curious article "*The symbolism of Hindu Caste marks*" by Kalki Das has reached us.] [vide pp: 299-303, Vol, XXII. Theosophist]

2. Curious to relate that early this morning (3-2-1902 A. C.), we had a dream as if we were travelling with our late mother Nrisimh-amba to *Tirumalai, the abode of Tiru-Vengadam-udaiyân*, or Venkatesa, the Lord of the Tirupati Hills, a Holy Place of very great renown (vide Table at end of St. Andâl's Life).

Near the very Holy Tank—that Yogi's birth-place,—he wished to abide for a time. Káñchî was no other than the Satya-vrata-kshetra, where Téva-pperumâl (Varada-Râja) is God-Resident, manifesting Himself to men visibly in all His glory of Person and Ornaments and Weapons, with His Lord Chamberlain,—the Archangel Vishvaksena,—and other Archangels, the Anantas and Garudas: and the Holy Consorts of Mercy,—Srî, Bhú and Nîla[1] Accordingly our Saint came and planted himself at the spot, going by the name of Tiru-vehkâ;—one of the twenty suburban shrines of To*n*da-country or Kânchî-Man*d*ala—presided over by Sonna-va*nn*am-seyda-Perumâl. or Yathokta-kâri, or 'the Doer of Behests' (of our Saint). (More of this anon.) Another seven hundred years were thus spent.

Now, the child Ka*n*i-kka*nn*ar, of the old couple who had daily carried milk to our Saint, had now grown up. He got scent of our Saint. Leaving his village, he came to Kânchî, fell at the feet of Bhárgava-Yogi,—seated near the Holy Tank—and engaged himself in his services.

An old woman of Kânchî also came and resolved to end her days in serving the hoary Saint in all the menial services, as for example taught by St: Nammâzhvâr:—

> 'List, heinous sins are best atoned
> By lowly service, door outside.'[2]

1. Read the opening paragraphs of Andâl's Life.

2. '*Kadai-ttalai sîykka-ppettâl kadu-vinai kalaiyalâme.*' Tiruvây-mozhi. X. 2. 7.

She would accordingly sweep the place, water and adorn it with artistic designs (*ranga-valli*). and do such other acceptable menialities. One day, the Saint woke from his Yoga-sleep, and seeing how the old woman was employed, asked her what made her do all that; and as he was pleased with her, she may beg of him any boon which he would gladly grant. She was overjoyed, and begged that her old age might depart and she be blessed with youth. The Saint eyed her with eyes brimming with mercy. Lo, she found herself in blooming youth as beautiful as a Deva-dame. Pallava-Râya, the King of Tonda Country, chancing to see her, was struck with her surpassing beauty, and begged her to become his bride. She consented. And the royal man found in her company such ravishing delights as he had never dreamt of before. They were exquisitely elysian, far above all human.

They were thus whiling away time, when old age gradually crept into the king's body: but his partner retained unfading juvenescence. The king was struck at this miracle. "How didst thou acquire it?" he asked her. "By the blest Bhaktisâra's grace," she replied, "But lord, do thou also acquire this super-human gift. Knowest thou Kanikannar? He comes to thy palace daily for alms. Get into his good-will: for he is a friend and devotee of the Yogi. Through his good offices, the saint may condescend to confer on thee also unwaning youthfulness.

Pallava-râya anxiously awaited Ka*n*ikka*n*nar's coming. When he came on his usual round, the king begged of him to invite his Master to his palace, as he wished to pay homage to him. "Impossible, Sir," returned Ka*n*ikka*n*nar, my Master goeth to no man's door, nor doth he care for even kings like thee." "Ka*n*ikka*n*nar, never mind that", said the king, "thou art a beggar at my door. Sing a verse in my praise." But sang Kanikkannar :—

"Oh, ne'er to mortal praise can stoop this tongue,
Most blest when sole the Lord Supreme it sings.
Oh, not for adulation made this mouth,
Nor I can bribe my muse for human use."

But the king would not let the poet go so easily. He insisted on his praising him by song. But Ka*n*ikka*n*nar did not heed the king, and sang instead :—

"Who own the lover's praise but his Beloved,
Full drenchèd revelling in Grace Supreme?
Beloved—who *Pâdag* sits, at *Ûrag* stands,
At *Vehkâ* sleeps—all Gems in Kânchi's groves."[1]

The King became wroth. "What" he broke out, when we commanded thee to sing *me*, thou singest thus? We banish thee from our realm. Get thee gone." As soon said, done; for like Vibhîsha*n*a, whom his demon-brother Râva*n*a rejected in this manner :—

1. "*Âdarargal ennai*" &c. *Pâdagam* is one of the 22 shrines in Tonda-Mandala where *Sri* Krishna (Pándava Dúta) is in *sitting* posture: *Ûragam*, where Tri-vikrama is in *standing* posture; and *Vehkâ* where *Sesha-sayana* is in *lying* posture.

"Soon as his bitter words were said
To Râm's and Lakshman's side he fled"[1],

our Kanikkannar with lightning speed fled to his venerable Master, our Saint, fell at his feet, related all that took place between him and Pallava, and begged his leave to depart. 'The Saint said: 'If you leave, my son, am I going to stay? When I stay not, will our God remain behind? When our God goes, how can his heavenly hosts remain without Him? Let me go to my Shrine Tiru-Vehkâ, and rouse the Lord and bring Him with me." So saying the Saint bent his steps towards the shrine and besought Him thus:—

"List, Lord in beauteous Kânchî sweet!
Forth goes our dear Kanikkannar,—
The sweet-tongued poet whom must I
E'er follow, Sapphire-Hued! do Thou
With us *depart*; thy snake-couch *roll*."[2]

As soon said as done. Without question or murmur—and not a word of explanation asked,—the Lord left the place and silently followed the lead of our Saint. Hence the Lord, the Tiru-vehkâ Nâyanár, is called

1. इत्युक्त्वापरुषं वाक्यं रावणं रावणानुजः । आजगाम मुहूर्तेन यत्ररामस्सलक्ष्मणः ॥ [Râmâyana: Yuddh: XVII—1.]

2. प्रयातिरोपात्काणिकृष्णकोविद स्तमन्वगेमित्यमिहास्पदं त्यजन् । फणीन्द्रतल्पं परिगृह्यमामनुव्रजेतिपश्चं सविधाय निर्ययौ ॥

[Divya-sûri-charitam III. 35]

Cp: the italics in this verse with italics in verse on page 110.

Sonna-va*nn*am-seyda Perumâl or Yathokta-kâri (vide ante). And, as when the glorious sun itself departs, the satellites cannot remain behind, so all the Yogis and Devas, and all the minor deities enshrined in various places of Kánchi, went after the Sovereign Lord, bag and baggage.

As when Srí Râma left Ayodhyâ for the wilds,

> "Each withering tree hung low his head,
> And shoot and bud and flower were dead.
> Dried were the floods that wont to fill
> The lake, the river, and the rill.
> Drear was each grove and garden now,
> Dry every blossom on the bough",[1]

So became the country of the foolish-proud Pallava-râya. It was found godless, bewildered, benighted and dreary and dead,—neither sun nor moon seeming to rise and gladden the hearts of men. A thick pall of darkness seemed to hang heavily over the land, dearth prevailed, and famine entered. Pallava found himself in straits; hastily summoned his ministers, and taking council, went in pursuit of the holy fugitives, and discovering them tarrying at a place called Órira-v-irukkai, fell prostrate at their feet, and implored them to return to his dominions. The Saint was appeased and condescended. Going to his Lord Yathokta-kâri, he entreated him thus :—

1. अपी वृक्षाः परिम्लानाः सपुष्पाङ्कुरकोरकाः । उपतप्तोदका-नद्यः पल्वलानिसरांसिच ॥ [Râmâyana: Ay. IX. 4.]

"List, Lord in beauteous Kāñchi sweet !
Back hails our dear Ka*ni*-kk*nn*aar—
The sweet-tongued poet—whom must I
E'er follow. Sapphire-Hued ! do Thou
With us *retrace*; thy snake-couch *spread*.[1]

As soon said as done; for Yathokta-kâri implicitly followed his beloved Bhakta's bidding, and returned to his native asylum. With the return came light and joy, and good seasons and all prosperity into the territories of the humbled Pallava[2]. The great spiritual truth of God becoming even a servant to His be-

---

1. पुनर्निवृत्तः कणिकृष्णकोविदः सभार्गवःकाञ्चयधिनाथमाधव ॥
इहत्वमास्तीर्य भुजङ्गमास्तरं कुरुष्वनिद्रामितिपद्यमातनोत् ॥
[Divya-sûri-charitam. III. 38.]

Cp. italicised words with those of similar verse on page 108.

2. Cp: "Idaikkâdar was a Yogi and was frequently moving in the society of the Professors of the Madura College. He is considered by some to be an incarnation of Vishnu just as Tiruvalluvar is considered to be an *avatâr* of Brahmâ. On a certain occasion, he wanted to have an interview with the Pândya, probably Ugra-pperuvâladi, to show his literary prowess and get the admiration of the King. Through his friend Kapilar who was one of the prominent members of the academy he had an interview. But the King gave a cold reception; and the irritation of the poet, according to *purânic* accounts, resulted in the evacuation of the God and Goddess of the local shrine from Madura to a place some distance yonder north, along with the Tamil academy. The wrath of the poet was subsequently appeased by the King, and God Somasundara, along with the academy, came back to Madura (Siddhânta Dîpikâ. Vol. IV. p: 88).

loved Bhaktas as illustrated by Yathokta-kàri to our Bhakti-sára, was immortalised by him in verse 36 of his Holy Poem *Námmukhan Tiru-v-andàdi*, and verse 63 of his other Poem *Tiru-cchanda-viruttam*. Settled down again thus, the ripe old Saint was again in Divine Thought enrapt. For a diversion, our Saint thought of presenting his homage to the Lord Resident at Kumbhaghona—the Ârâ-v-amudan—, and there spending some time absorbed in thoughts of the special graces and beauties of the Deity, as there made manifest. As soon the will was made, it was put into act. Rapidly the saint journeyed on to the shrine, and on the way he rested himself a little in the village called Perum-puliyûr, on the pial of a house. In that very house, it so happened, there were Brâhmanas assembled and were reciting the Holy Vedas. But on seeing a foreigner, they broke off. When they wished to take up the thread, their memory would not help them, do what they will. The Saint divined their perplexity and taking a black paddy grain under his finger-nails chucked it on the floor. This act immediately brought to their memory the thread of their broken recitation, for the passage ran to the effect that in performing the Ràjasúya Sacrifice, the master of the ceremony should take the grains of paddy which the huswife should husk with her finger-nails, then cook and oblate to fire[1] &c. At this they were wonder-struck, and exclaimed: "He

1. कृष्नानांव्रीहीणां &c [Yajus. I. 8. 9. 1].

may be a low-caste Sûdra, but he is not really one, being godly"[1], and they all came in a body, fell at his feet and atoned for their mistake.

When the saint went round the village on a self-imposed begging excursion, the Deity of the place, the worshippers observed, turned itself, face towards where the saint happened te be at the time. This miracle was whispered from ear to ear and the Bráhmana-fold of the place taking up the news fled to the Yágasâla Perumpuliyâr *Adigal*,—the Dikshit—and told him :—"Sire, a wonder have we witnessed. Our eyes are blest by the sight." On hearing this, he exclaimed :—

> "In troth the eye hath reaped its fruit
> When godly souls like these are 'spied:"[2]

And exulting stepped forth from his Yágasâla and fleeing to where the Saint stood, he was dazzled with the Spiritual Glory which presented itself to his sight. He supplicated the Saint to deign to visit his Sacrificial Yard (*Yâga-sâla*), and there seating him in the most worshipful seat, paid him all the worship due to the dignity of such extraordinary personage. The conductors of the ritual (the *Adhvaryus*)—Pharisaical in their spirit—took offence at their Dikshit (Master of the Ceremonies) paying honors to an unknown and undeserving individual—probably a low-caste—even as Dharmaputra of the Bhârata fame did thus to the

---

1. नशूद्राभगवद्भक्ता विप्राभागवतास्मृताः || [Bhârata]

2. [Meyyadiyâr tam &c.' (Perumâl T. Mozhi II. 1.)

cowherd Krishna in his Râjasúya Sacrifice!! Boisterous they cried: "Thou hast rendered Our Holy Sacrifice futile, by this wight polluting the place", and used such other reproachful language to the Saint that it made the Dîkshit's heart ache. He turned to the Saint and said: "Holy Father, it exceedeth my impatience to listen to this vile speech." Thereon the Saint thought it was time to teach the revilers wisdom by disclosing his hidden greatness:—

"Oh, who, the Heart-hid Holy Lord, can find
But he in Eight-limbed Yoga fitly trained?
But he in mental worship loving fixt?
But he whose End and Aim is Moksha sole?"[1]

"How can high-stringèd letters 'vail, O Lord'?
When pride of men in rules ritüal reek?
Ah, silence them, Thou Discus-handed God,
And prove my faith; declare Thy Hidden Face."

On this invocation reaching Him,—the High in Heaven—behold! there emerged from the Unseen, the resplendent Figure of God, recumbent on His *Sesha* couch, resting on the Milky-*Sea*, with *Srî* and Bhû on loving service bent. And the Saint's visible person was seen as enshrining in his heart this Divine Form. Wondrous to relate, they were all entranced, and the same Di-

1. अष्टाङ्गयोग सिद्धानां हृद्यागनिरतात्मनां । योगिनां अधिकारस्यादेकस्मिन्हृदयेशये ॥ [Pâñcharâtra.]

vine Form which shone enthroned in the saint's heart, seemed to be settled on each one of their devoted heads. Here was ocular demonstration before which controversy stood all silent and vituperation lost all its tongue. Astonished and astounded, the malefactors stretched themselves fully before the transfigured spiritual person of the saint, carried him in triumphal procession in a high car (*Brahma-ratha*), thus expiating for their rash conduct. The Saint, pleased, imparted to them the Truths of Divine Wisdom and pursued his way to his Goal, Tiru-kkudandai (Kumbhagô*n*am).

Arriving there, he enjoyed to his content the Blissful Visions of Lord Ârâ-v-amudan (= Ambrosia that satiates not); and as a result of his Divine experiences, he hymned the two works known as Nân-mukhan-Tiru-v-andâdi and Tiru-cchanda-Viruttam, and in dedicating the same he said :—

> " Ku*d*andai-Kâv'ri Bank Who sleep'st,
> Just let me see Thee rise and speak."

As bid, so did the Lord begin to rise. "Oh, pardon pray. Stretch theyself on they Sesha-couch as before", exclaimed the Saint, seeing now how willing ever is God to His loving slaves. The saint sang his benediction. Even to this day Ârâvamudan can be seen half lying and half risen. This position was made by the saint the concrete subject for his meditation, and he remained immersed in Yoga thus for 2300 years, discarding all solid food, and subsisting sólely on a little milk. For a total of 4700 years is Bhârgava-Yogi said to have lived. Leaving to posterity the two Holy Lays abovesaid, for their everlasting delectation, salvation and gratitude, the blest Yogi passed on to Nirvâna.

Blest be St. Bhaktisâra.

श्री.

THE LIFE OF

ST. KULASEKHARA ÂZHVÂR.

'Reverent bow I to Kul'sekhar—
The Royal Saint—whose Capital
Resounds with rumours recurrent :—
"*To Ranga's Shrine bound we for aye*"
"*To Ranga's Shrine bound we for aye.*"' [1]

Kula-sekhara Âzhvâr is thus a Royal Saint. He is the crown-gem in the Royal Pedigree of the Rulers of Travancore. They do not own the Kingdom. Their Dæmon God Ananta-Padma-Nâbha of Ananta-sayana (Travancore) owns it to this day. The Ruler for the time being is simply God's vassal and minister. Invariably twice a day the king makes his obeisances to Srî Padmanâbha ; and reads his reports to him of his daily administration of the country, of which he is but the trustee. Such is the Ancient Line of Hindu Kings, among whom our Kulasekhara appeared. His horoscope

1. घुष्यते यस्य नगरे रङ्गयात्रादिनेदिने । तमहंशिरसावन्दे राजानं कुलशेखरम् ॥ [Adoratory]

tells us the time of his birth as 27 Kali current, year Parâbhava, Punarvasu[1] Asterism; and born in Tiruvañjikka*l*am, of the Kolli Land (Malayâlam, the Western Ghauts and the Arabian Sea), of the *Sêra* Dynasty, spiritually descended from the *Kaustubha*-part of Srî Mahâ-Vish*nu*.[2]

As a Kshatriya of great prowess he shone; for our chronicles say that he was King not only of the *Sêra* Country, but of the Chô*l*as and of the Pâ*nd*yas. Our Text says:—He was *Kôlli-Kâvalan*, *Kûdal-Nâyakan*,

1. Punarvasu is the asterism in which Sri Râma was born. This has meaning as the Saint's life will show. The father of the Saint, Dridha-vrata is said to have been childless, and after intent worship and prayer, Nârâyana was pleased to accept it and provided for a saintly son being born. He was educated in all the arts of war and government, and all learning too, proper to the domain of the spirit such as the Four Vedas and the Six *Sâstras*. In short the father trained the heir-apparent in every way fitting the high position he was to occupy. When from boy he waxed into manhood, and wise and strong and fit to rule the Kingdom, Dridha-vrata who watched his son's development with great delight saw it was time to entrust him with the reins of Government. He duly installed him on the ancestral Throne, and as was the wont with the ancient Sovereigns, Dridha Vrata retired into forest life for contemplation on the eternal interests of his soul.

2. तस्मादभूच्छेरकुलप्रदीपश्श्रीकौस्तुभात्मा कुलशेखराख्यः । मही पतिर्माघपुनर्वसूद्यदिने हरेः पूर्णकटाक्षलक्ष्यः ॥

Kûdal=Madhura) *and Kôzhi-Kkôn* (*Kôzhi*=Uraiyûr)[1], The four-fold features of royalty he possessed in plenty, *viz.*, Infantry, Cavalry, Artillery, and the Commissariat Remount; and he held the neighbouring chiefs by the might of his arm as subject to his suzerainty. His internal administration was characterized by virtue, justice, piece and happiness; the weak feeling strong, and the strong weak, under his keen eye and watchful care. And magnanimity ruled his heart, like Srî Râma who gave :—

> " ...... all cows that wandered o'er
> The meadow far as Saryu's shore,
> At Râma's word the herdsmen drove
> To Trijat's cottage in the grove."[2]

And yet these were virtues which made him an all-round personage as far as this world's career went. What about the virtues which fits one for Heaven? King Kulasekhara, like every other man of the world, considered himself to be an *independent*[3] being, and *self-governor.*[3] In fact, he was worldly-wise but spiritually blind. Spiritual blindness consists in the self-conceitedness which ascribes all perfection, all thought, act, and even being, to one's one personality, forgetting the latter's unsteady and evanescent character; forgetting that

1. [*Perumâl Tirumozhi* II. 10.]

2. तंपरिष्वज्य धर्मात्मा आरात्मात्सरयूतटात् । आनयामासतागात्र त्रिजटस्याश्रमंप्रति ॥ [Râmâyana II. 39-40.]

3. I. E. *not dependent* on another Being; and *not governed* by another Being.

life on this globe is but a short lease, and that its secret strings and springs are elsewhere, in the hands of a Mighty Power, and Inscrutable Providence; in short forgetting that we really possess not independence absolute, but a small range of action assigned for a short time by another Absolutely Independent Sovereign of the Kosmos; and that we self-govern ourselves is an illusion,—which is amply daily illustrated by the incidents and accidents of life, over which no one can boast of having perfect control, *i.e.*, to stop, change, alter or create those events as one may at his good will and pleasure,—whereas really there is an absolute Governor above, who rules us and all the events which take place around us. As long as a man is worldly-wise, he will not perceive this truth; but when the truth happens to dawn on his spiritual vision, it is by God's Grace. We cannot bind God to manifest this free and sovereign Gift of His Grace at our bidding and at our convenience. Our duty lies in loyalty and allegiance which require a prayerful attitude of our mind, and a resigned and patient awaital of His own good time. This conduct comes as a natural sequel to the perception of the truth above-said, and which, postulated in other words, consists in the recognition on man's part of his true relationship to God, viz., that he is bound to God by dependence, and God is bound to him by Independence; that he is bound to God as the governed or protected; and God is bound to him as the Governor and Protector. Man is a *material* being in so far as he forgets this relation; and a *spiritual* being in so far as he remembers it.

Kulasekharar was to become a Saint and a Saviour for the uplifting of the evolving humanity. God's Free Grace began to operate on him, and he gradually felt a revolution working in his inner nature and his judgments and criteria of things undergoing a change. According to our philosophy, the soul and body are so intimately united that changes in the latter lead to changes in the soul. The change in the former case is a change of substance; in the latter of consciousness. According to our phraseology, the body is of a triune composition, Satva, Rajas and Tamas, of which the predominance of Satva tends to produce the spiritual mode of consciousness in the soul, as contradistinguished with the material modes which Rajas and Tamas tend to produce.[1] Thus, by God's Grace, Satva reigned now in Kulasekhara: as a consequence, spiritual perceptions dawned. He now began to estimate the world and its concerns at its true value. He began to recoginze that it was at best vanity and vexation of spirit. It deserved to be lightly treated, if not completly discarded. Added to these reflections, the blissful gleams of God's exquisite essence, nature, beauty and glory, that he was blessed with, made him a reformed and regenerated man. It is recorded that God in Heaven commanded his High Chamberlain,

1. On this subject, Lecture XIV, *Bhagavad Gîtâ* may be perused.

Vishvaksenar to proceed and administer to Kulasekharar the five-fold Sacrament called the Pancha-Samskâra and initiate him in the mysteries of Religion and return.

With this new vision, he looked on the world and on himself; and he exclaimed :—

" What madness, aye, doth mortals grip,
That lust and lucre turn their heads;
So prone are they to acts of vice,
With so much zest and will they 're done"[1]

"Oh! how men are slaves to their corpse-bodies! how they relish bodily joys! how they are alienated from God! how they identify body with soul; how given up to objects of sense are they! To remain in their midst, seems to me like being strangled in the gallows. To ride on the elephant's back,—an audacious Ruler of men—and enjoy all the delights of Royalty, seems to me like being enveloped in the burning flames of fire".

" In leaps and bounds, how fortune flows,
Yet all the more like fire it burns."[2]

" Desire not I detestful births,
Which pamper to the wants of flesh"[3]

---

1. अकृत्यकरणादावप्यत्यन्तोद्भटवृत्तिकः । अर्थकामाभिभूतोऽयमुन्मत्तइववर्तते ॥ [Adhyâtma-Chintá]

2. *Kollenru Kilarndu* [T-vây-Mozhi. IV, 9. 4.]

3. *Ûnéru selvam* (Perumál: T: Mozhi. IV. 1.)

"Desire not I delights of sense
Nor Sov' reignty o'er all this earth"[1]

Let me, like Vibhîshana who said :—

'From Lanka, friends and wealth, I fly;
And reft of all, on Thee rely;'[2]
'I left my children and my wife,
And flew to Raghu's son for life';[3]

abandon the world, and seek after my lasting God.[4] Let me journey on to where my Ranga-Nâtha of ocean-hue, lieth on His *S*esha-Couch in *S*rírangam; let me join the ranks of the Bhaktas, the enthusiastic devotees who ever teem the Holy Shrine. O! for the time when I will be a slave of theirs; O! for the joy when I will be one with them!!"

Love to God and contempt for the world did thus daily gain breadth and depth with our Saint; and it became his daily sigh and constant cry (read the Benedictory at the heading of this life) for journeying on to the Shrine of Ranganátha, and make

1. *Inbamarum* (Perumâl. T: Mozhi IV. 5.)
Vide Topic I Renunciation (*Divine Wisdom of Drâvida Saints,*)

2. परित्यक्तामयालङ्का मित्राणिच धनानिच ॥

[Râm: VI. 9. 4.]

3. त्यक्त्वापुत्रांश्चदारांश्च राघवं शरणंगतः॥ [Râm: VI. 17. 14.]

4. Cp: They (*i.e.* Nobili and his colleagues,) renounced all riches, dignities, honours, friends and kindred; they desired to have nothing of this world; they scarcely took the necessaries of life; attention to the body, even when needful, was irksome to them." [P. 174. *H. J. S. Cotton's New India.* 1886.]

it ever his dwelling place. He would sometimes sigh for the Holy Shrine of Tirumalai where Venkatáchala-Pati shines—the Shrine where both celestials and terrestrials equally pay the Lord homage,—the Shrine where the Holy Pond Svâmi-Pushkarinî is—the Shrine where :

> ' As herb or worm or stone or dust,
> 'Tis privilege high there so to dwell.'

He would sometimes sigh to go to another Shrine, and another, yet another, and at each place would settle down for ever.

He invited learned men, wise men and sages and Bhaktas to his capital and read with them all the Sacred-Lore, and all the Purânas Eighteen, and Sub-Purânas Eighteen and Itihâsas and Institutes, and taking the best gems out of that vast ocean, strung together into a garland of poems called the *Mukundamâla*, which to this day is extant. We can but translate one or two stanzas.

> " Cupid that kindlest carnal lust !
> No more defile my mind ;
> His Roseate Feet beware—the Lord
> Of Heaven and Earth there shrined ;
> Ere this singed art Thou once by ire
> Of Rudra's fiery eye ;
> Remember though the Chakra's fire
> Of Mura's foe for aye."[1] [V : 29.]

---

1. मदनपरिहरस्थितिंमदीये मनसिमुकुन्दपदारविन्दधाम्नि । हरनयनकृशानुनाकृशोसि स्मरसिनचक्रपराक्रमंमुरारेः ॥

"This frame, by time-wrought changes struck,
Unhinged of joints, will fall,
Oh, woeful shattered. Senseless fool,
Why mak'st thou drugs thee gall!
Drink thou that quintessence, Krishna,
To make thee well and whole,
And share for e'er the bliss reserved
In Heav'n for Angels sole."[1] [V: 31.]

From all the ocean of Holy Literature, he selected the Râmâyana for his daily recital; for according to the text:—

'When He, the High, the Veda-Known
Took form as Das'rath's son,
The Ved by Vâlmik's inspired tongue
Took form as Râmâyan,'[2]

Srî Râma was to him no other than God incarnate on earth, as Saviour of souls,—the same God whom the Scriptures spoke. In the course of the recital, to which he lent devout attention, there came the passage:—

---

1. इदंशरीरं परिणामपेशलं पतत्यवश्यं श्लथसन्धिजर्झरं । किमौषधैः क्लिश्यसिमूढदुर्मते निरामयं कृष्णरसायनं पिब ॥

For complete Translation of *Mukundamâlâ*, vide Pârthasârathi Yogi's New year's God-Send to the Maharaja of Travancore.

2. वेदवेद्ये परे पुंसि जातेदशरथात्मजे । वेदः प्राचेतसादासीत् साक्षाद्रामायणात्मना ॥

"There twice seven thousand giants stand
With impious heart and cruel hand:
Here Râma stands, by virtue known:
How can the hero fight alone?

On hearing the line: "*How can the hero fight alone?*" the King's love for his Râma was lashed into frenzy. He rose forthwith, commanded his army to proceed with him where Râma was fighting alone and helpless (as he fancied). In accents of frenzy he cried :—"Alone my Râma is fighting on the battle-field. Brother Lakshmana is left behind to gaurd my mother Sîtâ from dangers of solitude. Ráma single goeth forth to face the numerous demon-crew of four-and-ten thousand. My Râma is in peril. Should it go contrary with him, what dreadful consequences! With swords and bows well armed, how can he be in dearth of heroes to aid him? Shall not I, his Bhakta, go and guard his side, even though he lack not his fiery Wheel and pealing Conch? Quick, O Valiant Soldiers! march".

'What, has our Sovereign demented gone?' anxiously thought our King-Saint's men and ministers. "Oh Fates, how to calm him! How to bring him to sense! Oh Gods! How to rescue him from his impossible crusades, and infuriated resolves!" inquired they among themselves in great trepidation, and hit upon a device:—They should send a secret party in advance of the king, so instructed as to return and meet the king and his army from the opposite side while he was on his way. They should dissemble they were people coming from the battle-field where Râma fought, and deliver to the king the tidings that Râma won the field, single-handed, slewing all the vile crew of the 14,000 Râkshasas: and returned safe to his Sîtâ, and that:

> "When Sîtâ looked upon her lord,
> His foemen slain, the saints restored,
> In pride and rapture uncontrolled
> She clasped him in her loving hold." [1]

The secret party accordingly sped in advance unknown of course to the impassioned king, our Saint, and wheeling round at some distance, met the king marching on at an angry rate, and broke to him the gladsome news of Srî Râma's glorious victory and happy meeting with his darling Consort.

At hearing this, the king's joy was inexpressible. Of course, in his then mood, he believed their tale, and returned home with them.

The daily recital of Râmâyana went on as usual; and every important event which was read, was celebrated with great ceremony, pomp and rejoicings, and taking Srî Râma's Image (enshrined in his house-chapel and elaborately worshipped daily) in procession through the streets of his city with great eclat; ending with sumptuous feedings of Srî Vaishnava sages and gentry

1. तंदृष्ट्वाशत्रुहन्तारं महर्षीणां सुखावहं । बभूवहृष्टावैदेही भर्तारं परिषस्वजे ॥ [*Râm.* III. 30. 39.]

and with distribution of charities, and what not. Knowing the peculiar temperament of the king, and his keen spiritual susceptibility which carried him to the stigmata-stage, the reader (to the king) of Râmâyana exercised caution. For he enlarged on those events of the life of Ràma where Râma was happy; and only slightly touched, or slipped over such passages as treated of distress, fearing lest the king get excited and fired beyond bounds of ordinary reason.

One day however, the reader-Guru was obliged to absent himself, as other business called him elsewhere. He deputed his son to do the recital for him. The son was unaware of the king's abnormal religious fervour; and so he read and expatiated on all passages of the Râmâyana alike. And the incident of Sìtá's abduction by the vile Râvana, came to be read. Instantly, it lit fire to the King's imagination, his wrath roused, and his enthusiasm burst forth. "Immediately I must march, "across the ocean," he raved, "reduce Lanká to ashes; slay its ruler, Ràvana, with all his crew of brothers, friends and relations; rescue my weeping mother Sitâ; and join her with my Father Srî Râma." As he raved, he rose, armed himself, bid his army march, and sallying forth to the sea-shore, looking towards Lankâ, plunged into it without a thought of the dire consequences which must follow from such rash and reasonless act. The ministers and others were plunged in anxiety and dread, and wonder staring in their faces, eagerly watched the King's procedure. They were so staggered as not to be able even to think how to advise him against his head-strong impulses, nor dare to move to prevent him from giving action to his impulses. As they could not think anything at this critical juncture, they simply stared. As they stared, the King had already plunged into the sea, and was neck-deep in water, resolved to swim the vast stretch of the ocean beyond, to reach the shores of Lanka.

Srî Râma of the noble Kakustha pedigree installed in our Saint's Home-Shrine, and daily worshipped, was watching throughout, the course of events. Now matters had assumed a critical aspect. There was no alternative. Appear now He himself must. So Srî Râma thought, and lo! as the King was about to swim forward in the delirium of his frenzy, he saw before him the enchanting sight of Srî Râma approaching him, with his dear consort Sîtâ clinging to His powerful arm. Addressing his devout servant, our King-Saint Kulasekhara-pperumâl, Srî Râma spoke :—List, O my Faithful! We are returning victorious from the battle-field. Our foe-men have all perished. Our illustrious Partner we have rescued. Your venture for our aid has been forestalled, and your wish has been fulfilled. Pray let us all return to thy city. Let me lift and carry thee to the shore, even as souls are lifted and carried by us from the larger and deeper sea of Samsâra, to the shores of Heaven beyond." So saying, Srî Râma caught hold of His king-servant, brought him safe to the shore, and accompanying him as far as the city, vanished out of sight.

"God-sick is our king; what is the remedy for this disease? Let us diagnose. Ah, we find the cause now. It is the association with the Godly and the Saintly—the *S*ri-Vaish*n*avas—that has brought the king to this pass. Let us wean him then from such associations." Such were the cogitations of the poor ministers who surrounded the king. The king who, on the other hand, was daily sighing to go to *S*ríra*n*gam and live there for ever (read the Adoratory Verse), was now in earnest. He ordered preparations to be made for his bidding adieu to his kingdom and join the Kingdom of God[1]. The ministers thought:—"When the king is once there, he will never return. The association with the Godly there, is even of a worse (!) type than here. Irresistible associations abound there, let us devise a plan to foil the king's designs. He is so attached to Godly men—the Sri-Vaish*n*avas—that he looks upon them as God's own; and being so, worthy of first worship, or worthy of worship even before God Himself." So, whenever the king essayed to go to SrîRa*n*ga Shrine, the ministers had a batch of *S*rî-Vaish*n*avas ready as hailing from one Holy Shrine or the other. The king would postpone his journey on their account. In course of time, the ministers found that their plan proved but a case of 'out of the frying pan into the fire,' for the king's court, his palace, his private apartments as well as public places all became swarmed with the *S*rí-Vaish*n*ava gentry; and the

1. The British may build empires on earth, (says the *Arya*), but we Hindus build empires in Heaven.

king made no difference with them wherever they came and went, and whenever they came and went. They were allowed free access and familiarity, and the king literally venerated and adored them according to the Sâstric injunction that 'a *S*rîvaishnava even once worshipped' carried with it as much reward as worshipping God 60,000 years. The ministers found these Godly folk a nuisance and were in a fix as to what to do. They felt as between Scylla and Charybdis. If they tried to wean the king from his *S*ri-Ranga journey, they had to suffer the Godly folk to assemble and accumulate–but their crowd was becoming unmanageable–; but if they tried to eradicate this *root* of the king's divine ailment,—as they thought always,—by bringing about their evacuation from the country, the king would say farewell to his dominions and depart. "Supposing we could by some means calumniate these vile folk, in the king's eye," they thought, "then he would certainly awake from his delusion of believing: these are godly men. If the godly,– as *he* thinks–were proved ungodly, there is a good chance of reclaimimg the king from his odd ways." They thus hit upon a method:--Out of the box containing the valuable jewelry of the king's darling deity,—Image Sri-Râma,—they secreted a precious necklace, unknown to any one. It would be missed, and reported to the king of course. He would hold an inquiry. And who should be the felons? Surely these seeming Godly folk, who are the warders and guarders of the jewellery, the appointed priests as they were for fulfilling the function of daily worshipping Srí Ráma and therefore directly concerned in constantly ,using the jewellery. So, the necklace was missed and a report was made to the king that the Srî Vaishnavas who had the management in their hands of the worship-department, were culpable; and were to be subjected to trial and punishment. The king heard it all but at last exclaimed in a loud tone: "Hearken! O Ye ministers, Lovers of God are incapable of stealing. It is impossible that even a notion of vice can enter into their thought, not to say of act. Behold! I can swear to what I say. To prove this truth of my conviction and prove the falsity of your accusation against my Innócents, let a vessel, with a live venomous cobra imprisoned in it, be brought to me. I shall thrust my hand into it." As soon said as done. And the King, before his Court in solemn conclave assembled, said: "If my Innocents are straight in thought, word and deed, I cannot be bit by this cobra; but if they are crooked, let it bite me and kill." So saying, he fearlessly plunged his arm into the vessel of death, but drew it forth as clean as when he thrust in. The ministers were put to shame They hung their heads. It was useless, they thought, to dodge and trifle with the king, who was too much for them; fell at his feet, confessed their trick, brought the necklace and placed it before him in fear and respect. The king pardoned them even as Ráma pardoned the vile culprit Káká-sura, the crow,—and the King was Ráma's disciple—and bid them from that day forward to be the slaves of his Innocents.

"No more will I dwell with these vile and scheming ministers", the king thought within himself, "I am disgusted with them. Why them?—well the whole world is weary to me. With the world and with the worldlings I feel as if I would rather allow myself to be placed in the midst of flaming fire than keep company with them. Brutes are those who are turned away from God"[1] So determined, our Saint would no longer bear to remain in his kingly estate, but called his son named D*r*idha-vrata (so called after his grand-father), and entrusted him with the charge of his government, and accompanied by his daughter,—who, it is recorded, was a divine daughter of the *Amsa* of Nilá-devi (see St Ând*á*l's life),—went to the Shrine of Ranga,—his heart's Eternal Hunger. And there he gave his daughter in marriage to Ra*n*ganátha Himself and remained there for a length of time engaged in conducting manifold services to the Deity and His devout servants,—the Srî-Vaish*n*ava Brethren. At intervals he undertook pilgrimages to such Holy Shrines as Tiruvé*n*gadam (Tirupati), Ayodhya, Chitrakûtam, Tiru-kka*nn*apuram, Tiru-mál iruñjôlai, Tiru-vittuva-kkôdu &c.; and as an embodiment of the divine emotions and enjoyments which came to him on all these occasions, is left to us the Drávida Prabandha, called Perumá*l* Tirumozhi, consisting of one hundred and three stanzas, commented on by

---

1. वरंहुतवहज्वालापञ्जरान्तर्व्यवस्थितिः । नशौरिचिन्ताविमुखाजन-संवासवैशसम् ॥ [*Saunaka-Samhitá*]

Sage Periya-v-àcchàmbi*ll*ai. Perum*ál* is a title with which our saint is distinguished, in particular recognition of his unique disposition of the heart, feeling sorrow when God was in sorrow and happiness when God was happy (as in *Àvatàras*).

He undertook a pilgrimage to the Shrine of St. Nammàzhvàr, (Tirunagari near Tirnevelli), and went from there to the Holy place called Brahmadesa Mannár-Kôil and remaining there for some time doing services to the Lord Resident there—Ràja-gopàla-svàmi,—departed to Heaven at the age of Sixty-Seven. It was this Royal Saint who sang :—

> " What makes me king is not the crown
> Which men set on my head ;
> But king, when King of kings doth make
> His Lotus-Feet my crown."

(*Perumâl Tirumozhi* : *X*. 7.)

Blest be St. Kula Sekhara-Âzhvâr.

श्री.

THE LIFE OF

Sri. Tiru-ppâni Âzhvâr.

On the south bank of the sacred Kaveri River is Nichulâpuri or modern Uraiyûr. It was a thriving city in days of yore, ramparted and filled with palace-like houses. Belonging to the solar pedigree, the Chola King Dharmavarma claimed the city as his capital. His reign is recorded as one of peace and virtue. He was a pious devotee of Lord Ranganâtha, on the Northern bank. All these qualities prepared the way for a celestial daughter like Uraiyûr Nâycchiyâr (Vâsa Lakshmî) being born to him, like the very Lakshmî born in the Milky Main. Dharmavarma was in raptures over the event, and he reared up his rare child with all the doting affection of a royal father, even like Janaka of old, his pet daughter Sítâ. From childhood she was devoted to no other dolls than those of Ranganâtha. Even in her girlhood, that Holy Doll was her constant companion. To her it seemed instinct with life. Once on a day—now she was in her bright teens—she went out with her maids, riding in a sedan to the pleasure-gardens in the vicinity, on a pleasure excursion. The real prototype of her Holy Doll,—Ranga himself from Srírangam—chanced also to come to the place on a hunting-excursion[1]; and our darling dame's eyes fell on Him, rivetting them to His beauteous Person. She was in love. Her heart warmed and fluttered; and her will settled that no other than Ra*n*ga she would wed—as unshakeable a resolution as that of Saintess Â*n*dâl.[2] She returned home love-lorn and lost no time in opening her secret mind to her Royal Parent. He was in ecstasy at the rare fortune which was going to be yet his. As was his wont, he sped to the Holy Shrine of Srírangam and delivered to Ranga the proposals of marriage from his daughter. Of course, the King was assured that the proposals would meet glad acceptance at Ra*n*ganâtha's hands and the Lord would add too the title of father-in-law to His votary. Rejoiced, he flew back to his Divine daughter, and confided the gladsome news. Royal preparations were made for the godly marriage. Pennons waved and festoons sailed, tabours struck and music streamed forth; and good-folks sang and danced for joy. Both Uraiyûr and Srira*n*gam swam in decorations, and all people gathered and held high feast over the unparalleled event. In due pomp the marriage was celebrated, with all the ceremonies of pouring water, tying the necklace, binding the

1. See note 1, page 5, Life of Tondar-adi-ppodi *Azhvâr*.
2. Vide Life of *Andâl*.

colored thread, stepping the faithful stone, and propitiating all the Gods to bless &c. Three Hundred and Ten bags of golden rice-grains, Dharma-Varma gave as his daughter's dowry, adding priceless jewels of precious gems, rich wardrobe, herds of kine, elephants, horses, and other effects and equipage and what not. Not satisfied, the King made all his property God's own. Resigned thus he ruled in peace.[1]

St. Tiruppâni-Âzhzvâr, whose life we are going to relate, was born in Uraiyûr, of such holy repute and associations as delineated above. His horoscope tells us that he was born in Durmati, 342, Kali current; Vrischika month, Rohini asterism,—an incarnation of the Srîvatsa[2] mark on the breast of Mahâ-Vishnu. He took his birth in the Pañchama grade of society, called the Pânars, or a class below the Sûdras, who take to the profession of lute-playing, and who are not allowed to dwell with the high-class townsmen. His name was thus Tiru-ppân-Âzhvâr.[3] Not status in society but divine wisdom and spiritual illumination mark the saints.[4] Though low in society our Saint was

---

1. This event is annually celebrated, generally in the month of March. Is called the *Pangun-y-uttar-otsavam.*

2. For symbology, see *Vishnu-Purânâ*, *Astra-Bhûshana* Ch:

3. अयतत्रकुलेऽन्तिगेरमारमणोरस्थितलाङ्छनांशजः । समजायत-पाणसञ्ज्ञिकस्सुकविः कार्तिकमासिवैदभे ॥

[*Divya-Sûri-Charita.* VII-17.]

4. Read The Life of Nanda, the Paraya Saint.

greater than the highest in society, the priestly Brâhmanas. Apart from class or color, saints posses virtues as are sought after even by higher classes for their salvation, even as the divine Rhapsodist,—the low-class Nam-pâduvân of the Kaisika-Upâkhyâna—removed the curse afflicting the Brâhmana Somasarma.[1]

But our Saint was descended from no carnal parents. For outside the town of Uraiyur, he was discovered in a field with stalks of green and yellow paddy glowing. A man of the Pánar class picked up the heaven-dropt child, and felt inwardly glad that it should have been his good lot to possess such a child. Barren, his wife was; and this rare find removed that want. Both he and wife cherished and fondled the dear prize, and idolized it by cautiously shielding it from all deleterious influences such as indiscriminate food (proper to their class) and other professional abominations which might poison the baby's atmosphere, physical as well as mental. With pure cow's milk it was fed.

Being a Heaven-born child, all its instincts and tendencies were heaven-ward. The child grew. The boy evinced no taste for the glamour of the world.

1. Read *Kaisika-Purâna*(Varâha) with Bhattârya's gloss, and that wonderful work the *Âchârya Hridaya*, I. 85-86; and read these in connection with the efforts of Col: H.S Olcott, of the Theosophical Society, Adyar, for educating the *Panchamas*; and how much the higher classes of the Hindus are therefore in duty bound to help and strengthen his hands and the philanthropic ladies of America unselfishly labouring for this movement.

His love was pitched on The High. The boy became man. He would enter on no worldly occupation. As his sole avocation he would take up his lyre; and eternal strains from it, sing forth for the glorification of God. He realised his status in the society of men. He must respect its settled laws. Reform consisted not in defying, decrying or infringing the hoary conventionals and usages sanctified by the *Sâstras*, but in strictly respecting them and exemplifying their spiritual sense by exemplary moral conduct. "I am low-born by His dispensation", he soliloquized, "and that is a matter of the mere temporary *body*. But by His grace, my *soul* is enlightened and burns with love for Him. This, not the accidents of birth &c, constitutes my fitness for Môksha. I must abide strictly by the rules of society[1]. Here I am on the south bank of the Kaveri,—its south Branch. Between this and its north Branch, called the Kolla*d*am (Coleroon) is situate the Holy Island of Srî Ra*n*ganâtha,—my Life. I will dread to tread with my unholy feet, this sacred Land between the twin hugging streams. I will take my stand on the brink of the south bank of the south Branch, my face ever turned north towards where My Soul lies recumbent. I take up my sweet lyre, and draw out thrilling notes of His praise from its strings; and employed thus, I will:

1. Reformers, and Hindus who ape practices of the Europeans—and too under the cover of Christian *Religion*, and tempting snares spread by the foreign proselytizers—learn the spirit of this Paraya Saint.

"Aye muse and dote, e'er love and faint,
And faint and rally; rally, faint;
My palms in worship joined."[1]

Dharma-putra found *Srî* Krish*n*a seated silent and absorbed and absent-minded. "What is the matter with Thee, Lord?" Quoth he. The Lord thus shaken out of his slumber, said:

"There lies my Bhîshma on his arrow-bed,
As fading fire, his life fast ebbing 'way,
His mind and heart and soul on Myself fixt;
Hence, Lion of men! to him my mind had fled."[2]

Thus therefore, when Saint Tiru-ppâ*n*-Âzhvâr had lovingly fastened his thoughts on Ra*n*ga, Ra*n*ga's thoughts had more intensely fastened themselves on His beloved devotee, the Âzhvâr.

Tiru-ppâ*n*-Âzhvâr's love for God was more and more expanding. For hours he was lost in its ineffable intricacies. He would close his eyes and become utterly senseless and oblivious to the external world. He would be enjoying visions of God, in which he would see Him, approach Him and fear for His safety.[3] While the Saint seemed so dead to all outward objects there came one day Loka-Sâra*n*ga Mahâ-Muni to the river

---

1. 'Sindikkum &c' [*T'vây-mozhi.* VII. 2. 5.]

2. शरतल्पगतोभिष्म श्शाम्यन्निवहुताशनः । मान्ध्यातिपुरुषव्याघ्र ततोमेतद्गतंमनः ॥ [*Mahâ-Bhârata.*]

3. Expressed by the technical phrases: *Para-bhakti. Para-jnâna, Parama-bhakti.*

side, in order to convey the daily vessels-full of water for ablutory purposes of Srí-Ranga. But here he found Tiru-ppâ*n*ar seated almost like a lifeless statue, hallooed to him to move away and make way for him,—he being a holy person, a Brâhma*n*a and servant of Srî Ranga's Fane; and he (our Saint) being a Cha*n*dâla, an outcaste, deserved to stand at a distance. Tiru-ppá*n*ar heard him not, for his sense of hearing was suspended from functioning on account of his absorption. Misunderstanding this for indifference and stubbornness. with probable intent to scandalize his priestly person, Loka-Sárangar got incensed, and taking up a pebble flung at him. It hurt him in the face and brought down blood. He revived, oped his eyes slowly, and seeing Sàranga-muni standing at a distance fretting and frowning, realised the situation at once, moved away from the place, expressing his grief and repentance at the act of sacrilege which he committed—though unwittingly—in having remained unmindful of the reasonable warnings of Sârangar.

After Tiru-ppâ*n*ar betook himself to a respectful distance. Sâra*n*gar neared the water-edge, and after performing the daily round of caste-duties, duly carried his holy pails of water to Lord Ra*n*ga, in all due customary pomp of music, chowries, umbrellas &c. But on his arriving at the Temple, he met with neither reception nor countenance from the Lord as usual; and his services were not to be accepted. Sára*n*gar's countenance fell, his heart sank, and he fell to anguishful musing.

While so, he had a vision. *S*ri Ra*n*ga accosted him thus: "How darest thou hurt my faithful Tiru-ppâ*n*ar? Didst thou take him for a brute of low caste? We are sorely offended with thee." Sârangar's mind was puzzled. He knew not how to atone and pacify the Lord.

Meanwhile Ra*n*ga-Nâyaki, the Lord's Holy Consort remonstrated with Him as to why He delayed taking Tiru-ppâ*n*ar nearer to Him. "I have often tried to," answerd Ra*n*ga, "but as I advance, he recedes; and He is so sensitive of his humble birth and insignificance, that any contact with me, he looks on as contamination to My pure nature. I have thus been often jilted by this over-cautious self-abasing character of My beloved. Howbeit, my Queen! time has come for settling the matter amicably, and thou wilt see thy wish soon fulfilled."

Sâranga-Muni was now called. Tremblingly he answered the summons. "Thou shalt not think Tiru-ppânar low. He is my very soul. He is My intimate friend. He is my confidential servant. Hie thou hence to where he is. In due reverence and humility, lift him up upon thy shoulders, and make with him a triumphal entry into our Shrine; and let all the world witness this spectacle. This is our command. Let it be obeyed." Sârangar woke from his reverie, and felt relieved from a weight of sorrow, and exultingly ran saying;

"O That my life is blest!
O bliss! this morn has dawned!"[1]

1. अद्यमेसफलंजन्म सुप्रभाताचमेनिशा ॥
[*Vishnu-Purâna*. V. 17. 3.]

"Distances vast must travelled be,
To where do dwell great Godly souls."[1]

He ran and found the Saint standing as usual at a great distance, and conversing with his fond lyre-companion on the topic of God, in the language of music. Sârangar approached and fell at his feet; asked his forgiveness for injuries both physical and moral which he unwittingly indeed inflicted on his sacred person; and submitted to him humbly the wish of Srî Ranga that Tiru-ppânar should be hoisted on his shoulders and brought to Him. The Saint retreated to a distance and besought:—

"O touch not me, my profane self
Yet lower than the Four-fold Grade"[2]
"Oh list, not one of Four
My birth can claim."[3]
"I 'm low and base
Knowing no way."[4]
"Oh, how I with my foot
Can Rang-Land tread?"[5]

"But, Sire! you need not fear, for without your having to tread with your feet the Holy Land, I have commands to have the honor of carrying ye on my hould-

1. सुदूरमपिगन्तव्यंयत्रभागवतास्थिता: ॥ [*Bhdradvàja Samhità.*]

2. *Kulàm tàngu* &c. (T. V. Mozhi: III. 6. 9.)
3. *Kulangaliya* &c. (T. Ch. Viruttam : 90.)
4. *Nìsanén* &c. (T. V. Mozhi: III. 8. 1.)
5. *Tiru-v-arangu-pperu-nagar* &c. (Perumàl : T. Mozhi : 1.)

ers." So said Loka-Sâranga-Mahâ-Muni.[1] Tiru-ppâṇar saw now his position. Further resistance, he thought, would be construed into disobedience. "As the Lord wills," he said, "if He maketh the stalk to sprout from the plant, who could stop it? What *He* wills is our good and His pleasure. Be it then as He wills. Do with me, holy Muni, what thou wilt."

Loka-Sâranga Mahâmunigal delayed not; for he lifted our Saint on to his shoulders and like a victor returning home successful, like the Celestial Carriers (*Âtivâhikas*) who convey to Heaven the glorified souls who have passed the world, and amidst acclamations and applauses, Sàranga-munìndrar carried Tiru-ppàṇar[2] to the Lord's Shrine and was about to deposit him in one of the holy yards within, when lo! the Lord appeared in an aurora of celestial glory, surrounded by His Heavenly hosts, and Luminous attendants to his Holy Biddings, transplendant with Personal Embellishments and all the Consorts Holy. It was sunshine, moonlight and lightning, all blended in a Beauteous Blaze—a Blessed vision, Beatific spectacle,

1. This sage, it is said, belonged to the North of India; but had travelled to the Drâvida Land, attracted thereto by the sweetness of the Drâvida-Veda. (Read pp. 50 & 54 Foot notes, Vol. I. *Bhagavad Vishaya*: Telugu Edition.)

2. Hence the Saint is called Muni-Vâhana and Yogi-Vâha; and Sage Vedàntàchàrya has paid special homage by writing his Rahasya, the *Muni-Vâhana Bhoga*. The Saint also goes by the name of *Prâna-nâtha*.

which no eye ever saw before. Our Saint saw. He was bathed in glory. His devotion surplussed all limits. He broke out into a Song,—the Amalan-âdipirân,—descriptive of the condensed Universal God present before him—as in His eternal Now. And behold ! while all gazed and stared in astonishment, our Saint tarried not on the Earth to see any other sight, but melted and passed into the Lord's Substance in his 50th year of age. There are certain roots[1] which only smell *with* the earth particles adhering to them. So Saints sometimes pass into their God, body and soul.[2]

To us poor mortals, this Song of Bliss (in 10 Verses) is left for reading and ruminating ; and if God wills, for taking us into His eternal Fellowship likewise.

Blest be St. Tiru-ppan-Azhvar.

---

1. *Vetti-vér &c.* The plant *angelica* is said to have its root no less odoriferous and salutary than its stem and foliage.

2. Of the *Saiva* Saint Mànikka Váchakar, it is written that "on approaching the Sacred Idol (Natarájan) his corporal frame was absorbed in divinity and became invisible to the mortals present." (Siddh: Díp: p. 90. Vol. V.). Read St. *Andàl's* Life.

"The union is so close as to transcend our powers of language, no union on earth being close enough to represent it. Nevertheless the soul retains its personal identity, since the union is the union of Love, not of identification or annihilation".

श्री.

THE LIFE OF

St. Tirumangai Âzhvâr.

St. Tirumangai-Âzhvâr or St. Parânkusa is the last of the Twelve Canonized Saints of the Holy Church of the Srî-Vaishnavas. With him the Âzhvârs (Saints) end; and the Âchâryas (Sages) begin. He ranks as No: 17 in our Hierarchic Table. His date of birth is recorded in the Divya-Sûri-Charita as 397 Kali, current, year Nala, month Kárthika, and Krittikâ Asterism, spiritually descended from the Holy Bow Sárnga of Srî Mahá-Vishnu, and born in Tiru-kkuraiyalúr, near Tiru-Vâli (about 8 miles from Shiyàli)[1].

Legends tell us that this Saint, who was also called 'Nîla' or 'the black,' owing to his birth in the Fourth

---

1. समजायत तत्र पादजप्रमुखः कश्चन नीलनामकः । पुरुषोत्तम कार्मुकांशज स्फुरिते कार्तिक कृत्तिकोडुनि ॥

or *S*ûdra[1] class was no other than the Brâhma*n*a Kardama of the K*r*ita-age, the Kshatriya Upari-chara-vasu of the Tretá age, the Vaisya *S*ankhapâla of the Dvâpara-age, and made to take birth in the Kali age as Níla among the *S*údras; so thus to spread knowledge among all mankind, that all may,-without distinctions which society makes, merit Heaven. Not one method but diverse, doth God employ for salvation of mankind; one of them being that of our Saint having in each age been made to appear in one certain grade of society, and work there for the time being.

His father, who is said to have belonged to the Ka*ll*a-kkulam (Thief-class), was commander to the armies of King Chô*l*a; and gave the name of Nîla (or The Blue), after the Blue Color of *S*rî Krish*n*a. He followed the profession of his father, learnt the use of weapons and other military arts, helped his father in his duties, and in course of time, when he arrived at manhood, filled the same high office which his ageing father had held. He often followed the King in his military enterprizes, when he came to be distinguished for his martial qualities. The valiant soldier was recognized and duly rewarded. For not only did he hold the post of Commander of the armies, but was appointed ruler over a portion of Chô*l*a's Territories, the Tiruvâli-Nâd.

1. *Pádaja* = means foot-born=*S*údra (D: Siri: Ch: VII.34). *Sábara* (another version)=wild mountaineer tribe.
Mlechha (another version)=non-Hindu, or non-descript class.

He was yet unmarried. The hardy race in which he was born, the dash and intrepid nature, the heroic military achievements, added to power, wealth and flushing youth and exhuberant health, made him a champion in gallantry. In his private life he was thus a man after the pleasures of the senses. As described by St : Kulasekharar,

'He was a butt to cupid's bow'[1],

and as described by himself, he was ever

'Nestled in blooming damsels' breasts'[2].

In short, he was given to music, dancing. drama, and poetry; and thus as proficient in erotic feats as in military exploits.

Time glided on thus. There is a place in the Tiruvâli circle, called Tiruve*ll*akkulam, now Holy. It has a beautiful Pond over-grown with lotus blooms. A band of the celestial Apsarà-damsels descended into the pond in the course of their heavenly excursions; and wishing to have a bath there. One of them, by name Tiru-má-maga*l* busied herself plucking the gay lotus-blossoms; and the rest not waiting for her return, departed leaving her behind. Tiru-mà-maga*l* had assumed a human shape. Being thus left alone, she was puzzled as to what she should do; and as she was thinking, there chanced to arrive at the spot, a Vaishnava physician who practised

1. *Mànnàr erri reñjilai* &c [Perumà*l* T. Mozhi III. 3]
2. *Terirai már-ururaine maruwi* &c [Tiru-Mozhi : I. 1.3]

in the Holy Place of Tiru-nàngùr[1]. He was a holy personage. He came to the Pond for the purpose of bathing. He saw the lovely damsel and impelled by curiosity, asked her who she was and why she was solitarily stopping at such a place. She simply informed him that a batch of them came to the spot on a pleasure-trip, and that she was left alone by the rest as she was busy culling lotus-blooms. She appealed to him to take her to his house and to his care.

The visitor was delighted; for he was childless. He accordingly led her home and presented her to his good wife who was yearning for children; and the pair, thus providentially provided with an object of love on whom they could bestow all their affection,—doubled in intensity by their anterior childless state, and trebled by the miraculous nature of the child discovered,—conferred on her the name of *Kumuda-valli* in commemoration of the Lotus-flower having been the cause of her detention in the pond, separated from her play-mates,—the Apsarâ-Nymphs. The good pair brought her up as more than their own darling daughter and thought they were specially blessed in having their long-felt want satisfied in a way quite unexpected by them. The virgin grew and bloomed into a beautiful wench. And her adoptive parents were exercised sorely in

1. The details of the purpose for which all these events were brought about by Providence are recorded in the Sthala-Purána of Tiruvâli-Tirunagari.

their hearts as to where to discover a fitting mate for their love.

In the meanwhile, our commander Níla's spies who saw the flower-like maiden as perfect in person as in graces, carried the news to their chief, and gave him such a florid account too that his cupidity was excited, and his imagination thralled. In his chase after beauties, he cared not for the arduous duties of his office; and leaving them at sixes and sevens, started for Tirunâṅgûr in feverish haste; and he describes himself then as if his

'Heart was restive 'yond control '[1],

and that,

'To lust in female charms, I panted after them '[2]

He reached Tirunâṅgûr in such a state of mind; and immediately proceeding to the house of Kumudavalli's Guardian entered into conversation with him. His eyes were however on the look-out for obtaining a passing glimpse of the object of his passion. The nymph-like maiden chanced to pass before his view. To him she flashed like lightning. It sent a magnetic current into him. It set his frame thrilling and heart throbbing with love. For she was indeed a celestial looking dame, surpassing all human ideals of beauty. Need it be said that he was taken, especially one of his disposition and tastes? "Sire," he addressed the good guardian, "we knew you to be childless; and yet

---

1. *Ninraví Nillú* (T: Muzhi. I. 1. 4.).
2. *Avar tarum kalavi* &c. (Ibid. I. 1. 1.)

whence haileth this Treasure of charms we find in your house?" The guardian was good enough to give an account of all the incidents attending his rare find, to this illustrious visitor; and added:—"I was inconsolable in my grief at not possessing children. But this Gem of my accidental discovery makes my heart's joy complete. A fresh care has however taken possession of me now. She has come of age. It is time to marry her. We know not the circumstances of her family, Gotra &c; and where to find a suitable match for her is become a problem with us. Nila's heart leapt with joy at this information, and without further ado he said at once: "Gentle folk! be not anxious over this problem. For I offer myself readily as the solution. I will have the maiden given to me in marriage. Here is any amount of money you may need, jewels clothes &c." So saying, he used all his means and endeavours to ingratiate himself into the good graces of the guardian, pressed his suit earnestly, making at last formal proposals for marriage. The good couple submitted the matter to their deliberation, but they dared not promise acceptance or make refusal before the scheme was expounded to the damsel herself. They were willing, but what would the girl say? Duly they placed the matter before her, but she flatly refused to give her hand to any one but a Vaishnava, who must have undergone the Law-enjoined five-fold Sacraments[1],

1. तापःपुंड्रस्तथानाम मन्त्रोयागश्चपञ्चमः ॥

[Bhâradvâja Samhita. II. 2.]

which make a real Vaishnava, as she was too pure to be claimed by ordinary mortals. She was intended for a saint, or rather for one who would become a saint, before he could claim a saintess for his help-meet. She said :—

"None dare even breathe that I
will match myself to any other."[1]

This resolution of the maid was communicated to our Nilar. According to the saying :—

"No faint heart won a fair lady",

Nila was never faint. Any condition he willingly submitted to. Even if it costed his life, he would yet win his lady. And according to the text :—"The wise man shall never lose time over a good job"[2], he breathless winged himself to Tiru-naraiyûr and presented himself before Nambi, the Presiding Deity of the Holy Shrine, and prayed to him fervently to bestow on him the requisite Sacraments which his lady-love demanded of him. Behold, his fervid appeal worked a miracle. (Such is the strength of faith !! It will even melt *stones*!!!). For Nambi appeared to Nîlar in his real noumenal self (hidden so long by the phenomenal image), and administered to him the Sacrament of the Holy Wheel and the Holy Conch imprinted on either of his arms, and the vertical

1. *Matrornark-ennai* &c.

2 शुभस्यशीघ्रंप्रयतेतधीमान् ॥

marks—12 in number, reperesenting Him and His Mercy—duly labelled out on the several parts of His body. Already Nílar felt himself a peculiar being; and felt he was going in for a new variety in his adventures; he was, he thought, entering new fields, and turning new leaves in his career. Of course, these were but glimmerings, the meaning of which he had no time to inquire into, for the fair virgin occupied foremost his mental chambers. With her on his brain, he rushed back to her parents, with the visible banns of marriage bannered forth on his arms and limbs, and said: "Here I am, sire, to the *mark* exact, as your good daughter demands. Let me be exhibited to her, and learn her gracious will and pleasure. My fate is in her hands". He was presented in this style duly to the proud dame. And she said: "So far, so good; but thou shalt, good man, guarantee that for one year long, and daily, thou shalt sumptuously feed one thousand and eight Holy Men—the *Srí*-Vaishnavas-, thou shalt keep hungry till they are fed, then eat the remnants of their food, after previously purifying thyself by sipping holy water obtained by washing their feet"[1].

1. The ceremonial and sacramental washings of feet are often mentioned in the Bible. Cp: Cruden's Concordance under 'wash':—"The orientals were used to wash the feet of strangers who came off a journey, because they commonly walked with their legs naked, and their feet only defended with a sandal Thus Abraham washed the feet of the three angels, [Gen. 18. 4] The feet of Eliazar Abraham's steward and those that accompa-

"Agreed", said Nîlar. He was delirious with desire for Kumudavalli; and had it been asked, he would have laid his life down. On his giving guarantee for the due discharge of the obligation imposed, the proud dame at last signified her consent to be his own. Joy was every one's now. The anxiety of the parents to find a suitable husband for their fair flower ceased. The gallant Nîla had won his Love. The proud maiden was going to make a saint out of a sinner complete. Preparations for marriage were now made, and in all form and eclat, Kumudavalli was given in marriage to Nîlar. He was now Tirumangai-Mannan.

He was faithful to his promises to her. For he devoted all his means for the Holy *Fete* she had ordained, and one-thousand and eight godly souls were daily fed. "More than all worship is Vishnu's worship; more than Vishnu's worship is Vishnu-Bhaktas'

---

nied him, were washed, when they arrived at the house of Laban [Gen. 24. 32.]. And likewise those of Joseph's brethren, their feet were washed, when they came into Egypt. [Gen. 43. 24]. Our Lord Jesus, to give his Apostles an example of humility washed their feet [John. 13. 5.]. "After that he poured water into a basin and began to wash the disciples' feet. This washing as it was a servile employment denoted our Saviour's humility, which Christians ought to imitate him in." So far only, Christ took from India, whereas not only humility by washing, but the sacramental regeneration *(such as Baptisement)* is to be effected by sipping the washed water.

worship"[1], says a Holy Text. The Holy Kumudavalli had thus made her husband observe this injunction by actual practice.

We have already said that Nîlar had been assigned a tract of country, the Âli-nâd, to govern over. He was a subsidized potentate, and had to remit his annual subsidy to his Suzerain, the Chola-King. But the enormous drain on his purse caused by the daily feasting to which he had become bound, dis-enabled him to fulfil the terms of his compact with that Sovereign. The officials of the king reported the cause of failure on Nila's part to be due to his squandering(?) on festal viands. Messengers were dispatched to demand the sums due. "Come this evening, I will pay; I have no time now to attend to you. I am busy with my *fete*", he would thus say and send then away. When they came the evening: "tomorrow morning" he would say. When they came on the morrow, "this afternoon" he would say. The officials begining to distrust, began to coerce the defaulter. When he felt thus oppressed, he resorted to force and thrust them away from his door. Ill-treated and irate, the officials returned and reported to the King how matters stood. He, boiling with indignation at the contemptuous treatment his functionaries had received, sent for his new

---

1. आराधनानांसर्वेषां विष्णोराराधनंपरम् । तस्मात्परतरंप्रोक्तं तदीयाराधनंनृप ॥ [*Mahâ-Bhârata.*]

Commander-in-chief, and ordered him to proceed forthwith, capture Tirumangai-Mannan and bring him to him. With men and horses and weapons, they proceeded in cavalcade. Seeing this, Mannan ordered his army to meet them and give fight. They fought. Discomfited and beaten back, Chola's squadron returned with the sad news of their defeat. The King was mad with rage, his eyes becoming blood-shot. And he commanded all his infantry and cavalry, duly manned, to get ready and himself went forth in person to bring the holy swindler to his senses. They arrived and surrounded Tiru-mangai; but he was not at all taken aback. He and his men with swords and spears rushed against them riding on chargers and fought with a valour such that Chola's men felt as if they were churned like the Mandara mount in the ocean. They could not face the daring enemy, and were routed. They fell back on the King. He became now savagely furious, rallied his men, and cautiously returning to fight, encompassed our Mannar. But Mannar was equal to the occasion, for he fought like a demon, and sent a chill and dread into the hearts of Chola's men. Chola saw his situation. He admired the prowess of his old soldier, and ordered hostilities to be suspended. Advancing towards Tirumangai, he said:—"My old man, thy courage, thy chivalry, thy pluck and dash simply astonish me. I forget all thy injuries and disloyalties. Fear not. Come to me. I accord thee *friendship*. I grant thee safety. On my personal honor and the honor of all our gods and holy preceptors, I pledge: no harm shall be done thee." So, this truce gave our Mannan credence. He ceased from fight and sheathed his sword; and approached Chola. Chola received him with every mark of assurance and said: "We forgive thee for thy riotous conduct, but advise thee to reimburse our royal treasury with thy arrears". Nila did not suspect Chola; but in his professions of faith there was perfidy; for he circumvented Tirumagnai thus, and catching him, handed him over to his ministers with orders to recover dues from him.

Chola returned to his Capital. The ministers taking Tirumangai-Mannan as a prisoner, immured him in a temple under custody. For three days he remained thus without food and sleep; the one thought alone racking his mind, viz., the fate of his *fete*. He had a vision. VaradaRÂja Svâmi, the Lord Resident at Kâñchi, appeared to him and said: "Take heart, O my faithful! Promise arrears in my Land". When, according to custom the ministers came in the morn to reiterate their demands for rents due, Mannan boldly said:—"I have my secret store in Kâñchi. Go thence with me and take your dues". This confession was duly communicated to Chola. He ordered that it be so done, but warning that strict vigilance be maintained over Mannan's person, lest he escape and evade. Under strong escort, then, he was led to Kâñchi. At random he showed a certain spot to be excavated. *They did* so but found no money there. They asked him, but he was silent and pensive. They let a day or so pass. He became more and more pensive and puzzled; and drowsed away in the depth of his anguish. The Merciful Lord of Kânchi again appeared to him in a dream and said :—"Proceed to the riner Vêgavati, and dig at *this* spot". *That* spot remained a clear picture in Tirumangai's mind. For on waking, he bid Chola's men to go forth there and dig. They did so, and lo! they struck upon a trove. Dismayed and delighted, they unearthed the thing, and to their utter astonishment, they discovered it to be a large treasure. 'Tirumangai-Mannan disbursed out of it the King's due and retained the rest for his Holy feting of the Holy men. The King's officials of course released him and taking their share proceeded to the King. Placing the sum before him they related to him all the adventures connected with its finding, and the divine intervention in the affair, which they had learnt was the secret influence helping to Mannan's solvency.

The king was struck dumb at the wonderful narration of his officials and thought to himself that Tirumangai-Mannan could be no ordinary mortal. He was god-blessed and godly. Even like Draupadi's garment which miraculously grew in her hour of dishonor and distress in the court of Dhritarâshtra, did money miraculously grow for St. Tirumangai. The money that came to him was thus sacred and he ought not to let it be deposited with his worldly treasury. So musing, the King invited Tirumangai-Mannan to his court, received him with every mark of respect and veneration, begged his forgiveness, and despatched him loaded with honors. The money that had been forced from our Saint was too good to be used for mundane purposes. He therefore spent it on Holy Feeding.

Meanwhile Mannan had spent all the money, that VaradaRâjar had given him, on his wife's fancy-dinners. He was again indigent and insolvent. He pondered over. The year-long dinners must be maintanied at any cost. For he would rather die. he thought, than break his solemn promise to his Kumudavalli before he wedded her.

He would take to robbery, plundering and way-laying travellers, he thought, and leave no stone unturned to maintain his Holy dinnering to the end of its days. For this purpose, he entertained into his service four consummate rogues, called *Nir-mèl-nadappàn*[1], *Nizhal-odunguvân*[2], *Tal-ûduvân*[3], and *Tôlà-vazhakkan*[4]. With such picked men, Tirumangai-Mannan launched out on his depredatory expeditions, and all the ill-gains he so obtained were to a pie strictly devoted to the Holy Banquet, he had undertaken at the bidding of his spiritual wife.

---

1. The water-walker. 2. The shade-glider (meaning a pick-pocket and such other shady acts) 3. The lock-breather, (i.e by breathing, any locked door would unlock). 4. The indefeasible wrangler.

God Nârâyana was from the beginning watching the development of this soul, under the stress of varying emotions, beginning with love; then valour, determined will, suffering and endurance, earnestness and strong faith; and an iron-will which suffered no opposition to baffle its resolves. For the one righteous resolve he formed—in obedience to the dictates of his divine wife,—of feasting so many Godly men daily for a long time,—which exceeded the limits of all his means—he sacrificed all. Under seeming ruffianism and reckless daring, precious qualities were developing. The ordinary man who proved a success in the field of matter, was to become the extraordinary man fit to be a success in the field of spirit. The hero of the world was to turn a spiritual hero. All the character which formed under worldly impulses was to be applied to higher uses. In short the consummate rogue was to become the consummate Saint.

God's ways are really inscrutable. Bumper crop doth He grow out of manure. Into a mould of clay, He could breath a spirit. Out of a stone (bone) he could make a woman.[1] And why not then a Saint Tirumangai Azhvâr,—worshipped by all the high-caste Brahmans to this day in India's Temples–out of a Nila born of a low-caste *Kallar* band? God's grace alone is our Refuge. Otherwise, how are we sinners on earth, to merit heaven? Unless God gave signal instances of His conversions by

1. The *stone* is in allusion to Ahalya. The *bone* to Eve.

operations of His infinite grace, such as on those of St. Tirumangai Âzhvâr (and St. Augustine) how are we, enveloped as we are, in ignorance and darkness and sin, to be reassured in hopes, to cross the ocean of pain, and suffering and vanity and ephemeralness, and reach at last that Empyrean, where we may ever dwell with our God, to see and know and love and serve our Father there, never more to fall? Unless our loving Parent gave us Saints after Saints and Saviours after Saviours, how can we hope to be lifted from the abysmal depth of worldliness, we find ourselves plunged in? Such Saints anb Saviours come to us of different patterns; and St. Tirumangai Âzhvâr is a model of his own, and God began his conversion through means quite unknown to him and unsuspected by him; and our Mother Kumudavalli-Nâycchiyâr was chosen as His instrument of converting this splendid soul, though for a time made to dwell in a habiliment of the most forbidding and repulsive type, and yet possessing qualities which were to become useful in another direction.

Lord Nârâyana, we said, was watching the development of our Saint under peculiar environments and varying conditions. It was an interesting series of dramatic and trajic display of the life of the spirit combating with external forces. The Lord was now going to open another scene; and in which He would directly, take a part. Tirumangai was devoted to the *feting* of God's own elect, and for this purpose he embarked on a course of raiding and lawlessness, as as he had no other alternative. God's own and God's elect, worshipped and pleased, is God Himself worshipped and pleased. Aye more. For, our *Sâstras* declare that between these two modes, God's worship is but the First Step (*Prathama-Parva*), whereas the other is the Final Step (*Charama-Parva*). Whereas in the former case, God is invisibly and therefore indirectly worshipped; in the latter, he is visibly and therefore directly worshipped. This is a Grand Truth, the apprehension, appreciation, and practice of which is given only to a few and rare souls.[1] To such a practice, Mannan was heartily devoted. Though the End was the Highest and most Exemplary, the Means he employed was out of fashion. In God's sight it was pleasing, but not in man's sight. Spiritually Mannan was right, but his moral procedure was against Law. This must be set right, the Lord thought; and He would Himself be waylaid by this Robber-Saint. Theodicy justifies God to us in all His Mysterious deportment in the drama of the universe. 'The end justifies the means', has so far been the theodicy for our Robber-Saint.

Tirumangai-Mannan one day waited for his usual prey. He was now established near Tirumanankollai (near Tirunagari), and ensconced himself among the leaves of an Asvattha-Tree (which to this day exists, and where the event is annually celebrated), and ready

1. आराधनानांसर्वेषां विष्णोराराधनंपरम् ।। तस्मात्परतरंप्रोक्तंतदीयाराधनंनृप ॥ [Maha. Bhârata.]

with his men and means to pounce upon people just at the fitting moment. He waited thus, with all his signals arranged.

According to the text :—" Nârâyana Himself, though God, taketh on flesh like the human ; and out of mercy, lifteth (redeemeth) sunken worldlings, by His hand of Law ",[1] the Lord Resident, the Vayal-âli Manavâlan, put on the guise of a Brâhmana, improvised a wife, and designed a pageantry which was to be a grand wedding-procession in which He was to be the Chief Personage,—the Bridegroom,—and his wife the Bride, both bedecked with priceless jewellery ; and the retinue was to carry with them other invaluable valuables. This procession was to pass by that way of course where our Robber-Saint, with his select gang, was lying in wait.

From the top of the tree, our Robber-Saint sighted the grand procession creeping towards his ambuscade. It was nearing. It was time for action. To his men, he gave the alarm. All armed themselves with their weapons ; and growling and muttering menaces, surprized the approaching party, by suddenly falling upon them. They were unprepared for such an attack ; and the gang, without opposition or murmur on their part, abstracted all the precious articles on the Persons of the Bride and Bridegroom, and stripped others of all their priceless possessions. The Bridegroom had a

1. साक्षान्नारायणोदेवः कृत्वामर्त्यमयींतनुम् । मग्नानुद्धरतेलोकान् कारुण्याच्छास्त्रपाणिना ॥ [Naradiye.]

signet ring on His finger, which could not be easily taken. But the Robber-Chief would not let it go. He applied his teeth and extracted it by force, when the Bridegroom-God exclaimed in admiration: 'Art thou not our Kaliyan?'[1]

Kaliyan bundled up all his rich spoil, but when he wished to lift them off the ground and run away, the bundles would not lift. They stuck to the ground as if by magic. "Ah: knave Thou art, Thou seemst a wizard, a man of incantations and magic formulæ". cried Kaliyan, "else how could these bundles stick? The disguised Lord said: "I will teach thee the Holy Formula[2] (Mantra), come near, bend thy head, and lend thy ear". "What!" vociferated the Robber-Chieften Kaliyan, 'How audacious! Thou askest *me* to bend my head and lend my ear for Thy *mantra*! But look". So threatening, he drew his sword, and said: "Now, wilt thou reveal the Mantra at once, or shall I employ the sword against thee, O Brâhmana wretch! Come out with it sharp, or—". "Here it is, my good old soul. Take it", said the disguised God, and repeated the Holy Eight-Syllabled Mantra, which Kaliyan repeated after Him. Kaliyan put the Mantra to test

1. That is the last Azhvâr or Saint of the Kali-age. Admiration is for the work of *extraction* of souls form evil which this Saint was hereafter going to do in the same determined manner as the *extraction* of the ring.

2. Read Topic 14 of The Divine Wisdom of the Drâvida Saints by the Author.

by uttering it and lifting the bundles. Lo, they came up. What resisted before now easily gave way.[1] Kaliyan was about to depart.

"But stay," the Lord cried, 'Thou shalt have more." Kaliyan stopped. "What more"? he asked." "A good deal more, listen," the Lord continued: " 'All the four Vedas, *Rik*, *Yajus*, *Sâma* and *Atharva* are enclosed (as in a nut-shell) in this Mantra. All else is mere verbosity.'[2] 'This Mantra is the essence of the Teachings of all the Vedântas ;-the Raft which carries souls across the ocean of Samsâra: the Means for men to reach the Bourne of God from which never more to return.'[3] 'This Mantra can confer this world's prosperity, and of the celestial worlds; it can grant the Kingdom of Soul or the Kingdom of God.[4] 'It is the Mantra declared in the Nârâyana Upanishad, as

---

1. On the efficacy of *Mantra*, Holy Name, the Word &c, the reader may well read the scientific explanation as furnished by Mrs Annie Besant [Pp: 22-25, *The Building of the Cosmos.*]

2. ऋचोयजूंषिसामानि तथैवाथर्वणानिच । सर्वमष्टाक्षरान्तस्थं यच्चान्यदपिवाङ्मयम् ॥ [Páñcharátra.]

3 सर्ववेदान्तसारार्थः संसारार्णवतारकः । गतिरष्टाक्षरोनृणां अपुनर्भवकांक्षिणाम् ॥ [Ibid.]

4. ऐहलौकिकमैश्वर्यं स्वर्गाद्यंपारलौकिकम् । कैवल्यंभगवन्तञ्च मन्त्रोयंसाधयिष्यति ॥

composed of Three terms and Eight Syllables.' 'It is the Mantra which has received the sanction of all Holy Souls.' 'This ancient root-Mantra of the Mantras, is the Secret of Secrets, the Purifier of Purifiers.'[1] I had no one deserving to be taught this, and had therefore in days gone by to split myself into Nara and Nârâyana in the Badarî Âsrama of the Himâlayas, and thus teach my own half, the Nara.[2] This precious Mantra has now been imparted to thee. All this time I felt grieved that I had not a second soul to receive the Mantra. Thou hast removed that grief; for even by force hast thou extracted it from me."

Kaliyan received the sermon, and lo, he found himself a transformed creature. It seemed as if his old savage nature left him, giving place to penitence, piety and love to the Preceptor. In fine he was now feeling as if he had turned from the ordinary man to the saint. As this revolution and regeneration were still working in his inner being, it seemed as if a new vision was developing in him. And it did. For the disguised Brâhmana and his wife were transfigured before his vision into a most indescribably thrilling and exalted sight.

The sight was of Hrishíkesa with His consort Lakshmî,—the mother of Mercy—riding on the gold-

---

1. मन्त्राणांपरमोमन्त्रो गुह्यानांगुह्यमुत्तमम् । पवित्रञ्चपवित्राणां मूलमन्त्रस्सनातनः ॥ (Pâñcharâtra.)

2. *Vide* note 2. p. 572. of our Bhagavadgítâ.

winged Garutmàn, in His resplendent yellow-hued Raiment (*Pitâmbara*). It seemed as if a noble blue-tinted cloud,—levin-picked—rode aloft on the peaks of a golden hill[1]. At this rapturous sight, he felt blessed and beatified. He was now finally converted. He was now a full-fledged and full-blown saint. In the paroxysm of his ecstatic delight, he poured forth his divine emotions in sweet rippling song, as has been handed down to us in the form of the Six *Prabandhas*, called :—

(1) Periya Tirumozhi,
(2) Tiru-kkurund-Â*nd*agam,
(3) Tiru-ne*d*und-Â*nd*agam,
(4) Tiruv-ezhu-kûtr-irukkai,
(5) *S*iriya-Tiruma*d*al, and
(6) Periya Tiruma*d*al.

said to represent the Six A*n*gas to the Four Vedas of St Nammàzhvàr's Four Prabandhas[2].

A man of fierce passions and filled with worldliness, became a saint of deep divine devotion, and full of spiritual illumination. Says Henri Joly: "We may expect, therefore, to meet with these latter virtues in the lives of the saints, even while, as yet, they have given small sign of their future sanctity.. Not

---

1 सुपर्णपृष्ठेप्रबभौ श्यामःपीताम्बरोहरिः । काञ्चनस्यगिरेश्शृङ्गे सतटित्तोयदोयथा ॥

2. Read his life, *following*.

that these virtues are at that time fully or even equally developed, for sanctity often requires conversion and the abandonment of the state of life up till then adhered to. The saints have not all begun life like St. Aloysius Gongaza. Take, for instance, St. Mary Magdalen, St. Mary of Egypt, St. Afra, St. Margaret of Cortona, who were courtesans, St. Paul, who was a persecutor, St. Augustine, who had many sins on his conscience, St. Francis Borgia, whose ingenions method of curing himself of an immoderate love of wine, Liebnitz is so fond of quoting. There are saints too, who did not wander quite so far, but who, neverthless, had to struggle against fiery passions. Bernard, the future Abbot of Citeaux, in order to get rid of a temptation caused by a single look, threw himself into a pond and stayed there until the icy water had cooled the ardour of his senses. St Vincent of Paul, incredible as it may seem, was "naturally of a bilious temperament and very subject to anger." We should be inclined to doubt his testimony of himself, if his friend and disciple, Abelly, did not tell us the same thing. St Francis of Sales, as every one knows, was naturally extremely passionate."

"We see by these examples, and many more which we have not time to quote, that easy temperance and absence of desires and passions are not necessarily among the natural virtues that sanctity builds upon. M. Renan has tried to make out that David was a ruffian, but he has been unable to deprive him of his largeness of heart and his tenderness, so wisely and sincere, even in the midst of crime. Christ, when he was on earth, forgave the debauchee, far more readily than He did the miser, and St Augustine was only interpreting His Doctrine when, later on, he dared to write, "Love God and then do what you like." The meaning of the saint's words is not difficult to understand. Love alone can suggest sacrifices and love alone gives the soul strength to carry them out."

* * * * *

"If, as we have seen, grace finds more to work upon in the saints than an empty receptacle or inert and passive material, we must expect to find that each saint has his own individual character and temperament." [1]

One such was our Saint Kaliyan. God's Grace, symbolised as *Srî*, had fully operated on Kaliyan's soul, and accordingly he received the Title of *Arul-Mâri* or 'The Grace-Cloud,'—either he on whom the Cloud of Grace had rained, or he whose Cloud of Grace raineth on us. In the first outflush of his soul brimming with gratitude and love for his Saviour-God, he exclaimed :—

(1) "Oh withered I; withering agonized in mind; and in bottomless depths of misery flung;

(2) For to clay was I joined; and joined I with wenches blithe, as if joys of cupid were the sole end and aim;

1. Pp. 47...50. "Psychology of the Saints."

(3) Roved I thus; roving found I Saving Grace, which illumed me; and woke I to my high estate.

(4) And searched; and searching I did discover the Holy Name of Nârâyana."[1]

And thus beginning, he wound up the First Decad of his First Outburst of love by confessing that every good is conferred by this Holy Name:—

(1) High birth it bestoweth, and prosperity; and all the pains God's servants suffer

(2) Are razed to the ground; Heavens High are granted and privileges there of Services Great;

(3) Capacities given, aye more: what the mother doth, even greater doth It do;

(4) Bliss it giveth. Such Holy name discovered I and that is Nârâyana." [2]

Thus giving vent in song to the nectareous delights of the Deity who had now permanently taken His abode in Arul-Mâri's heart, our Saint started out on a visit to Holy Shrines. In his rounds, he dedicated a decad of verses to such Holy Shrines in the North as Tiru-ppirudi, Badarik-âsrama, Sâlagrâma, Naimisâranya, Singa-v-êzh-kunnam, and Tiru-vêngadam; and

1. *Vâdinén, vâdi &c.* [Tirumozhi I. 1. 1.]. (1), (2), (3), (4), show the 4 lines of the original verse, of which this is a rendering.

2. *Kulam tarum &c.* [*Ibid.* I. 1. 9.] (1), (2), (3), (4,) [see note 1.]

coming to the south, paid homage to Tiru-vevvuḷûr, and came to Tiru-ninravûr[1]. But the Lord Resident here, Pattar-âvi[2], gave him no countenance, as He chose to be otherwise engaged. The saint left the place and proceeding to Tiru-valli-kkeni[1], made his obeisance to the Five Lords there enshrined. Thence he hied to Tiru-nîr-malai; and on to Tiru-kkaḍal-mallai[1], where he sojourned. Wherever he went he dedicated a hymn there, but he had left Pattar-âvi of Tiru-ninravûr without one. Lord Pattar-âvi's Consort was indignant with her Spouse for the cold treatment He had shown to the Saint, and said: "Unless Thou also art hymned by this Saint of rare quality, Thou art not glorified." On hearing this, the Lord went to Tiru-kkaḍal-mallai, and there appeared to our Saint,—when he sang both the Holy Shrines together in his Tiru-mozhi. II. 5. 2.

Then the divine Rhapsodist travelled on to Shrines in the Tonda-Land and arrived in the Land of the Cholas. By this time his fame had gone in advance of him, and he had become known as the *Nâlu-Kavi-pperumâl*, or 'the Lord of the Four-Fold Poetry',—(1) Âsu, (2) Madhuram, (3) Chitram, (4) and Vistâram. He had a great following too; and as they travelled the country abroad, the air resounded with the praises and titles of our eminent Saint. In the towns and villages, they wended their way in processional style,

1. For these and other Holy Shrines, consult the Table at end of St Andâl's Life. 2. Means: *Bhaktas' Life*.

exclaiming at the top of their voice : "Here comes our Nàlu-kavi-pperumà*l* ;—here goes our great Kaliyan ;—here marches our Âli-Nàdar ;—here walks our Aru*l*-mâri ;—here paces our Ko*n*gu-malar-kuzhaliyâr-vè*l* ;—here steps our Mangai-Véndar ;— here passes our Parakâlar ;— here proudly treads our 'Lion to the rutting Heretic-Elephants'[1] &c.

They had now arrived at *Sígâli* (Shiyali) where the *S*aiva Pa*nd*it Sambandhar lived at the time. His disciples, hearing the acclamatory resonance of our Saints' followers, came in a body, opposed them, interdicting them to sing his praises while their own distinguished and matchless poet lived there. Our Saint Parakâlar [= Enemy of heretics] proposed a debate with Sambandha Náyanâr; to which they agreed, and led him to where Sambandhar was. As he was treading his way, he found *S*ígà*l*i full of Pàshan*d*is[2] ; there were no Vaish*n*avas,—not to speak of even a roof belonging to them where Parakâlar could rest a while—where then an image of Vishnu ? Parakàlar, as soon as he smelt this atmosphere,. is said to have felt as if his tongue cleaved to the roof of his mouth, as if it threatened to refuse to function, in the pending dispute with Sambandhar. By chance, a *S*rívaish*n*ava dame passed by him. He saw her and asked for a loan of her Vish*n*u-Image. She gladly lent her Lord Tá*d*à*l*an (or Krish*n*a). Armed with this Power, which seemed

1. I.E. *Para-vàdi-matta-gaja-kanthìrava.* 2. Heretics.

to restore his tongue and whet his wits, he proceeded to Sambandhar, and began the debate. On seeing Parakàlar, Sambandhar composed a sang but which Parakâlar condemned. Sambandhar then begged Parakâlar to frame one in his turn, to which he responded by a Decad of verses which form the Tirumozhi: III-4, in praise of Kàzhi-cchîRàmar [= *S*ri Râma of *S*îgâ*l*i]. At hearing this, Sambandhar was delighted, and admiring the Saint for his qualities as poet, saint, and philosopher, and confessing that he was beaten, declared that he full-deserved the Title of Nàlu-kavi-pperumàl; gave him his trident (Vêl) as a sign of his homage to his greatness, and paying him all honors, escorted him some way on his journey and returned taking his leave. In all the Temples where Saint Parakála is enshrined, this victory-lance is borne on his Person.

From *S*igâ*l*i, Saint Parakàlar passed on to Tiruvàli,—his native place—and visiting Tirunán*g*ûr and other shrines on the way, reached Tiruvinda*l*ûr. The Lord Resident here appeared to the saint; but disappearing immediately, threw him into a mood of grief. But when he composed his carol:—

" Vási vallîr Inda*l*-ûrîr
Vázhnde pôm Nîre,"

the Lord's heart was melted, and He re-appeared to him in His full glory and let the Saint enjoy the Sight as long as he wished. Proceeding thence to other Shrines, the Saint at last reached Namberumà*l* Sannidhi [=*S*rî-

Rangam] and here to *Srî* Ranganátha, he dedicated more than one panegyric of verses. The Lord was mighty pleased, and vouchsafing to appear to him spoke thus:—"Beloved Son! no more shalt thou wander. Thou shalt stay with us evermore. The rest of thy sojourn on earth, thou shalt devote to the strengthening of Our Temple, by enclosing it with ramparts, raising splendid towers and adding other corridors, chambers, aisles and recesses to our Holy Premises.

Parakâlar received the command with due submission. He called together his men and consulted them as to how to find the wherewithal to undertake such a gigantic business. One Yatirâsan—the husband of his sister Ândâlammai—suggested a visit to Nâgur-Nâgapatna, for he had heard there was a priceless golden Idol of Buddha there. The information was welcomed with joy and the party sallied forth. Arriving at Nâgapatna, Parakálar set about inquiring for the place; when a goodly woman gave him to understand—as a matter of secrecy confided to her by her mother-in-law—the whereabouts of the place, but it had such secret passages and mechanical contrivances, she said, that it was inaccessible to strangers. The architect however lived out in the sea in an Island (Bay of Bengal). Parakâlar with his party took ship forthwith and sailing to the shores mentioned, discovered the architect's dwelling. Parakâlar fixed upon a plan by which to draw out secrects from him. They would all loiter near his house as if way-farers met and exchanged intelligence of far-off countries. Of course they would place themselves near enough so as to be within hearing. They would wait till the architect had dined and sat down to munch his betel and nut. They would then start a conversation amongst themselves thus :—"Ah! friends, what a fate has overtaken Nágapatna! What a fall of gloom has spread over that fated Temple! A horde of Turks have raided the place! The Temple has been reduced to atoms! The beautiful golden Buddha has been made away with! Comrades, how is it we still live, after this misfortune! and so on." With their plan ready, they waited; and when they saw the architect seated and discussing contemplatively his betel and nut, they began their ready-made speech. This fell into his ears. It put him into fright, sorrow and shivers. He started, and joined the tattlers outside his house, and eagerly learnt from them more details—of which there were numerous, of course. What good novelist is in want of materials? The architect was greatly affected, shed tears, and rolled on the ground. "Sires," he wailed, "who could have been that architect, cleverer than myself indeed, to have been able to disclose to the Turks the secret clues to the Temple?, the whirling wheel at the main entrance, the secret chain hanging from the top of the Tower and fastened to a pin hidden under the heavy stone-pavement where the Gomukhi-waters drop?". And so on the poor stricken man lamented. The detectives learnt all the secrets thus, looking at each other secretly, and laughing in their sleeves at their project so well succeeding. "Take heart, O good man", they consoled the architect, "what is past cannot be recalled. Why dost thou vainly cry over spoilt milk? Be quiet, poor soul!. Go home. we bid thee good-bye. Thanks."

The party arrived at the sea-shore and saw a ship laden with areca-nut about to weigh anchor for Nâgapatna. They found the merchant and, like devout mendicants, blessed him and asked him to give them a passage back chargeless. He gladly assented; and they were all on board. While they were fairly out on the main, Parakâlar took a full nut, cut it into two halves, and dropping one half, said to the merchant who was watching:—"Sir, will you let me have my *half the nut* on arrival at the destination?" "Certainly" replied the merchant. "But give me a written chit to that effect", asked the Saint. The chit: *'half the nut* yours', the simple merchant gave. But on arriving at the harbour of Nâgapatna and unloading, the Saint claimed *half the* (*whole cargo of*) *nut*. The trader remonstrated, the saint challenged. An appeal was carried to the chamber of commerce. The headmen there decided that as the written document executed by the trader and exhibited by Parakâlar was quite clear as to its meaning, the trader was bound in all probity to clear off half the cargo for the chit-holder. The merchant was sorely puzzled at the chicanery practised on him; but though grieved in his heart, he had to relinquish *one half of (all) his nut*.

He gave him the cargo-half, converted in money, consoling himself with the reflection that this was a pre-natal debt he had to discharge. The Saint took it and inwardly wishing the merchat *Heaven* as his reward,[1] threaded his way into Nâgapatna.

They hid themselves in the enclosure of the temple through the clue a dame had already given; and at midnight, they began their burglaring. The heavy pavement stone near the Gomukhi was lifted, and the secret pin discovered. The chain attached thereto was released. Then they mounted up the tower, the cap of which, to which the chain had been fastened, was now free. They opened it and looking down saw the Buddha gold idol dazzling like the sun. Parakâlar on seeing it exclaimed :--

1. This act may be considered covert. But it suited the time, men and circumstances. If the merchant had been preached a Vedântic Sermon, or even if God had been presented to him in person, he would not have parted with his areca-nut. On the principle of "material loss is spiritual gain", which God is every moment proving in our world, and which is stated in such Scriptures as "*Yasy-ânugraham-icchâmi tasya vittam harâmi*", and which is reiterated often by Jesus, as for example *Matt*: XIX. 24: "It is easier for a camel to pass through the eye of a needle, than for a rich man to enter the Kingdom of Heaven": and *Rev*: VI. 15: "And the Kings of the earth, and the princes, and tribunes and the rich and the strong &c. hid themselves in the dens and in the rocks of mountains," the merchant spiritually gained. At any rate our saint's process was much better than the process by which mission funds, are said to be collected in America for the conversion of the Hindus!

"Was such pure gold required to make thee with?
Enough if tin had usèd been for thee,
Or iron say, or one of el'ments five,
Or brass or copper worn out from use!"[1]

There was the teethed whirling wheel, which prevented approach to the idol. They brought a number of plantain trunks, and cast one after another at the wheel. The bark sticking in the teeth of the wheel and becoming tangled, stopped its movement. Parakâlar then let down his brother-in-law Yatirâsan into the aperture. When Yatirâsan laid his hands on the idol, it escaped; and he ran and it ran, round and round the compartment. Parakâlar suggested Yatirâsan's spitting on it. He did so and the mantra-power which gave the idol motion vanished by this act of pollution. He then clutched the idol and hoisted it up to the aperture and Parakâlar lifted it out. He then drew up Yatirâsan, but lo! he had become somewhat bloated by this time, and the hole was too small for him to get out, do what they will.

"Alas! Yatirâsan, what shall I do?" cried Parakâlar in agony, "what a narow pass this? How can I go without thee? How can I live without thee? And yet I must go; and must live, to do the services laid on my head by Srî Ranga. But what services these? What *do I want* to do with this golden idol, if I have to cut *thy head* off—to escape discovery—and make my

1. *Iyyáttál áhádo* &c.

godly sister *Ândâl* a widow thereby? Is this what Ra*n*ganátha wills?" Yatirâsan saw his brother-in-law thus lamenting in great anguish of heart, when he addressed him thus: "Brother-in-law, dear! art thou not a Mahátma? Dost thou forget thy divine orgin from *Srî Sâr*n*ga*? Hast thou forgotten thy mission on earth, —incarnated here as a saviour of mankind? Is not Divine service of the foremost importance? Is not Ra*n*ga's Commandment to be obeyed at any cost? Again, are not our 'life on Earth, of lightning-duration'[1]?, is not this body perishable, subject to hunger, disease and a series of calamities? Is it not but a stinking mixture of flesh and nerve and blood and bone? My time is come to pass out of this dismal prison of urine and fæces, and pass on to the exquisite spiritual body in heaven, and there serve our Eternal God in full blessedness. Hence why dost thou delay, my saviour? Canst thou not extened thy vision beyond matter and all temporal interests, and deign to despatch me soon? Saint, art thou not? Why then like a mauling dost thou weep for my fate? Envy me not the high state to which I become heir by one stroke from thy hand. Cut my head off, pray. It is dawning already. We may be discovered, and all our plans for Ra*n*ga's Service baffled. Make me Ra*n*ga's victim. Isn't it His worth? Pray now, at once let me be off to Heaven. Surely, gladly, I shall wait for thee there.

1. *Minnin nilai-y-ila* &c [T. V. Mozhi. I. 2-2].

Now, don't give way to human weakness; lay aside mortal considerations. Revive to the Higher Law thou hast to carry out, to which all mundane laws had better be sacrificed". At hearing this discourse, our Saint rallied, summoned up superhuman courage, and crying: "Oh, my Yatirásan, if any one deserves Heaven indeed it is you", and invoking: "Great Ranga, in Thy name I do this," he flashed his scimitar and by one stroke took Yatirâsan's head off[1]. Merciful Heavens! This scene of unparalled martyrdom for the cause of God was witnessed by all the Gods of the blue celestium. The party now descended from the tower readily packed; and laying Yatirâsan's head in a stretcher, covered it as a corpse and ranging themselves into a funeral procession, with fire-pot, wood, and sobbings, slipped out of Nagapatna, their atrocious deeds never in the least suspected by anyone. Going far away, beyond human sight, they deposited Yatirasan's head safely in a thicket and carrying the gold idol pursued their journey onward.

Our Divine mother, Mercy Incarnate, She who stands to God as light to sun and scent to flower,—*Srî* Ranganâyakî of *Srîrangam*[2], She was embittered in her heart that one of her sons, Yatirâsan, should meet such a horrible death. She expostulated with her Lord *Srî* Ranganâtha thus:— "How canst Thou, O

1. Cp: the priest who said to the martyred king on the scaffold: "Son of St. Louis, ascend to heaven".

2. Read Topic 17: "Virtue of Mediation" in our *Divine Wisdom of Drâvida Saints.*

cruel Lord! silently witness such occurrences? Have omniscience and omnipotence taken leave of thee? Didst thou not raise to life the whole army of Sugríva when it lay dead on the battle-field under the fierce arm of Indrajit? Many years after the Demon Pa*n*chajana carried away Sândîpin's son into the sea, didst Thou not recover him for Sândîpini, thy Âchárya? Like Vibhíshana and Gajendra, poor Yatirâsan had no selfish end in view, but sarificed his life solely for Thy service. And yet how canst Thou vouchsafe to those but be indifferent to him? Strange indeed are thy ways; inexplicable Thy dispensations! I cannot, Lord, suffer my Yatirâsan to be dead, and my daughter Â*n*dâ*l* made a widow. If thou wilst revive him for me, how will Thy universe suffer on that account? I plead, I pray: grant his life, O Lord!"

The Lord became affected on hearing these pleadings of his tender-hearted consort, and summoning Garutmân, bid him go at once to the tower of Buddha's temple and rescue the trunk of Yatirâsan's body, join it with the head in the thicket, breathe life into it, and leave the revived Yatirâsan with Parakâlar. Garutmán blessed himself to be deputed to such a worthy task, for he was going to see a martyr to God's cause—a rare commodity to be found in all the three worlds. He flew to the tower, reverently lifted the trunk lying there, and carrying it to where the head lay, united them and breathed life. Yatirâsan opened his eyes and seeing the feathered Archangel, fell at his feet and learning from him all the events which led to his resuscitation said :—"What a sinful creature I am, that I have been denied heaven; and Oh, all its celestial enjoyments I have forgone! Oh, God Great! Hast Thou no will yet to take me to Thee?" So saying, he took to wailing. But Garutmân never stopped to reason with him, but lifted him on to his shoulders, and flew to where Parakâlar was, and safely dropping him there, explained to the Saint all the circumstances of Yatirâsan's return, and winged his way to his Lord *Srí* Ranga and gave an account of all his doings.

Parakâlar's joy knew no bounds when his beloved brother-in-law was restored to him. He and his ministers embraced him, kissed him, wept tears of joy and jumped and danced with him. And our Saint broke out into a discourse thus;—What, my Yatirâsan, thou daredst to go and have all the Heaven for thyself? Served right, thou hast been sent back to us! What is celestial joy after all to the joy of serving God right here in this land of darkness! It is higher privilege to serve the Lord here where servitors are scarce. There is no need for such in Heaven; for there their name is legion. The want is here; and it is given to us to supply it. Our royalty is here. Our crown is with Ranganátha. To Him annd His service, I am entirely sworn. Not all the gods of the sky above, Brahmas, Rudras and Indras can band themselves against our *work here.* For I feel I could in an instant quell them *all, only* to be left here undisturbed in order to carry out my programme of erecting towers and pavilios and ramparts and what not for my beloved Spouse, Srî Ranga." Maddened with such outflush of divine enthusiasm, they minded not night, for they rose and pushed their journey forward with all speed.

They had now reached Tiru-kka*nna*n*gudi*. Parakâlar saw he was dogged by some one. He looked back. It was the village-watchman of the Pariah caste. "What dost thou want with me?" asked our Saint. "Holy sire," he said, "we have no good drinking water here." The Saint took up a stone, and gave it a throw. "There," he pointed out, "you have water." The watchman ran and lo, found a sweet-water pond there in front of the Temple of Tiru-kka*nna*n-gu*di*, and the good-folk to this day drink the waters thereof.

Hastening onwards, they were near an Agrahâr. As daylight was breaking, it was necessary to conceal the gold idol. They found a ploughed field, and slushy, close by; and it was buried there. The owner chanced to come with a bundle of crops for transplanting the same at the very same spot. The party obstructed him saying:—"We own this field. You cannot transgress here." Taken thus by surprise, he retaliated;—"How, Sirs? I hold documents from my ancestors' times!" "So be it," replied they, "bring the documents to-morrow, and we shall settle the dispute." He went home to fetch the papers. But darkness fell in the meanwhile, and disinterring the idol, Parakâlar went his way, leaving the undisputed possession of lands and papers to the cultivator himself. Arriving at Uttamar Kôil, and hiding away the idol, they sojourned.

Meanwhile, there was great commotion at Nâgapatna. The Buddha temple had been broken open and sacked. The idol was missing. A search-party was despatched. Gathering information about the fugitive gang, they traced them out by means of the incident of the landlord and his bonds; and overtaking the Saint at Uttamar Kôil, demanded the idol from him. "What do we know about it?" opposed Parakâlar. "Will you swear then?" demanded the search-party. "Never mind," coolly returned the Saint, "we shall restore to you the idol—*not less than our small finger*—next year, Pa*n*guni month, Rohi*n*i. Here take this slip to that effect." They returned.

Fearless now, Saint Parakâlar's myrmidons reached Srirangam, melted the gold idol, which placed ample funds in his hands, added to his income from the arecanut traffic. He began the construction of the formidable towers, ramparts and other necessaries of the great Fane; and when the alignment of a rampart fell across the spot where St. Ton*d*ara*d*ippo*d*i daily weaved his floral wreaths for the Lord, Parakâlar reverently altered the line. St. Ton*d*ara*d*ippo*d*i blessed him for his considerateness, and in token of the incident gave he his flower-knife the name of "Aru*l*-Mâri."

It was now the year, month and date promised for

the Nágapatna people. They came and presented the slip. Parakâlar received it duly and said:—"Here, take it," and *cut his small finger and threw it.* That was the idol, *not less than the small finger.* They, struck mute at this act of martyrdom and finding it was useless to deal with such a wild and desperate character, quietly went back as they came.

The Saint nearly completed his grand project of the construction. Funds ran short, and the workmen became boisterous for their arrears of wages. "Fear not", the Saint told them, "a very treasure-trove I have for you in an island. Go on board this brig." They all did so, and when the craft had gone to the midstream of the Kâveri (north branch), he beckoned the paddlesman to tranship him and himself to another raft, and commanded him to overturn the boat with all its crew into the hissing billows of the holy river.[1] The couple rowed themselves back to Srîrangam shore.

The sons and grandsons of the workmen, finding their sires missing, beleaguered the saint, and bellicosely enough demanded of him an explanation. "O, clamour not, my sons! Your elders are quite safe in the island. Such a find of fortune there, aye! And they are so busy collecting, and packing." "Cheat thou art," bawled they, "thou hast emptied them into the river.. We know it for a fact. Unless thou restorest them to us as

1. To this day, Kaveri here goes by the name of Kolladam or Konnedam (Colcroon).

they were, we will let thee not an inch budge." Our Saint was thus beset and plagued. He laid himself down in their midst and sent a secret cry of anguish. Thus :— "Ranga! what a hecatomb of victims for Thy sake! Oh, for *Thy* sake! To what plights and passes are thy servants brought! To what straights they are reduced! Not for *me* have I done all these mighty feats, but for *Thee.* Let Thy fair name suffer not. Glory to Thee, O Lord!"

He had a vision. *Sri* Ranganâthan appeared and spoke :—"Be not distressed, my faithful! Rise and tell these men to stroll to the river Kâveri, bathe there, and pick themselves with the Holy Vaishnava Symbols[1]. Bid them come thus to the Holy Azhagia-Manavâlan-Pavilion, and invoke their dead ancestors by their names." Our Saint recollected and confidently begged them to follow the course as traced out to him by his Lord. They dispersed, and preparing themselves in the fashion dictated, ranged themselves in the Holy Pavilion; and one by one called his ancestor by his name. Merciful Heavens! Behind the Holy Image of Ranganâtha, appeared the spirit-forms of the ancestors with their Paternal Deities (Pitri-Devatas), and answered :—"Dear children, we are here safe. We have reached the other shore, by the grace of that Saint over there. We are harboured in blessedness in the

1. About the *Vaishnava-Lingas* generally, *Sàtyàyaniy-upanishad* may be read.

Holy feet of the Great Lord. Waste no time nor grief for us. There, to that blessed Saint Parakâlar, be obedient and humble, and a little while more live to earth; and through the power of your Saint's saving grace, you will be re-united to us. We wish you well." And so saying the spirits vanished out of sight.

Some time elapsed. St: Parakâlar felt he had nearly fufilled his mission. He promised himself a little rest from his indefatigable toils and turmoils; and composed his Lyric the Tiru-ne*d*un*d*-*ân*dagam (already noticed along with his other works)—and dedicated it along with himself to Lord Ra*n*ga. He sung it to celestial music (*deva-gâna*). Srî Ra*n*ga was pleased and His voice asked the Votary to ask for any boon he wished. "Lord," he prayed, "I have only two boons to ask. St: Nammâzhvàr, our Patron Saint, sang his four famous Prabandhams,[1] representative of the four Vedas. Every year during the festival called the Adhyayan-otsava, these Drâvida Scriptures must be recited along with the Gîrvâ*n*a Scriptures. During this celebration, St: Nammâzhvâr must be invited from Tirunagari to be present and witness." This was granted, and our Saint escorted St: Nammâzhvàr to and from Tirunagari annually, and thus celebrated the Adhyayan-otsava with great eclat.

"Lord! I have the other boon to ask," said the Saint, "let me feast my eyes by sighting Thy Ten Avatârs."

1. Read St: Nammàzhvâr's Life.

The Lord said:—Proceed to our South House (Terku-vídu), viz., Tiru-kkurungudi, and there have Thy wish, entering Archa-Form. The Saint made his obeisance to Sri-Ranga, and departed with his Queen Kumuda-valli Nâcchiyâr(his Saviour[1])to the place named—a veritable Siddhâsrama, skirt by the famous Mahendra Hills of the Western Coast reaching to Cape Comorin. There he paid his homage to the Five Nambis, and by the side of the Hill Stream, called the Sindhu Nadi, lived the life of a recluse with his Saintly Queen, absorbed in meditation; and in that Great Stage of complete absorption, called Samâdhi, passed out of this earth and attained beatification, after carrying out his vocation here as saviour, for upwards of one hundred years and more. He was exalted to the eternal Empyrean of the Infinite Now, where he witnessed not only the Ten Avatârs, but God Himself in Essence and what not.

Yatirâsan was called. Srî Ranga said:–our Kali Kanri (or he who by his works hâs routed the demon of Kali-age) is thy Âchârya (Master). We bid thee go to his native place Tiru-kkuraiyalûr, and instal his Archa there in a duly erected Temple; and let, for all time to come,—and that mankind be blessed,—be his daily, monthly and yearly solemnizations inaugurated." Yatirâsan carried out the Lord's behests and in due time joined his master in the spiritual Realms.

1. In many Shrines, she is always by the side of her saintly husband.

Before closing this life teeming with bold adventures, we may add another word to the justificatory passages already written in regard to the seemingly wrong conduct on the part of St: Tirumangai Âzhvâr :—He acted on the Principle of "End justifies the Means". His end was Divine Service, from which therefore all trace of selfish purpose or egotism was absent. He espoused His cause; and to that cause, he would sacrifice himself and all the world. Worldly considerations were to him worthless. To him, their sacrifice was well; and Heaven was clear to his vision. Though he stripped men here of their worldly goods, and earthly lives, their rewards were great; for in lieu of worldly goods, their gain was the Kingdom of God; and in lieu of earthly lives of short span, they obtained Eternal Life. Such deeds as he did, only a Saint and Martyr like him could be permitted to do. To other than a Saint and Martyr of his type, most of the deeds indeed would be heinous and could never be permitted. A brigand and a pirate and a swindler have motives of their own for their acts; but this Saint had no motives of himself. Perfect self-abnegation ruled his mind, and sole service to God swayed his heart. If it pleased God to effect human salvation by curious modes and methods, who to question Him? If it pleased Him to constitute this Saint different from others, and work His ways through a bravo and a desparado, who to prevent Him? God Himself works out salvation by pain, and misery, by fire and water and hurricane, by catastrophes and catalysms. What then can we say against His ambassadors of the type of our Saint? Indeed His ways are mysterious and His plans inscrutable. Modern-day moralists might be inclined to put our Saint down for a sinner; but without regard to such irresponsible opinions, all the same, the ancients had sufficient reasons for them to canonize him as a Saint and idolize him in all the temples. Though Paul of Tarsus felt that he was "the chief of *sinners*", yet admiring men have named him *Saint*[1].

St: Francis de Sales said: "Love God and do anything." And our Saint loved God too, not for his sake, but for His sake. In the same strain, voice forth our Scriptures:—

For example: *Bhagavad-Gîtâ*: *IX*. 30 *ff*:—

" ... ... Nay Prince!
"If one of evil life turn in his thought
"Straightly to Me, count him amidst the good;
"He hath the high way chosen.

* * * * * *

"Though they be born from the very womb of sin,
"Woman or man; sprung of the Vaisya caste
"Or lowly disregarded Sûdra,—all
"Plant foot upon the highest path."[2]

---

1. Vide Carlyle's *Sartor Resartus*, Ch: VII:—"The Everlasting No". And read to what tactics Cecil Rhodes resorted to in Africa in order to accomplish even his *worldly* ends.

2. अपिचेत्सुदुराचारो &c.

Mahâ-Bhârata :—

"Though of evil ways, of indiscriminate food, ungrateful, and athiest,—but if he lovingly seeks the Ancient Lord as his Rest—know he is rid of sin, for Great is God.[1]"

Vishnu Sahasranâma (Mahâ-bhârata, Ânusâsanika Parva *132*):—"Not the least stain remains on the lovers of Vâsudeva. From him, all birth and death, and age and ailment—and all fear—flee."[2]

Blest be St. Parakâlar.

1. दुराचारोपिसर्वाशी कृतघ्नो नास्तिकः पुरा ॥ समाश्रयेदादिदेवं श्रद्धया शरणं यदि ॥ निर्दोषं विद्धि तं जन्तुं प्रभावात्परमात्मनः ॥

2. न वासुदेवभक्तानामशुभं विद्यते क्वचित् ॥ जन्ममृत्युजराव्याधिभयंवाप्युपजायते ॥

श्रीः

THE LIFE OF

St. Nammazhvar.

or (St. Sathagopa[1])

and of his disciple

St. Madhurakavi-Âzhvâr.

Reference is made in *Srî* Bhâgavata, Ch. V, verses 38 to 40[2], propheysing the birth of Holy Saints in the Drâvida Land (or the south of India) by the side of the Holy Rivers. These verses inform us that—

---

1. A name of St. Nammàzhvâr, so called because of his conquest of the *Satha-Vâyu*, or the materializing magnetism of the world-atmosphere, which, it is believed, obstructs the spiritual vision of souls. To overcome this and recover the spiritual, becomes the work of life. Another name is Máran meaning: He who is cross. *i. e.* he who is cross to the ways of the world. Nammázhvâr means "Our own Saint," a title given by Lord Ranganâtha [Read Kamban's Sathagopar-Audádi. Pâyiram 3]. Also called Parânkusa meaning the 'Victor over false faiths.' Other names are Vakulâ-Bharana and Kuruhaip-pirân &c. Kulapati, Kútastha are other names signifying 'the Holy Head' of the Sri-Vaishnavas.

2. कृतादिषु महाराजन् कलाविच्छन्तिसम्भवम् । कलौ खलु भविष्यन्ति नारायणपरायणाः ॥ क्वचित्क्वचिन्महाराज द्रविळेषु च भूरिशः । ताम्रपर्णीनदी यत्र कृतमाला पयस्विनी॥ कावेरी च महापुण्या * * *

"Men born in the Krita, Trêta and Dvàpara ages, wished to take birth in the Kali age(the so called dark age), because they knew that in this age would be born great souls devoted to Nârâyana." [38]

"But these souls would be thinly scattered about here and there[1]; but in the Dràvida Land, they would be found in some numbers, living by the side of such rivers as Tàmraparni, Kritamâlá (Vaigai) and Payasvinî (Pâpanàsinî)" [39]

"And where the Holy River Kâveri flows......" [40] St: Nammàzhvâr, one of these Mahàtmas whose place in the galaxy of saints may be found in the Hierarchic Table (No 11), was accordingly born in the Kali Age, B. C. 3102, or just 43 days[2] after the retirement of Lord Krishna from the world or at the end of the Dvàpara age.

---

1. The reason for this sparseness is given in Vishnu-Puràna thus :—

कलौ जगत्पतिं विष्णुं सर्वस्रष्टारमीश्वरम् । नार्चयिष्यन्ति मैत्रेय पाषण्डोपहताजनाः ॥ "In the Kali age, the heretics who are wedded to false doctrines do not worship, Maitreya ! the Lord of the Universe, the Creator of all, Vishnu." (VI. 1-50) And Harivamsa says (I. 54-61):—

महेश्वरं कुमारं च द्वौ च देवौ समाश्रिताः । भविष्यन्ति नरास्सर्वे लोके न स्थविरायुषः ॥ (In the following Kali) short-lived do men become and depend on the two deities Mahesvara and Kumâra.

2. For Lord Krishna's age see Introduction.

This saint's life comes to be written last as he is considered the chief Saint to whom others are like his limbs.

The Bhavishyat Purâ*n*a prophesied that :—

"In the beginning of Kali Yuga, on the day when the full-moon day is in junction with the constellation Visâkha, Senesa or Vishvak-sena,[1] the Archangel-chief, will himself incarnate (as Nammâzhvàr) in order to revive and emphasize the Way of Love to Vish*n*u."

Brahmâ*n*da-Purâ*n*a fixed the place of birth thus:—

"In the Pân*d*ya Land there is a town called *Srînagari* (Tiru-nagari) situated on the banks of the river Tàmrapar*n*î, where the 'Conqueror of the senses,' (Hrishìkesa) is himself seen (in the image of Nammâzhvàr)."

The rank of our Saint thus is in a line of Hierarchy, the members of which are staunch adherents of Vish*n*u or Nárâya*n*a—the one God; and he is to be the spiritual Head of a spiritual body, consisting of all the other Saints and sages and their followers.[2] So far for the

1. Vide Hierarchic Table (No. 5).

2. For these names, consult Hierarchic Table. "The Vedas are the Revelations which refer to Purá*n*as and Itihásas. To the latter class belongs the Mahábhárata called the *Fifth Veda*. The Mahábhárata and the Vedànta-Sùtras refer to Pàncharàtra Âgamas. The latter such as Îsvara-samhita refer to the Âzhvâras." Says Pàrthasârathi Yogi (page 206 of his English Tatva-traya):— As S_3 we reckon the Drávida Saint Parànkusa or Nammàzhvâr and in *his* wisdom we regard as included. the wisdom of *all* the other Drâvida Saints (who are eleven in,

Saint's Spiritual heredity. The bodily kinship borne by him, has been traced for us in a race of rulers, thus :—

1. Tiruvazhudi-va*l*a-nâdar (The king of Kurugu-nàdu, of which Tiru-nagari is capital)
2. A*r*am-Tà*n*giyár (or Dharma-varma).
3. Chakra-Pá*n*iár.
4. Achyutar.
5. *S*en-tâmarai-kka*nn*ar.
6. *S*en-ka*nn*ar.
7. Por-kàriyâr.
8. Kâriyár.
9. St : Nammázhvàr.

The grandsire Por-kàriâr, wishing to marry his son Kâriàr in a way befitting his rank, proceeded with him to the place called Tiruva*n*-parisâram, where lived a Holy man of the Vaish*n*ava Faith by name Tiruvàzhmârbar with whom Por-káriyàr considered a matrimonial alliance quite respectable. Entering his

number). and also of the Dràvida Saintess Ândâl whom we regard as a goddess incarnate. Saint Paràṅkusa's life and psalms and the admirable commentaries in ten huge quartos which these psalms have produced, may be advantageously compared with the life and psalms of David, the Royal prophet of the Hebrews and the commentaries on that prophet's psalms in the seven Octavo Volumes of Spurgeon's Treasury of David. I have no doubt whatever that, whoever honestly makes such a comparison as I have suggested, will pronounce the life and psalms of Saint Paràṅkusa, and the commentaries on these psalms to be in every *respect far* superior to David's life and psalms, and the commentaries on those psalms'. (Ibid).

residence where also the elders of the neighbourhood had assembled, Porkâriyâr formally opened negotiations of marriage in their presence and begged of Màrbar to give his daughter Udaiya-nangaiyâr in marriage to his son. Márbar most heartily gave his assent to the proposals; and without loss of time ordered grand pavilions to be erected, bedecked with pearls, and ordered bands to discourse sweet music, and with various other rejoicings, gave Udaiya-nangaiyâr[1] in marriage, with all the Âryan models of ceremony such as pouring water &c., duly observed.

Kâriyàr with his new bride proceeded to the Holy Lord of Tiruvan-parisâram,—and after duly paying their homage to that God, returned to his native town Kurugûr (or Tirunagari). The high priests and other residents of the place welcomed them in due style, by decorating the town with banners, water-jugs &c., in the manner, so to say, of the good-folk of Ayôdhya welcoming Srî Ráma on his return from Mithila, after marrying King Janaka's daughter Sítá :—

" And soon Ayôdhyá's gates be viewed
High over the roofs gay pennons played;
Tabour and drum loud music made,
Fresh water cooled the royal road,
And flowers in bright profusion glowed,
Glad crowds with garlands thronged the ways
Rejoicing on their king to gaze." [Râmâyana I. 77].

After making such a triumphal entry into his native

1. Natha-Nayika in Samskrit.

city, Kâriyâr lived with his spouse for some time discharging duly all the righteous duties incumbent to the station in life, of a Householder (*Grihastha*). Some time after, he paid a visit to his father-in-law's house at Tiruvan-parisâram accompanied by his wife Udaiya-Nangaiyár; and on his way back, visited the Holy Shrine Tiruk-kurungudi—a charming spot, near the Mahendra Hills of the Western Ghats, abounding in groves infest with buzzing bees and cooing birds—and paid his honors there to the Nambi or the Lord resident there. [Read the closing paras of the life of St. Tirumangai-Âzhvâr]. He prayed to the Lord for an issue to him. Thereupon the Lord signified to him through his officiating priest that His own self would become incarnate through their medium, and so saying, blessed the pair, bestowing on them as a sign of His Divine favour the holy basil-garland worn dy Himself, and bestowing other honors such as Tírtha and Prasáda. Kâriyâr's heart overflowed with joy. Taking leave, the favoured pair returned to their native place Srínagari (or Kurugûr). Some time after, Nangaiyàr was found carrying, for Nàràyana (same as Nambi) had commanded His own High Chamberlain, Senesa or Vishvaksena to become incarnate on earth, as His representative and a saviour of mankind. In due season he appeared as our infant Saint.[1] His appearance is figuratively

1. The date of his birth is recorded in the Divyasûri Charita as follows:—राधे कलिदिने लाभे वैशाख्ये काव्यवासरे । लग्ने कर्कटकेऽसूत तनयं नाथ नायिका ॥

described as the sun rising in Nàtha-nàyikà's Horizon—the sun adorned with Vakula[1]-blossoms, chasing the gloom of spiritual darkness, drying up the waters of the ocean of births and deaths (transmigration), and making the closed lotuses of men's hearts to open into full bloom.

When at Nárâyáṇa's bidding, Senesa incarnated as our Saint, Âdisesha,—His Holy couch—had preceded him and was born in the form of a Tamarind Tree[2], to be the Blessed Tree of Shade under which our infant Saint was to make his abode.

St: Madhura-kavigal.

Like dawn,—the harbinger of day,—Saint Madhura-kavigal had already taken birth on earth in order to foretell the event of our Saint coming[3]. St Madhura-kavi is said to be spiritually descended from the Angel Kumuda-Gaṇesa, a subordinate functionary under the High Lord of Hosts, Senesa. He was born in a Bráhmaṇa family of the Sama-veda and Pûrva-Sikha and his time of birth is recorded in Divyasúri-charita as:—

1. The fragrant flower of Mimusops Elengi, the characteristic mark for our Saint.

2. This Holy Tree is to this day seen flourishing. It is said to bear no fruit like other trees of its kind.

3. Like Âlavandar before Ramanuja; and John the Baptist before Jesus.

गणेशः कुमुदोनाम्ना कविर्मधुरसंज्ञिकः ।
चैत्रमासि शुभेच्चित्त तारकायामजायत ॥[1] [IV-28].

As Brâhmana, all the sacraments such as the Upanayana &c. were duly administered to him; he became well-versed in all the Fourteen subjects which make the wise man: *viz.*, the six Angas (Síksha, Vyàkarana, Chandas, Nirukta, Jyotisha and Kalpa-sûtra), the Four Vedas (Rik, Yajus, Sáma and Atharva), the Mîmàmsa (the Pûrva and the Uttara Divisions), the Nyáya or Logic, the Puránas (eighteen in number) and Dharma-Sàstra or the Laws. Once upon a time, he proceeded to the North of India on a holy pilgrimage to Ayodhya, Madhura, Màyá, Kàsi, Kánchi, Avantikà, and Dvàraká &c., a visit to which is said to possess the efficacy of securing salvation. Madhura-kavi was keeping himself thus employed. We shall leave him for a moment and return to our Saint.

St. Nammázhvär (resumed)

He was born, it was said, just 43 days after the exit of Lord Krishna from the stage of this world. As soon as the child was born, it never cried, but smiled a heavenly smile, never sucked the mother's milk and showed itself to be an extraordinary child maintaining wonderful silence and serenity. The parents were not only awe-struck but racked their wits as to what

1. Born in the month of Chaitra under the constellation Chitra [Vide Hierarchic Table No. 10.]

measures should be adopted towards such an inexplicable prodigy. In the end, however, they simply resigned themselves to the good will of God, thinking in their minds: "Lord! what may be Thy mysterious design?" Ten days passed thus in the infant's chamber. The eleventh day, according to Hindu ordinances, the parents bathed, and taking the child to the Holy Lord of *S*rînagari[1] situated on the Southeren Bank of Tàmrapar*n*i, fondly and reverently disposed it in a gold gem-made cradle under the Holy Tamarind Tree (already alluded to). They named the child Mâ*r*an and looked upon it no more as their own, but as a miraculously born heavenly child destined to become the (spiritual) king of their Holy race.[2] Sixteen years did thus pass by, and the child would neither open its eyes nor its mouth[3]. It seemd as if it mused within itself thus:—"Except Thee I shall see no one. Except

---

1. The full description of this Lord is given in:—

शंखतीर्थसमीपेतु ताम्राया दक्षिणेतटे । सुस्थितं पुण्डरीकाक्षं शंखचक्रधरंहरिम् ॥ वरदाभयहस्तञ्च रमया धरया सह । नव नीरद-नीलाभं पीतवाससमच्युतम् ॥ [Brahmâ*n*da Purâ*n*a.]

2. That is taking the chief place in the Hierarchy. Consult the Table.

3. That our Saint would behave thus was foretold in:—

सुज्ञानघनपूर्णत्वात् तिंत्रिणीमूलसंश्रयः । बाल आषोडशाब्दात्तु मूकभावं गमिष्यति ॥ [Bhârgava Purâ*n*a].

of God what is there I can tell others?"[1] But that such were the inner thoughts of the boy, how could the astonished parents divine? They were simply (agreeably) distressed in their hearts, and curiously thought within themselves as to what peculiar fate submitted them to such decrees of God (the Lord of Tiruk-kurungudi) as to subject them to such unusual test and tribulation! We shall now revert to

Saint Madhurakavi (*ga*l).

In the course of his travels in the north of India (as already described) he was now on his way back from Badarikásrama to Ayôdhya. Madhurakavi was somehow aware of the greatness of this born Saint. On a certain night he awoke and went into the open ground to answer calls of nature. As he lifted his gaze, behold! he saw in the Southern direction, a supernaturally strange light, which electrified and staggered him and filled him with wonder and joy. "What could this be?" he pondered in his mind, "could any village have caught fire? or is any forest in flames?" In his contemplative reverie he would fall to dozing, and would, startled, open his eyes. but find the same strange light steadily enchantingly dancing before his vision and entrancing his spirit. Furthermore he sighted the same glory steadily blazing every night in the same Southern direction. He was now resolved to find out the mystery of this marvellous glory and he therefore bent his steps at once towards

1, *Arukk-en-sollugên.* [T-vâi-mozhi, IX. 9. 7.]

the south; determined to go wherever the light might lead. All day he would rest and as soon as darkness fell, he would travel fast in that direction, guided by the brilliant light. He thus trod from one Holy place to another, till he arrived at *Srîrangam*, the Metropolis of the *Srivaishnavas*. But still more south to that shrine, the star receded. He pursued it steadily, and reached Tirunagari, where at last the star seemed to settle down somewhere and disappear.[1]

Madhurakavi now felt certain that if he should inquire and search about this place diligently, he would probably discover the clue to the marvellous blessed vision. He made local inquiries and was informed of all the incidents connected with a wonderful child, which oped neither eye nor mouth; and its abode under a Tamarind Tree &c. Madhurakavigal fell impelled to visit the Tree, and lo ! when he went and reached the spot, he saw his star there in the person of our Saint Nammâzhvâr absorbed in meditation, seated in the posture called Padmâsana. His eyes were closed, his

1. *Cp*: "Behold there came wise men from the East to Jerusalem". (1) "Saying:—where is He that is born King of the Jews? For we have seen His star in the East and are come to adore him." (2) "Then Herod privately calling the wise men, learned diligently of them the time of the star which appeared to them. (7) "And behold the star which they had seen in the East, went before them, until it came and stood over where the child was". (9) "And seeing the star, they rejoiced with exceeding great joy." (10) (Matt: II.)

right hand was half-raised, the palm open, and thumb and first fingers joined (called *jñána-mudra*) proclaiming the spiritual teacher. Madhurakavi doubted—despite the living radiance of the sixteen-year old youth eloquently proclaiming to the contrary—whether there was any life at all in the seated statue-like Figure before him, not to speak of the sense of hearing. He would test, he thought. And so he lifted a big stone and let it drop on the ground so as to produce a noise and startle the motionless Figure, if it had life. A thud—and behold, the Figure opened its eyes and beamed on Madhurakavi with heavenly grace. But its mouth? It remained sealed as before. "He might be dumb after all", thought Madhurakavi, "let me test him". So saying, Madhura-Kavi put him the question :—

> "S*ettattin vayitril siriyadu pirandàl*
> *Ettai-ttinr-engè kidakkum*".

I.e. "If in the womb of what is dead, a subtle thing be born, what doth it eat, and where doth it abide"?[1] Hearing this—a riddle—our saint instantly opened his mouth and answered :—

---

1. प्रकृतेरुदरे जीवो यदि जातस्तदाऽनघ । किं भक्षयन्वा कुत्रार्य वर्तते स पुमान् गुरो ॥ [*Prapannâmrita Ch*: 164] Born &c = soul inhabiting the body. The meaning of this is follows :—

"*What is dead*", dead matter (*achit*) = body.
"*Subtle thing*" = Immaterial formless soul.

"Attai-ttinr-angê kidakkum" *i. e.* "It eateth *that*; it abideth *there*."[1]

When he heard this, Madhurakavi was transported with rapturous devotion to the Saint, who—he had now no doubt left—was a great-soul born on earth endowed with God-knowledge; and he was a prophet and spiritual guide whom, he felt, he was bound to follow in order to effect his own salvation. The pious joy so much overpowered him, he threw himself on the ground, feet together and hands clasped—all signs of humility, reverence and adoration—and he worshipped the Saint with his heart overflowing with ineffable love. The love poured into his speech ending in hymn, and animated the body so as to mak it perform all kinds of

---

1. तद्दस्तु भक्षयन् सम्यग्जीवस्तत्रैव वर्तते ॥ [Prapannámrita: Ch: 104.]

The meaning is as follows:—

"*It eateth that*"=The soul enjoyeth the body and experiences pleasures and pains derived through that vessel.

"*It abideth there*"=The soul lies bound in the prison of the body, incapable of escaping therefrom. Another interpretation is given with reference to the Saint Himself, living and growing as he was without any material nourishment. Then the purport of the answer is that the food of the soul is God Himself; and its place of abode is God Himself. Hence it requireth nor material food nor place.

Cp: "But he said unto them: I have meat to eat that ye know not of" [John IV. 32.] Cp: Gabriel saying to Tobias:—"I use an invisible meat and drink, which cannot be seen by men.' [Tob: XII. 19.]

divine service, the whole being of Madhurakavigal being thus entranced, and thrilling with divine life. Ever did he devoutly dwell on His lotus-feet; ever did he invoke on His Holy names; and thus did he even divinely deceive time in the delightful enjoyment of the company of his Master. It was thus with the disciple.

And with regard to his Master, St. Nammâzhvâr, it now entered the will of God—the Lord of Heaven and Earth—the Ancient, the All-Pervading, Four-armed Vishnu[1]—to reveal himself to him in all His divine glory. Accordingly He rode on Garutmân[2], with His Holy Consort Srî by His side. Blessing the Saint with sights of unutterable spiritual sight, the Lord revealed Himself to him, in the plenitude of all His divinity—His Esseuce—His Attributes,—His resplendent Person,—His Cosmic glories and Harmonies of law, order and economy—and what all may lie in the infinite depths of his infinite Bosom. Our Saint was so enraptured with this awful beatific vision, was so animated and transported, felt so blessed and so afflated with divine ecstasy that he expanded beyond the limits of his own being; and his heart poured forth its uncontainable contents of love and

1. Read:—"आदिदेवो जगन्नाथो वासुदेवो जगत्पतिः ॥ चतुर्भुज श्श्यामळाङ्गो परमे व्योम्नि तिष्ठति" ॥ [Jaya Samhitâ].

2. Read:—"अथागतं गरुड समुं पुरस्स्थितं महागिरिं जलद इवाश्रोह सः" ॥ [Paramêsvara Samhitâ].

wisdom into song[1], melodious and mellifluous, and brimming with all the varying phases,—joys and sorrows, nights and days, of the soul in its journey towards the Divine—in its progess towards the Goal of Infinite Bliss. These constitue the Four Hymns extant, viz.,

(1) Tiruviruttam=the Essence of Rig-Veda.
(2) Tiruv-âsiriyam=the Essence of Yajûr-Vẹda.
(3) Periya-tiruvandâdi=the Essence of Atharva-Veda.

(4) Tiru-vây-mozhi=the Essence of Sâma[2]-Veda. Into these mysteries of divine Love or Love between God and man, Madhura-kavi—who knew no God other than his master (the Âchârya)—was initiated and instructed, that by means of his first apostleship, the Word of God as revealed through him be proclaimed to the world. The Saint's highest ambition, it may be noted, was not his own individual salvation, but redemption and salvation of every soul, past and future. That was his ideal. Nothing short would satisfy him. To this end, he would forfeit and forsake his own individual beatitude.

Not only did the Lord Transcendent in Heaven, but his representative Lords on earth in Holy shrines

---

1. Cp: St. John the Apostle and Evangelist, who 'replenished with the clearest and fullest revelation coming from Heaven' burst forth into: "In the beginning was the Word:"

2. The most pleasing to the Lord as said in Bh: Gita: X. 22. वेदानां सामवेदोऽस्मि.

resident, such Lords as abide in what are called *the Pavilion of Flowers*[1], *the Pavilion of Bounty*[2], *the Paviloin of Bliss*[3], *the Pavilion of Wisdom*[4], reveal themselves to the inner vision of our saint, as he sat meditating under the Holy Tree. As in grand order they passed before his vision, he glorified them by his immortal song. Not only did they thus present themselves, but all the celestial Hosts of eternal Thrones and Dominions, the Dèvas of the distant White Island and other Innumerable Estates and Hierarchies teemed to have a sight of this Saint-gem of rare water. On them all, he bestowed benedictions. And in the height of his joy and glory he exclaimed:—

" Who is there a peer on all this globe
To me, in blissful Krishna-love ! "[5]
"In all the wide expanse of Heaven,
Who can with me equal claim ? "[6]
"In Thee is all, but Thou in me,
Say who is great, or Thou or I ?"[7]

Neither on earth nor in Heaven, it is said, can there a Saint like Nammàzhvâr be ? This is proved by his life, character and work. For what the Avatâras (or God Himself incarnate) left incomplete, (read

1. Holy Tirupati (*Pushpa-Mantapam*)
2. Holy Kánchì (*Tyâga-Mantapam*)
3. Holy *Srirangam* (*Bhoga-Mantapam*)
4. Holy Tirunàrâyanapuram (=Melkote) (*Jñana Mantapam*)
5. *Mär-ulado* &c [T : Vây. Mozhi. VI. 4. 9]
6. *Ini yàvar nigar* &c. (T : Vây : Mozhi, IV. 5. 8)
7. *Yân periyan* &c. (Peri : T. Andâdi, 75.)

Introduction), this Saint completed; viz., the work of redemption and salvation. Before the Glory of this Saint, the glories of other Saints pale. All the other saints form, as it were, his limbs. Here is a Saint who never tasted the so called sweets of this clayey globe, but ever tasted Lord Krishna as his food, his drink and all manner of luxury[1]. This Saint is the fountain-source of all Revelational Truths. To cut a long theme short, it is this Saint who clearly formulated, in his famous Prabandha, the Holy Tiruvâi-Mozhi[2],—the essentially five-fold[3] Truth of the Veda, and the Sublime Doctrine of Trust, of Faith and of Grace as taught in the Holy Dvaya-Mantra,[4] the essence of the Vedas; not by precept alone but by practice, he showed to the world the nature of the three-fold love

---

1. "He afflicted thee with want, and gave thee manna for thy food, which neither thou nor thy fathers knew, to show that not in bread alone doth man live, but in every word that proceedeth from the mouth of God." (Deut VIII. 3.)

2. Chaitanya of Bengal is said to have visited Tirunagari (Âdi Kesava or Âdinâtha) and taken a copy of *Brahma Samhita*, (or the Drâvida Brahma Samhitâ, as Tiruvây-mozhi is called.) (P: 45. 'Life of Chaitanya' by D. N. Ganguli.)

3. Called the Artha-Panchaka epitomized in the verse:—
प्राप्यस्य ब्रह्मणोरूपं प्राप्तुश्च प्रत्यगात्मनः । प्राप्त्युपायं फलं प्राप्तेस्तथा प्राप्तिविरोधिच ॥-(Hárita-Samhita.)

4. Read` द्वयात्परतरं नांस्ति मन्त्रं वेदेष्वपि द्विज । केशवाच्च परो देव ऊपायश्च भरार्पणात् ॥ (Srî Vâsishtha.)

to God,[1] and thus raining nectar as it were, (or laying unction) to all thirsty souls in search of God, our Saint cast off the fleshy envelope in which he appeared to men (though the Lord would take him with it to Heaven) and re-entering the celestial Realms of the Blessed, was beatified. He has been canonized to us as the Head of all the Saints and Sages, *Prapanna-jana-kûtasthah.*

Throughout, in the manner of birth, character and work, this Saint is unequalled. His whole career is a miracle. Many miracles are related, but one alone will be written here. Once upon a time there lived a Yogi (hermit) on the north bank of Tàmraparni river (our Saint being enshrined on the South Bank). He had a dog, which, about midday daily, crossed the river to the Southern Side, roamed through the streets of Holy Tirunagari, and ate of the leavings of the Vaishnavas residing there. One day the dog did not return in time. So the Yogi walked down to the river-side to ascertain the cause. To his consternation and regret he saw that the dog had as usual left the south bank, but when it had performed about half its journey across, a flood suddenly came down. The dog swam but its strength failing, it got drowned. The Yogi anxiously watched. The dog now floated up. It was dead; but as he observed, its head, burst, and the

1. Read दर्शनं परभक्तिस्स्यात् परज्ञानन्तु सङ्गमः । पुनर्विश्लेषभीरुत्वं परमा भक्तिरुच्यते ॥ (By Sage Àlavandár.)

soul, like a glory of light, flew heavenward, as if a thousand lamps were lit on the pitch-dark night of a new moon. The Yogi sang of this event thus:—

" Ocean of Drâvid-wisdom! whose lyrics make even the crowned head of Lord God to nod to their sweetness! what harm if the ghost that I am, be saved even like the dog[1],—the dog that ascends to Heaven, by the mere virtue of its eating the leavings of food scattered in the Holy streets of Holy Kurugûr (Tirunagari) ?[2]

To enter here into a long account of the Doctrines

---

1. The following reflections from the Holy Bible are useful in this connection :—

"Consider the ravens, for they sow not, neither do they reap, neither have they storehouse, nor barn and God feedeth them. How much are you more valuable than they ?" [Luke XII. 24].

" Consider the lilies how they grow :—they labour not, neither do they spin. But I say to you, not even Solomon in all his glory was clothed like one of these." [*Id. XII. 27.*]

" Now if God clothe in this manner the grass that is to-day in the field, and tomorrow is cast into the oven; how much more you, O ye of little faith ?" [*Id : 28.*]

2. " Vúikkum kurugai ttiruvídhi yecchilai vári yunda
Nàikkum Paramapadam alittáy anda náyód-inda,
Péykkum idam-alittár pazhudo Perumàl-makudam
Sáykkum-padikku-kkavi sollu fiána-ttamizh-kadale."

[Vide p: 11 "Tiruviruttam" by S. Rámánujáchár, 1900.]

This incident of the dog &c. is sculptured on a stone pillar of a mantapam which stands in the middle of the Tâmraparni river to this day. [Personally witnessed by us in March 1901]

held by the Âzhvàrs, and numerous other points raised in connection with them, would be out of place. These matters must be left to be dealt with separately. Having therefore space only for briefly touching on a few interesting points, we shall do this and close the present sketch.

After the exaltation of our Saint to Heaven, Madhura-kavi, his first disciple and apostle, lived for several years perpetuating the memory of his master, by construction of suitable temples, the inauguration of his Holy Images therein, and the establishment, on a royal scale, of daily, monthly, and annual solemnizations of his glory and works; and at the same time, as became his First Apostleship, proclaiming far and wide, eternal truths embodied in the four Dràvida Vedas, already mentioned; and with cymbals in hand ever chanted forth[1] the charming melodies of his Master's Hymns on Divine Love.[2] There lived a royal poet (whose name is not known but is guessed or wrongly called as Kamba-Nátt-Âzhvàn) with a council of three hundred learned men under him in the old Sangha days of Pândya Kings of Madhura. Every poet in those days was obliged to pass the ordeal of a critical test of his works by this

1. Cp. "And David and all Israel played before God with all their might with hymns, and with harps, and with psalteries, and timbrels and cymbals, and trumpets". (I Paral: XIII. 8)

2. Our Saint Madhurakavi was to St. *Sathagopa* as Svàmi Vivekânanda is in our days to Paramahamsa Ràmakrishna [Vide P. 77 ff. Brahmavàdin, Vol VI].

council or academy before he could be declared a poet. Some of these members of the council heard of the fame of our Saint and his inspired greatness, proclaimed by trumpets by his disciple Madhurakavi. They took objection to this unlicensed procedure and demanded of him to produce his master and his productions before the august members of the Pândyan Academy, so that they may receive the formal *imprimatur* of the literary luminaries there assembled. "My Saint will not deign to stir from his place.[1] Take ye this scrap," rejoined Madhurakavigal, handing a palm-leaf fragment with the 1st words of our Saint's Hymn X. 5. 1. of Tiruvâimozhi,[2] written thereon. They did so, and the Pîtha,[3] as soon as the Holy slip was placed thereon along with

---

1. Our Saint had departed this life by the time. So, calling him to come up, is a figurative way of throwing down the gauntlet and challenging his *party* to rise and defend him.

2. This verse runs as follows :—

"Kannan-kazhal inai
Nannu manam udayir
Ennum Tiru-nâmam
Tinnam Nâraname."

"For meditation take this Holy formula; ye whose hearts are in love with Krishna's Holy Feet. It is the Holy name Nârâyana indeed (revealed in the Upanishads and Vishnu-Gâyatri)"

3. This is a magical plank (or stool) left to float on what is called the Padmasarovara (lotus-pond) in the temple of South Madhura, capital of the Pândya potentate. As soon as the literary specimens were placed thereon, the plank began to

(*Continued.*)

other literary specimens submitted to its judgment, retained the Holy fragment and threw the others overboard. Kamba-Nátt-Âzhvân with the 300 poets under him, it is said, was at once convinced of the eminently God-inspired character of our Saint and his immortal utterances. And he and others testified to their admiration of the work and submission to the saint's greatness by bestowing on him poetic eulogiums and becoming his followers :—

Of the many spiritual truths revealed by our Saint—a few of which now find light in English dress in the book called the "Divine Wisdom of Dravida Saints"—the foremost truth established is the oneness of God, whose highest and most complete conception is even etymologically enshrined in the Holy name of Nárâyana (= the Deity combining within Himself the Emanative, Preservative, Regenarative &c. powers.), whose temporary functional forms for the projection and retraction of the kosmos, being Brahmà and Rudra[1] respectively and

oscillate, and by its motion retained what was meritorious and eschewed the comparatively inferior productions. M.T.H. Martyn says:—[*Theosophy in Australia, July* 1901] :—"That the Gospels were finally selected by having recourse to magic. The various scriptures in dispute were placed under the communion Table in a church, and prayer was offered to the Lord that he would cause the inspired writings only to remain on the Table and according to this authority (Nicean Council), it was so."

1. (*a*) As expounded for example in Vishnu Puràna :—

(*Continued.*)

the permanent preservative principle, assuming the name of Vish*n*u subsisting directly as Vish*n*u-principle, and indirectly so through the partial functions represented by Brahmâ and Rudra—

This being the chief Teaching, or rather the *Fundamentals* on which all other teachings are based, St. Nammâzhvâr further teaches as follows (we can only give a few) :—

" The Navel-Lotus,—the source of Brahmá, *S*iva, Indra and all,"[2]

स एव सृज्य स्सच सर्गकर्ता स एव पात्यत्ति च पाल्यते च । ब्रह्माद्यवस्थाभिरशेषमूर्त्ति विष्णुर्वरिष्ठो वरदो वरेण्यः ॥ [II. 70.]

" Vishnu is both the material as well as the effective cause of the Universe. He is the Creator, Protector and Destroyer, by evolving from his all-comprehensive Form, the special forms of Brahmâ, Rudra &c. He is the Supreme, Giver of all food, and the Fountain of bliss."

सृष्टिस्थित्यन्तकरणीं ब्रह्मविष्णुशिवात्मिकाम् । स संज्ञां याति भगवानेक एव जनार्दनः ॥ [II. 66.]

" It is Blessed Janârdana (Vishnu) alone who puts on the signs of Brahmâ, Vishnu and *S*iva according as he fulfils the functions of making, preserving, and unmaking the universe."

(*b*) Also see Manu I- 10 *Âpo* &c. with which, Cp: "And the spirit of God moved over the waters." (Gen : I. 2.)

(*c*) For other meanings implicated in this Holy Name, read for example V. 8 of Pramêyasâra by *Arul-âla-pperumâl* Emberumânâr. (Contemp : and disciple of Râmânuja) :—*Vittam* &c

2. (Tiruvâi-Mozhi X. 10. 8.)

"The Four-faced Brahmà and all his creation hath his abode in the Navel-Lotus (of Nârâyana), and He, who burst the three cities (Rudra) hath his adode in his right side.[1]

"The Bull-Rider(Rudra), The Flower-born(Brahmá), and the Flower-daughter (Srí),--He keeps in Himself, without difference"[2]

"Sri abides in His breast, Brahmá in His Navel, and Lord Siva in His side".[3]

"O, the mystic one! Siva, Brahmá, Indra, and all celestials, approach the Holy Feet of Thee, the Garuda-Rider, and praise Thee thus:—"O Thou who hast manifested all the Seven Worlds and us all in Thyself." [4]

"If eelestials, Saints and Sages all,—in love,—body-melting and mind-liquifying—approach Thee with articles of worship, wreaths, and scented waters and incense, and bow to Thee, O The first of all (&c.,)! will not Thy greatness suffer thereby?"[5]

"Thou pervadest and art Thyself Ether, Fire, Air, Water and Earth. Thy subtle pervasion is like that of the soul and the body. These Thou devourest. Thou art the meaning of the Srutis."[6]

We cannot expatiate here on the other Seeret Doctrines taught,—the evolution of the Spiritual life of the

---

1. (Tiru-váy Mozhi I, 3. 9.)
2. (Ibid. II. 2. 3)
3. (Tiruvidame &c.)
4. (Tiruvày Mozhi II. 2. 10)
5. (Ibid I. 5. 2.)
6. (Ibid I. 1. 7.)

Saint and the development of his devotional feeling to the heights of Para-Bhakti &c. It must be reserved for a book by itself (D.V).

As to the authoritativeness of the Drávida Revelations, a word is necessary. Through Agastya Rishi, the Drávida Language, it is said, was by God revealed to the world[1], and in this ancient tongue, He thought it fit to proclaim to the world the eternal Truths of the spirit, through His chosen vessels, the Âzhvárs, so that all men without distinction of race or country may through them, learn how to know, love and serve God, thus obviating the strict and hard course otherwise, of having to learn the Gírvàna (Samskrit)-Vedas, not to say of the special qualifications of High Birth, special Sacraments &c. demanded on the part of a postulant to find entrance thereto.

1. Vide Authorities from *Sambhu Rahasya* in Samskrit and English published in Siddhanta Dîpika: Vol. IV. 1,900 p. 34-35. Those who may be disposed to consider Tamil as modern or rather posterior to Samskrit may read the following:—"The existence of Bahuis to the west of the Indus, whose language shows clear indications of Dravidian descent, is supposed by some to be an evidence in favor of the view that the *Dasyus* with whom the Aryas fought in the Panjab, were all Dravidians. It is said that Spiegl has shown that Dravidian grammar has had some influence on Samskrit Grammar, and Dravidian phonology, on Samskrit phonology. Dr. Caldwell also holds a similar opinion. He says that the Dravidian languages "appear to have been spoken throughout India prior to the arrival of the Âryans," and that Samskrit has not disdained to borrow from the Dravidian languages, words as well as sounds." (P. 22. *The Function of Religion*, by Prof. M. Rangacharya, M. A.)

The Dràvidá Vedas have thus as high a sanction and authority as the Gìrvàna-Vedas. The truths eternally lying in the bosom of God's will were revealed to mankind in different forms, in different times, by means of His different chosen instruments or apostles[1].

As to the institution of Visible Images adopted for man's adoration and worship in our Holy Temples, it receives special recognition and emphasis at the hands of the Âzhvârs, so much so that all critical inquiry into their nature and efficacy is forbidden as blasphemous in the extreme. It is said that such inquiry is beyond the capacity of unilluminated souls, and that the Holy mystery involved is revealed to Initiates only, when their faith is supreme and their heart cleansed.[2]

As regards the nature of realization of God by the Âzhvárs, while their souls abode in the material habitations, it has been settled that all spiritual realisation of God is revealed only to the interior or spiritual vision; and even then they are only temporary rush-lights. They experienced the interior vision so

1. Cp: (*a*) "Because that which is known of God is manifest in them. For God hath manifested it unto them." (*Rom. I. 19*)

(*b*) "And there are diversities of ministries, but the same Lord." (*I. Cor: VII. 5.*)

2. Cp: अर्चावतारोपादानं वैष्णवोत्पत्तिचिन्तनम् । मातृयोनिपरीक्षाया स्तुल्यमाहु र्मनीषिणः ॥ (*Brahmánda-Puràna.*). Image worship is not the worship of the mere symbol, but what it imparts. The

(*Continued.*)

vividly that it was almost akin to a materialized or objectified vision, so much so that they believed that their senses could realise the same in the exterior world. But when they opened their eyes, and wished to see and talk and otherwise completely sense God outside them, and out of love embrace Him, and kiss

---

visible symbol, to the knower of the secret thereof, becomes the very transcendental person of God. Otherwise, it is idolatry which Hinduism deprecates. The misunderstandings on this Doctrine has led to so much bloodshed. *Matt.* III-9. reads: 'For I tell you that God is able of these stones to raise up children to Abraham'. If this is granted, it is no more impossible or profane for God Himself to manifest through stones. Also Cp: (*a*) 'And Jacob, arising in the morning took the stone, which he had laid under his head, and set it up for a pillar, pouring oil upon the top of it.' [*Gen*: *XXVIII*-18] (*b*) "I am the God of Bethel where thou didst anoint the stone". [*Gen*: XXXI. 13.]. (*c*) "But he set up a monument on the place where God had spoken to him: pouring drink-offerings upon it, and pouring oil thereon." [*Gen*: XXXV-14.] (*e*) Read Dr. G: U. Pope's remarks in his Tiruvâchakam:—There is in them (hymns) a strong combination of lofty feeling and spirituality with what we must pronounce to be the grossest idolatry. And this leads to the thought that in the *Saiva* system of to-day two things that would appear to be mutally destructive are found to flourish together, and even to strengthen one another. The more philosophical and refined the *Saivite* becomes the more enthusiastic dods he often appear to be in the performance of the incongruous rites of the popular worship". [Pp: XXXIV-V]. (*f*) "Both within and without, that which Mystic wisdom reveals exists unvarying; to those who have obtained it, no

Him and otherwise fondle and play with Him in a thousand ways, they found it impalpable. This drove them mad again and they then suffered acute pangs of separation from God. When this agony became insuppportable, they were again blessed with a spiritual vision and so on till final beatification was attained. Or these alternate moods caused by union with, and separation from, God-bliss, lasted till the gross body, in which the spirit remained bound, and which they felt as a load set on their eternal freedom, was completely shuffled off, and they found themselves clothed in a spiritual or celestial body,[1] which helped more than obstructed their unrestricted enjoyment of Divine Blessedness for ever afterwards. This truth is confirmed by Scriptures, a few passages only being here quoted ;—

---

means of communion with Him, even through the senses, must be despised. This shows us that to mystically enlightened, the phenomenal universe is only seen in God. [Cp. *Siva-Pra*, p: 369:— 'To those who have attained to *Jnânam* (mystic wisdom) *Sivan* is revealed within, and is seen equally in forms, such as the Lingam &c, in which he reveals himself. The perfected mystic despises not any means of realising the presence of the Immanent Infinite'.] [*P*: IX. *Foot note*: *Ibid*].

If in the place of *Siva*, Vishnu be substituted, the remarks apply to Vaishnavism. *verb. et. lit.*

1. Cp: "And there are bodies celestial, and bodies terrestial; but one is the glory of the celestial, and another of the terrestial." [I *Cor*: XV-40.]

न मांसचक्षु रभिवीक्षतेतम्,

'Him no fleshy eye can perceive'.

तदीक्षणायस्वाध्याय श्चक्षुर्योगस्तथापरम् ।

न मांसचक्षुषा द्रष्टुं ब्रह्मभूतस्सशक्यते ॥

[Vishnu-Purána. VI. 6. 3.]

"Through the eye of Scripture-Reading, we see him; the other eye is of meditation; but not by the fleshy eye can the searcher see Him" As to what constitutes a Jívanmukta, or who realises God while yet living on earth, or realises Him to that extent only as can sublunary conditions permit, is embodied in the Usanasa Smriti thus:—

" न शब्दशास्त्राभिरतस्यमोक्षो ।
न चैवरम्यावसथप्रियस्य ॥
न भोजनाच्छादनतत्परस्य ।
न लोकवृत्तिग्रहणे रतस्य ॥ "

" एकान्तशीलस्य दृढव्रतस्य ।
पञ्चेन्द्रियप्रीतिनिवर्तकस्य ॥
अध्यात्मविचाररतमानसस्य ।
मोक्षोध्रुवो नित्यमहिंसकस्य ॥ "

"Not to the learned in all the learnings, is salvation:
Not to the lover of delightful houses of dwelling:
Not to the lover of dinners and dresses,
Not to the rover in the business of the world."

"To him is salvation sure, who is fond of retirement and austerity;

To him only who has abstained from loving the five objects of sense;

To him whose heart is set on the science of the soul;

To him alone who is ever a stranger to cruelty."

To such souls, the full light of wisdom enshrined in the out-pourings of the Âzhvârs will shine, and be their constant guide to lead them to the final end and meaning of existence, viz., the knowing, loving, seeing and serving our loving Creator and Father in Heaven for ever and ever.

We here add a few specimens of our Saint's Teachings:—

1—(*Poy-ninra* &c)

"Eternal angels' Lord! who yet dost deign to veil Thy Form
In all Creation's varied state, for saving souls,
Vouchsafe in all Thy grace to stay and hear Thy servants' cry,
That we be saved the dire return to former wretchedness,
When we mistook the body for our souls and sinned all sins
Which clung to us and fixed us ever more to mortal frames."

(*Tiru-viruttam, 1st verse*)

2—(*Kàviyum* &c)

"Lo! here's my Soul—a virgin bride of God,
A gay-winged lady-swan, who casts her eyes,
Fish-shaped—never-fading blushing blooms—
—Ah! Sapphire eyes with ruby fitly dight—
—Ah! darts that plunge within the inmost soul

Of Garud's Lord, the Lord of even blessed *Srí*,
The Fear of foes, the faithful's constant Joy!"

(*Ibid*, *67th Verse.*)

3—(*Ulagu-padaittu* &c.)

"My Father, Lord of worlds evolved, involved! Breaths there a man
That sees thy lotus feet with royal signs adorned, which stride
The triple worlds[1] at once, and seeing will not melt away
In bliss, ambrosial sweet,—his heart immersed in joy supreme—
—A sweetness ravishing,—a feeling rare? Or else Ah, fool!
He knows not, what for him is highest good, save love for Thee!
Ah! fool, to lose this wealth and strive his every nerve to win
With mountain-labour, short-lived joy or power o'er mortal things
Albeit he sways the spheres three, or sleeps in swarga's[2] shade."

4—(*Muyatri &c*)

"Alas! my heart, wouldst thou now start ahead
Of me to reach His feet and praise His grace

---

1. Cp. Purusha Súkta:—"त्रीणिपदा विचक्रमे विष्णुः &c"

2. (*a.*) To intense devotees, Heaven-going too is an object of indifference". (Epistle d/ 14. 12. 1900, from S. Pârthasârathi Yogi).

(*b.*) "Aspiring to go to *Paramapada* (Heaven) is also set down by the ripest sage among his childish prayers". (*Ibid*, d/ 22. 9. 1895).

So fired by zeal, so goaded by thy love?
But tarry now, I prithee, let us work
Together up to Him of hue of pûvai flower;
And weave into wreaths of honied song
Which welleth forth from tongue, unhelped by mind."

(*Periya-Tiru-v-Andâdi. v.* 1)

5—(*Uyarvu* &c)

"Serve, heart, His bright ills-chasing feet and live:—
That Lord of bliss surpassing glories all—
That Lord who darkness chasing, wise love grants—
That Lord who rules supreme o'er deathless souls."

(*Tiru-vây-mozhi I.* 1. 1)

6—(*Vâne-taruvân* &c.)

"O Lord of holy Tiruppèr
Engirt by honey-flowing groves!
How pledgest now to grant me Heaven
And enterest this cage of flesh
To chase the sins that part us twain"[1].

(*Tiru-vây-mozhi* X-8-5.)

7—(*Talir-nadi etc.*)

"Who lonely on the Fig-leaf[2] lay

---

1. Compare the Christian idea of the sanctification of souls by the infusion of divine grace.

2. The chronicle of Mahâ-Vishnu lying on a fig leaf at the time of universal flood, keeping all things in their potentiality in His Body and showing Himself as an infant to the sage Markandeya, is described in Srimat Bhagavata: XII. 8. (Cp. the Noah's flood of Hebraic tradition). About the fig-tree symbol, compare the Perfect Way or the Finding of Christ: "Wherefore then, saith the Lord, that the budding of the fig tree shall foretell the End."

The symbol of the All
The moon-decked Siva, Four-faced Brahm
And Indra, king of Devs;
All things of life and lifeless things
Earth, Water and the Fire
And Wind and Ether luminous;
All else of light and life—
The least not missed and all entire—

---

1. 'The Fig is the similitude of the matrix, containing inward buds, bearing blossoms on its placenta, and bringing forth fruit in darkness. It is the Cup of Life, and its flesh is the seed-ground of new births.'

'The stems of the Fig Tree run with milk: her leaves are as human hands, like the leaves of her brother the vine'.

'The Fig is often made mention of in the Holy Bible. Zecharias says in one place (10): Ye shall call every man under the *Fig*.'

The following notes are found in Cruden's Concordance:—

'Our first parents covered their nakedness with *Fig*-leaves. (*Gen.* III. 7)

'This tree hath in it a milky or fat-oily liquor; it is very fruitful. M. Tournefort says, that in the islands of the Archipelago, one of their Fig-trees generally produces two-hundred and four-score pound-weight of figs'.

'The Prophet Isaiah gave orders to apply a lump of figs to Hezekiah's boil; and immediately after he was cured'

(*II Kings.* XX, 7).

'Physicians agree, that figs are employed with good success in bringing imposthumes to a ripeness, to healing ulcers, quinsies, and sore throats.'

(*Continued.*)

Most subtly enter Him.
Ah! who will own another Lord
Save Him alone, the Mystic God?[2]"

The sacred Fig is the only Tree which increases by itself *ad: infin:*, by its droppings taking root.

The Akshayavat is worshipped from immemorial time in Prayág (Fort Allahabad). All Hindus offer food to their manes under the Vat at Holy Gaya. Every *Sráddha* ceremony closes with a formula referring to Vat and Vishnu-Páda.

Saint Poygai Âzhvâr in his *Tiruvandádi, verse* 69 (Pálan tamadu &c) exclaims his wonderment at the Vata-dala-sâyi form of manifestation of the Deity at the close of cosmic manifestation; also our Saint Nammâzhvâr in Tiru-váy-mozhi, verse IV. 2. 1. (Pâlan-ây &c.)

2. As to Mahá-Vishnu or Nárâyana or Hari being the Source or Fountain of all the Three-fold Energies of manifesting (Brahma), Sustaining (Vishnu), and withdrawing (Rudra or Siva), that He is the One God (to whom our Saint owes allegiance) the Védas have conclusively declared. The following interesting extract from V. Gopâlâchârya's (M. A., B.L.) learned M. A. Dissertation on the Púrva-Mímâmsa is here annexed:—

"The works of the ancient writers of the Visishtâdvaita School refer to the last 4 Adhyáyas (of the Púrva Mimamsa) as the Devatâ Kända. They quote the concluding Sûtras of the Devatâ Kanda. ... ... Vedânta Desika says that the 1st Sûtra of the Devatá Kända is नानात्वा देवता (there are *numerous gods*) ... ... The Adhikarana Chintâmani quotes *an old verse which* states in general the contents of the Devatâ

(Continued.)

St. Madhurakavigal is distinguished from all other saints, in having preached to mankind not the Greatness of God (*Prathama-Parva*) but the Greatness of God's Elect, God's Servants, God's Saints, God's Sages,—God's own godly souls (*Charama-Parva*). In elucidation of this Truth, he sang the Ten Verses of

---

Kända :—"The nature of the Devatas, their varieties, their worship and the fruit they give are told in the Devatà Kànda. This verse is quoted in Appayadikshita's Naya-mayúkha mälikà in which the Sútras of the Devatà Kända quoted by Vedánta Desika, Naindchärya and others are also cited ... . There is no elaborate discussion of the Devatas in the first twelve Adhyäyas and it is just possible therefore that there was a Devatä Kánda devoted wholly to the discussion of the Devatas as there is a separate Kânda for Devatas in the Nirukta (of Yâska) ... ...The Sûtras cited as from the Devatà Kànda are out and out Vaishnava and may therefore be suspected to be the fabrication of some Vaishnava writer, but in fairness to the Vaishnava authors, it must be said that their quotations have not drawn any protest from their opponents and that even Appaya Dikshita, who quotes the same Sûtras, does not raise his voice against them." (P. 5. Dodson Press, Trichinopoly). The concluding Sútra of the Pürva Mímâmsa, runs as follows :—

अन्ते हरिस्तद्दर्शनात् ।
स विष्णुराह हि ।
तं ब्रह्मेत्याचक्षते ।
* तं ब्रह्मेत्याचक्षते ॥

* *Kureso-Vijaya* may be studied. Also see *Introduction Page* i. for foreign opinion on Vaishnavism.

Kanninun-Siru-ttâmbu (11 verses), the closing verse declaring :—

"Mark! High Heaven do those attain
Who, reverent faith, place in my lay;
For, Him I love, who 's Nagari's Lord".[1]

In the words of sage Ma*n*avâ*l*a Mahâ-Munigal :—

"*Azhvârgal Vâzhi Aruli-cchaiyal Vâzhi*"

"Blest all Âzhvârs be, and blest be their Grace-Utterances."[2]

करारविन्देन पदारविन्दं मुखारविन्दे विनिवेशयन्तम् ।
जगद्वटे तं पृथुकं शयानं प्रपन्नसन्तारमहं प्रपद्ये ॥

Blest be All Saints.

1. (Verse 11): *Anbantannai* &c. The high discourse, *Division 6*, Sentences 436—494, treating of '*The Teachers' Saving Power*,' may be read in this connection, in Pârthasârathi Yôgi's *Good-Word-Jewel*.

2. (Upadésa-Ratna-Mâlai. V. 3.)